I0592984

"I celebrate this collection of incisive and animated essays by some of the sharpest scholars of literary studies in India; but even more, I salute the man who has inspired it.

GJV Prasad—longtime friend and colleague, sharer of laughter and bon mots at so many locations over the years and finally at JNU offices two doors apart—has worn both his erudition and his popularity with a rare, and equal, lightness. It may be said with certainty that an overwhelming number of English teachers and students across India know him slightly or well: and not merely for his translations, his academic writing, his courses and his talks, but for the generosity of his time, humour, advice and affection. All of these—with the exception of his hugely anticipated classes each semester over an eventful forty-one years at Jawaharlal Nehru University, whose Centre for English Studies he grew synonymous with—should remain unaffected by his retirement from teaching.

Yet, the retirement of a stalwart teacher and mentor such as GJV Prasad is a moment of pleasant pause for all the minds he touched and shaped over decades. This volume of essays in honour of him is timely, thoughtful and fitting. It traverses the wide reach of his scholarly interests in the collated work of his friends, students and colleagues; they pay tribute to his place in their intellectual lives through this gesture that will speak the most eloquently to him, as well as to all those who occupy the field of English literary studies in contemporary India. It is a public encomium that carries with it a scent of friendship: there could hardly be a better gift."

Brinda Bose, *Jawaharlal Nehru University*

"An extraordinary tribute to teacher, translator and creative writer Prof. GJV Prasad, the book *From Canon to Covid: Transforming English Literary Studies in India* tracks every significant signpost in the evolution of the most 'aspirational' subject in the country. From questioning the canon to offering insightful readings of Indian writing, from analysing syllabus change to noting corresponding developments in translation and publishing, from creative writing to theorisations, the essays constitute a comprehensive understanding of literary studies in the context of national dynamics. Scholars of renown, associated with the long and illustrious career of GJV, have come together in a remarkable expression of solidarity to create a book of outstanding quality and significance."

Malashri Lal, *Department of English, and former Dean of Colleges, University of Delhi*

FROM CANON TO COVID

This multi-genre collection of chapters presents the dramatic transformation of English Studies in India since the early 1990s. It showcases the shift from the study of mainly British literature and language to a more versatile terrain of multilingualism, culture, performance, theory, and the literary Global South. Tracing this transition, the volume discusses themes like Indian literary history, postcolonial theory, post-pandemic challenges to literary studies, the state of Indian English drama, vernacular literature in English Studies and pedagogy, translations of feminist writers from South Asia, caste, and othering in literature, among other key themes. The volume, with contributions from eminent English Studies scholars, not only reflects the altered terrain of English Language and Literature in India but also invites readers to think about the transformative potential of the present juncture for both literary imagination and literary studies.

This timely book, in honour of Professor GJV Prasad, will be of interest to scholars and researchers of English Studies, cultural studies, literature, comparative literature, translation studies, postcolonial studies, and critical theory.

Angelie Multani is Professor of Literature in the Department of Humanities & Social Sciences, Indian Institute of Technology (IIT) Delhi, India.

Swati Pal is the Principal of Janki Devi Memorial College, University of Delhi, India, where she is also Professor in the Department of English.

Nandini Saha is Professor in the Department of English, Jadavpur University, Kolkata, India.

Albeena Shakil is Professor of English at the O.P. Jindal Global University, India.

Arjun Ghosh is Professor in the Department of Humanities & Social Sciences, IIT Delhi, India.

FROM CANON TO COVID

Transforming English
Literary Studies in India

Essays in Honour of GJV Prasad

Edited by Angelie Multani, Swati Pal,
Nandini Saha, Albeena Shakil, and Arjun Ghosh

Routledge
Taylor & Francis Group

LONDON AND NEW YORK

Designed cover image: © Suvadeep Mondal / Getty Images

First published 2024
by Routledge
4 Park Square, Milton Park, Abingdon, Oxon OX14 4RN

and by Routledge
605 Third Avenue, New York, NY 10158

Routledge is an imprint of the Taylor & Francis Group, an informa business

© 2024 selection and editorial matter, Angelie Multani, Swati Pal, Nandini Saha, Albeena Shakil and Arjun Ghosh; individual chapters, the contributors

The right of Angelie Multani, Swati Pal, Nandini Saha, Albeena Shakil and Arjun Ghosh to be identified as the authors of the editorial material, and of the authors for their individual chapters, has been asserted in accordance with sections 77 and 78 of the Copyright, Designs and Patents Act 1988.

All rights reserved. No part of this book may be reprinted or reproduced or utilised in any form or by any electronic, mechanical, or other means, now known or hereafter invented, including photocopying and recording, or in any information storage or retrieval system, without permission in writing from the publishers.

Trademark notice: Product or corporate names may be trademarks or registered trademarks, and are used only for identification and explanation without intent to infringe.

British Library Cataloguing-in-Publication Data
A catalogue record for this book is available from the British Library

Library of Congress Cataloging-in-Publication Data
A catalog record has been requested for this book

ISBN: 978-0-367-76834-8 (hbk)
ISBN: 978-1-032-50843-6 (pbk)
ISBN: 978-1-003-39992-6 (ebk)

DOI: 10.4324/9781003399926

Typeset in Sabon
by Deanta Global Publishing Services, Chennai, India

for Prof GJV Prasad,
beloved and inspirational Professor who taught at JNU

CONTENTS

CONTRIBUTORS

Mohd Asaduddin is author, critic, and translator in several languages; he writes on literature, language politics, and translation studies. Currently, he is the Dean, Faculty of Humanities & Languages, Jamia Millia Islamia, and Advisor to the Vice-Chancellor. He was a Fulbright Scholar-in-Residence at Rutgers University and a Charles Wallace Trust Fellow at the University of East Anglia. Among his books are *Complete Premchand Stories* (PRH, four volumes), *Premchand in World Languages* (Routledge), *Filming Fiction: Tagore, Premchand and Ray* (OUP), *A Life in Words* (Penguin), *The Penguin Book of Classic Urdu Stories* (2006), *Lifting the Veil: Selected Writings of Ismat Chughtai* (Penguin), and *Image and Representation: Stories of Muslim Lives in India* (OUP). He is the Chair, Indian Association for Commonwealth Literature and Language Studies (IACLALS). Awards: Sahitya Akademi, Urdu Academy (Delhi) and Crossword Book Award.

Meenakshi Bharat, published writer, translator, reviewer, and cultural theorist, teaches at Sri Venkateswara College, University of Delhi. Her wide and variegated writing, both creative and critical, spurred by contemporary concerns, includes three monographs: *The Ultimate Colony, Troubled Testimonies: Terrorism and the English Novel in India*, and *Shooting Terror: Terrorism and the Hindi Film*. Her love of the short story form took her to co-editing five successful Indo-Australian short fiction anthologies, which too have variously taken on burning contemporary issues. She has served the cause of literatures and languages as the President of the International Federation of Modern Languages and Literatures (FILLM, UNESCO) and is on the advisory board of the FILLM Series, John Benjamins, the Netherlands.

Radha Chakravarty is former Professor of Comparative Literature and Translation Studies at Dr. B. R. Ambedkar University Delhi, has co-edited *The Essential Tagore*, nominated Book of the Year 2011 by Martha Nussbaum, and edited several anthologies of South Asian writing. She is the author of *Feminism and Contemporary Women Writers* and *Novelist Tagore* and has translated the works of major Bengali writers from India and Bangladesh, including Bankimchandra Chatterjee, Mahasweta Devi, Syed Shamsul Haq, and Selina Hossain. Her poems have appeared in numerous books and journals. She has contributed to *Pandemic: A Worldwide Community Poem*, nominated for the Pushcart Prize 2020.

Keki N Daruwalla writes poetry and fiction. He is awaiting his next poetry volume from Speaking Tiger Publishers. He has given up writing his fire-and-brimstone political columns.

Mahesh Dattani, a Sahitya Akademi awardee, is a playwright, stage director, and drama teacher. He is the Artistic Director of Playpen Performing Arts Trust, a group dedicated to developing and producing new writings for the theatre. He lives in Mumbai.

Arjun Ghosh is Professor in the Department of Humanities & Social Sciences, Indian Institute of Technology Delhi, India. He has a PhD from the Centre for English Studies at Jawaharlal Nehru University (JNU), New Delhi. He has contributed articles to journals like *Asian Theatre Journal* and *Drama Review*. He has worked on organized cultural movements and political open space performances with special reference to the Jana Natya Manch, Delhi. He has authored three books, namely *A History of the Jana Natya Manch: Plays for the People*, *Freedom from Profit: Eschewing Copyright in Resistance Art*, and *Nabanna: Of Famine and Resilience: A Play*.

Suman Gupta is Professor of Literature and Cultural History at the Open University, UK. He has coordinated several international collaborative projects with partners in China, India, Iran, Nigeria, Morocco, South Africa, Bulgaria, Romania, and the USA. He has held visiting positions at Wolfson College, University of Oxford, UK; CRASSH, University of Cambridge, UK; Harry Ransom Centre, University of Texas at Austin, USA; Institute of World Literature, Peking University, China; English Department, University of Delhi, India; State University of Campinas, Brazil. He is Honorary Research Fellow at Roehampton University, UK. His books include *The Theory and Reality of Democracy: A Case Study in Iraq* (2006); *Social Constructionist Identity Politics and Literary Studies* (2007); *Globalization and Literature* (2009); *Imagining Iraq: English Literature and the Invasion of Iraq* (2011); *Contemporary Literature: The Basics* (2012); *Consumable Texts in Contemporary India*

(2015); *Philology and Global English Studies* (2015); *Reconsidering English Studies in India* (2015, co-authored with Allen, Chattarji and Chaudhuri), and a co-edited volume *Academic Labour, Unemployment and Global Higher Education* (2016, with Habjan and Tutek).

Achingliu Kamei is Associate Professor in the Department of English, ARSD College, University of Delhi. She is a short story writer, poet, and author of *Naga Tales: Dawn* (2017), *Songs of Raengdailu* (2021), *Liangtuang Pu: Illustrated Novella for Children* (2021), and *Headspace* (2022). Her next collection of folktales titled *Naga Tales: Morning Blush* is due for publication shortly. Her poems and haiku have been published in several journals and anthologies. She has presented several papers at national and international seminars and conferences. Her area of interest is literature written in English from North East India. She is also an ultra-marathon runner.

Tabish Khair is an Indian writer and Associate Professor at Aarhus University, Denmark. His studies and novels include *Babu Fictions*, *Filming: A Love Story*, and *The Body by the Shore*.

Udaya Kumar teaches at the Centre for English Studies, Jawaharlal Nehru University. He has previously worked at the University of Delhi and the Centre for Studies in Social Sciences, Calcutta. His publications include *Writing the First Person: Literature, History and Autobiography in Modern Kerala* (Ranikhet: Permanent Black, 2016), *The Joycean Labyrinth: Repetition, Time and Tradition in Ulysses* (Oxford: Clarendon Press, 1991), and papers on modern literature, literary theory, and the cultural history of modern Kerala. His recent research has focused on death and contemporary culture, forms of life writing, cultural histories of the body, and idioms of vernacular social thought. He writes and publishes in English and Malayalam.

C S Lakshmi has been an independent researcher in Women's Studies for the last more than 40 years. She has a PhD from Jawaharlal Nehru University, New Delhi. She writes under the pseudonym Ambai in Tamil about love, relationships, quests, and journeys, and her short story collections have been published in Tamil and also translated into English. She was given the Sahitya Akademi Award in 2021 for her book *Sivappuk Kazhuththudan Oru Pachaip Paravai*. She is currently the Director of SPARROW (Sound & Picture Archives for Research on Women).

Somdatta Mandal is former Professor of English and Chairperson at the Department of English, Visva-Bharati, Santiniketan. She has held several administrative posts and has lectured widely in national and international fora. A recipient of several prestigious international fellowships and awards, her areas of interest are American literature, contemporary fiction, film and culture studies, diaspora studies, and translation. A detailed list of her publications can be accessed by visiting her website http://sites.google.com/site/mandalsomdatta

B Mangalam is Professor in the Department of English, Aryabhatta College, University of Delhi. Her research work pertains to gender and caste intersectionality in Tamil Dalit fiction. She has published critical editions of *Pride and Prejudice* (1999), *Paradise Lost, Bk IX* (2000), *The Balcony* (2001), *The Book of Vanci* (2015; rev.2023), *Ilango Adigal's Silappadhikaram* (2021), Worldview Publications, Delhi. She has published articles on Dalit literature and contemporary Indian theatre in journals and books. She translates from Tamil to Hindi and English. Her translations of Indira Parthasarathy's Tamil play *Mazhai* as *Baarish* and Plautus's *The Pot of Gold* as *Fakirchand* have been performed by professional groups in Delhi Hindi theatre circuit. She collaborates with NGOs on gender equity at workplace.

Anuradha Marwah is Professor of English at Zakir Husain Delhi College and is the author of three novels, *The Higher Education of Geetika Mehendiratta*, *Idol Love* and *Dirty Picture*, and five plays that have had several public performances. Her play *Ismat's Love Stories* was shortlisted for the Hindu Playwright Award 2016. She directed *Medea* (Hindustani) in 2019 and toured with it in rural Rajasthan where she runs a community NGO. She is a recipient of the Charles Wallace Writer's Residency (2001) and Fulbright-Nehru Academic and Professional Excellence (FNAPE) fellowship to the University of Minnesota–Twin Cities (2017). More information on her work is available at anuradhamarwah.com.

Jisha Menon is Professor of Theatre and Performance Studies and, by courtesy, of Comparative Literature at Stanford University, where she serves as the Fisher Family Director of Stanford Global Studies. She is the author of *Brutal Beauty: Aesthetics and Aspiration in Urban India* (Northwestern University Press, 2021) and *The Performance of Nationalism: India, Pakistan, and the Memory of Partition* (Cambridge University Press, 2013). She is also co-editor of two volumes: *Violence Performed: Local Roots and Global Routes of Conflict* (with Patrick Anderson) (Palgrave-Macmillan Press, 2009) and *Performing the Secular: Religion, Representation, and Politics* (with Milija Gluhovic) (Palgrave-Macmillan, 2017). She is currently working on a new book at the intersection of law and performance.

Angelie Multani is Professor of Literature in the Department of Humanities & Social Sciences, IIT Delhi. Her research interests are in Indian theatre, contemporary novel, gender and queer studies, along with fantasy fiction. She has published extensively on the works of Mahesh Dattani and on Indian novels in English.

Rukmini Bhaya Nair is Honorary Professor of Linguistics and English, IIT Delhi, and Global Professorial Fellow, Queen Mary University of London (QMUL). She received her PhD from the University of Cambridge. She has taught at several universities including the National University of Singapore and Stanford University. Author of 10 books and about 175 articles, Nair was awarded an honorary doctorate by the University of Antwerp for her contribution to narrative studies. Her most recent book is the 2020 reference volume *Keywords for India*. She is on the boards of many international journals. The Department of Science and Technology and the Indian Council of Social Science Research awarded Nair major grants to conduct research on 'Language, Emotion and Culture' and the 'Capabilities Approach to Education'. Recipient of several awards (the Tata Scholarship, Hornby Memorial Award, Dorthy Leet Grant, Charles Wallace Award, the US Subcommission on Education and Culture Grant, etc.), Nair is currently Indian Team Leader on a University of Pittsburgh multi-country project titled 'The Geography of Philosophy'. Profiled as a 'Face of the Millennium' by *India Today*, she also won the All-India Poetry Society/British Council First Prize and has since published three volumes of poems. Nair's writings, creative and critical, are included in courses in Chicago, Delhi, Harvard, Kent, Toronto, and other universities.

Mala Pandurang is Principal and Professor at Dr BMN College, Mumbai. She is a postdoctoral fellow of the Alexander von Humboldt Postdoctoral Foundation and is its 'Ambassador Scientist to India' for 2022–2024. She is also Fellow of the first Humboldt Residency Program in Berlin for a project on social cohesion. Her research grants include Dr Aroon Tikekar Research Fellowship of the Asiatic Society (Mumbai); Fulbright Visiting Professor at the University of Texas at Austin; recipient of the Charles Wallace In-UK Research grant; Major Minor research grants from the UGC; and Inlaks Fellowship in Social Sciences from the Asiatic Society (Mumbai). Her areas of research are postcolonial, gender, and diaspora studies.

Swati Pal is the Principal of Janki Devi Memorial College, University of Delhi, India, where she is also Professor in the Department of English. Her research interests include performance studies, academic and creative writing, and education. She is the author of the book *Look Back at Anger: Agit Prop Theatre in Britain from the Sixties to the Nineties* and a co-author of the books *A Handbook of Academic Writing and Composition* and *Creative Writing: A Beginner's Manual* prescribed by the University of Delhi. She has edited a volume of essays titled *Modern European Drama: From Ibsen to Beckett* as well as a volume of essays on Australian Literature. She has translated a number of Premchand's stories into English published by Penguin. Several of her newspaper articles articulate her views on education and her research in drama.

Meena T Pillai is Dean, Faculty of Arts, Professor, Institute of English and Director, Centre for Cultural Studies, University of Kerala. A former Fulbright Visiting Professor to the University of California, Los Angeles; she was also a Shastri Fellow at the Mel Hoppenheim School of Cinema, University of Concordia, a Commonwealth Fellowship at the Centre for Media Studies, University Sussex, and a Fulbright Doctoral Fellow at the Ohio State University, Columbus. Widely published, her latest book is *Affective Feminisms in Digital India: Intimate Rebels* (London: Taylor & Francis, 2022).

K B Veio Pou is Associate Professor in the Department of English, Shaheed Bhagat Singh College, University of Delhi. He is the author of *Literary Cultures of India's Northeast: Naga Writings in English* (2015), and his debut novel *Waiting for the Dust to Settle* (2020) won the Gordon Graham Prize for Naga Literature (Fiction category). He likes to engage on various contemporary issues that relate to literature, culture, society, and faith.

Nandini Saha is Professor, and former Head, Department of English Jadavpur University, Kolkata. She was formerly also the Head of the Department of English, University of Kalyani. Her doctoral research was on John Fowles. She has taught courses on Indian writing in English, translation, modernism, and postmodernist fiction. Her research interests are in the areas of translation, Bengali Dalit writing, and cultural studies.

Santosh K Sareen retired as Professor from the Centre for English Studies, School of Language, Literature and Culture Studies, Jawaharlal Nehru University, New Delhi, in October 2010. He taught English language and literature, including English poetry. He taught and guided research in Australian literature for more than 15 years and is President Emeritus of the Indian Association for the Study of Australian Literature (IASA). He has published *English Reading Texts, A Socio-Cultural Study, Intellectual Publishing House*, 1992, and a number of articles on cultural relationships, history of English in India, English literatures of South Asia and the Pacific and translation studies in various journals and books. He has edited *Australia and India: Convergences and Divergences*, Mantra Books, New Delhi, 2010, *Australia and India Interconnections, Identity, Representation and Belonging*, Mantra Books, New Delhi, 2006, and *Contemporary Australian*

Short Stories, Affiliated East-West Press, New Delhi, 2001, and co-edited *Of Sadhus and Spinners: Australian Encounters with India* together with Bruce Bennett et al., Harper Collins, 2009, *Sabda: Text and Interpretation* with Makarand Paranjape, Mantra, 2004, and *Cultural Interfaces,* together with Sheel C Nuna and Malati Mathur.

Albeena Shakil is Professor of English at the O.P. Jindal Global University, Sonipat, Haryana. She is the author of *Understanding the Novel: A Theoretical Overview* (2015), guest editor of three issues of *Summerhill: IIAS Review*, and guest co-editor of *JGLR: Women, Law and South Asia*. She is a former Fellow of the Indian Institute of Advanced Study, Shimla.

FOREWORD

Suman Gupta

Reflecting on his career around 40 years after he enrolled as a university student reading English, G.J.V. Prasad (2013) summed up the situation of English departments in India with these words:

> English departments are places for significant contestations, and the major difference that makes them so, as compared to the 1970s and 1980s, is that literary studies and humanities are now seen as exciting and politically relevant spaces, under attack but to be defended stoutly. English departments are at the forefront of this struggle for the survival of humanities in many of our leading universities, mainly because they have translated themselves into transdisciplinary centres of cultural studies, almost representing all Humanities. No longer do English departments see themselves as irrelevant in India, they only contest the terms of their relevance.
>
> *(49)*

He felt that English departments had become not merely spaces for, as Gerald Graff (1992) had put it, 'teaching the conflicts' but also for engaging with conflicts. For those in English departments, such conflicts were not ivory-tower squabbles. They were grounded in the everyday and social life of the Indian demos and, therefore, of the world at large. G.J.V. Prasad also suggested that to designate these spaces as '*English* departments' is to court a misnomer in India. These departments centre deliberations of considerably wider scope, 'almost representing all Humanities'. In practice, pedagogy and scholarship in English departments range across the languages of the subcontinent and the geopolitical zones of the world. Even with broad characterizations of linguistic and literary studies in mind, received disciplinary boundaries are as often infringed as respected in English departments – as G.J.V Prasad saw it, they are akin to 'transdisciplinary centres of cultural studies'.

It is entirely fitting that this volume on concerns currently being debated in English Studies in India appears as a *Festschrift* for G.J.V. Prasad. Few have made as wide-ranging and sustained a contribution to the fluid boundaries of this space, as a teacher, researcher, administrator, creative writer, translator and public intellectual. When he wrote the article quoted above, he still had a decade of his formal career before him. This volume marking its distinguished conclusion gives a strong sense of the preoccupations of students and scholars now and of the authors and readers who feature in their discussions. Some of the papers acknowledge a vestigial rooting in the disciplinary designation of 'English', more as an institutional formation than as a well-defined subject area. But that is only to radiate out towards the many regions, identities, languages and identities of India and the wider world. The protean scope of this volume is captured in its alliterative title *From Canon to Covid*. At one end there's a narrow and conservative disciplinary core and at the other there's a global contingency that upended every area of human coexistence. Somewhere between those, this volume offers some purchase on English Studies in India. If there's a point at which the 'English' in English Studies becomes meaningful here, it's as a via media rather than as a theme. English flickers in the transactions between many languages and texts, in deliberations amidst numerous locales and standpoints. English appears on the pathway or at the sidelines of these, or perhaps as a prop in the backdrop of various performances. Perhaps 'English' is ultimately meaningful here because this volume appears in English, with articles by contributors who acknowledge some connection to 'English Studies' simply by contributing.

For an area as contested and effervescent as English Studies in India, naturally this volume is not a singularity. It should be considered an intervention in a continuing scholarly conversation. Shortly before G.J.V. Prasad wrote that essay, important reconsiderations of the history of English education and English Studies in India had been published (notably Mukherjee 2009, Dash 2009). Since its publication, reckonings with the place of the English language and the scope of English Studies have appeared at regular intervals: to name a few, Gupta et al., *Reconsidering English Studies in Indian Higher Education* (2015); Gupta and Garg edited, *The English Paradigm in India* (2017); Mahanta and Sharma edited, *English Studies in India* (2019); Tasildar, *English Studies in Indian Universities* (2019); Sethi and Khanna edited, *Dialogues* (2020); Saxena, *Vernacular English* (2022); Dutta edited, *English Teachers' Accounts* (2022). In various ways, the present volume resonates with these, advancing the conversation.

Naturally, much remains to be covered in such deliberations. For instance, the political economy of English Studies in India could be woven more closely with the cultures of reading and writing, pedagogy and scholarship that are predominantly foregrounded. At the interstices of these ongoing deliberations, governmental and commercial rationales can be discerned. These rationales have a bearing on higher education in general and, in traceable ways, specifically on English Studies. For instance, public and private education providers present some distinctions in their curricular offerings and teaching methods. Uneven investments in higher education according to regions and categories of institutions play a tractable part. Policy drives to promote applied knowledge and skills-based learning have put particular pressures on areas like English Studies. The market calculations of literary and academic publishing have an obvious bearing on what is more or less easily available. Media and publicity industries have a similarly determinative role therein. International investments in education, publishing and media have impinged significantly on practices in these sectors. The effects of changing conditions of employment in and the funding of universities, shifts in the socio-economic backgrounds of student constituencies, strengthened top-down bureaucratic and management regimes, exacerbated political polarization in campuses and so on are obviously germane. And, in fact, they are all discernible in deliberations on English Studies presented in the volumes cited and in this one. But they are often found between the lines, in fleeting observations, in variously muted and backgrounded ways. Undoubtedly, these will come to be reckoned with more explicitly as this conversation unfolds and the impact of these developments become clearer. The ideological self-awareness of the space thought of as English Studies has evidently not diminished since 2013, quite the contrary. What G.J.V. Prasad saw as the propensity of English departments to 'contest the terms of their relevance' seems to me to bring inquiries into texts and languages, socio-cultural analysis and political-economic critique ever closer.

Such political-economic developments have, in fact, had a palpable effect on English studies in various higher education contexts, internationally. The conflicts that are studied and encountered in India are as much national as international. Engaging with English Studies in India inevitably implicates much more than India. This is evident in most of the contributions to this volume. The fluid boundaries of English Studies are constantly and numerously subjected to assessments of its 'global', 'transnational', 'planetary', 'cosmopolitan', etc. scope – arguably more so than any other Humanities area. Such assessments appear from an extraordinarily diverse range of socio-linguistic zones around the world, many of which are not ordinarily Anglophone or do not designate English an official language. In every instance, a balance is struck in taking possession of the area in terms of its local nuances and, thereby, placing that locale in the wider world. This balance is invariably extended in an inclusive spirit, keeping the self and all possible others in view. The more the boundaries of difference proliferate within the field, the more expansive and interconnected the field becomes. At this current juncture of expanding ethno-nationalist conflicts and nationalist protectionism around the world, this spirit of unbounded inclusiveness is very much worth underlining. That spirit is well exemplified in this volume.

As through much of her post-Independence history, the place of the English language in India continues to be beleaguered and yet irrepressible. On 7 April 2022, Union Home Minister Amit Shah rekindled anxieties about the status of English by proposing in a public address that people of different states should communicate with each other in Hindi, not in English. He observed: 'Now the time has come to make the Official Language an important part of the unity of the country. When citizens of States who speak other languages communicate with each other, it should be in the language of India' (quoted in Express NS 2022). Since this was directed against the use of English, it was understood that English is not a language of India. There are many across the country who do not share this view. In response to Shah's exhortation, misgivings about the imposition of Hindi as a national language were expressed. Linguistic diversity, some reiterated, is a constitutive feature of the national formation. And some observed that the version of Hindi that Shah promotes has itself been deliberately alienated from the languages of India, for instance by being implausibly distanced from and promoted at the expense of Urdu. Whether the status of English in India will be reconsidered and pinned down in some formal way is, however, of little moment for the accommodative pursuits of English Studies. Rather, such debates are grist to the mill of English Studies in India, which seem likely to prosper in the foreseeable future.

10 July 2022

References

Dash, Santosh (2009). *English Education and the Question of Indian Nationalism: A Perspective on the Vernacular.* Delhi: Aakar.

Dutta, Nandana ed. (2022). *English Teachers' Accounts: Essays on the Teacher, the Text and the Indian Classroom.* Abingdon: Routledge.

Express News Service (2022). 'People from different states should speak in Hindi, not English: Amit Shah'. *Indian Express*, 9 April. https://indianexpress.com/article/india/people-different-states-should-speak-hindi-not-english-shah-7858861/

Garg, Shweta Rao and Deepti Gupta eds. (2017). *The English Paradigm in India: Essays in Language, Literature and Culture.* Singapore: Springer Nature.

Graff, Graff (1992). *Beyond the Culture Wars: How Teaching the Conflicts Can Revitalize American Education.* New York: W.W. Norton.

Gupta, Suman, Richard Allen, Subarno Chattarji, and Supriya Chaudhuri eds. (2015). *Reconsidering English Studies in Indian Higher Education.* Abingdon: Routledge.

Mahanta, Banibrata and Rajesh Babu Sharma eds. (2019). *English Studies in India: Contemporary and Evolving Paradigms*. Singapore: Springer Nature.

Mukherjee, Alok (2009). *This Gift of English: English Education and the Formation of Alternative Hegemonies in India*. Delhi: Orient Blackswan.

Prasad, G.J.V. (2013). 'English Studies: A Personal Journey'. *Australian Literary Studies* 28:1–2. 40–49.

Saxena, Akshya (2022). *Vernacular English: Reading the Anglophone in Postcolonial India*. Princeton, NJ: Princeton University Press.

Sethi, Rachna and A.L. Khanna eds. (2020). *Dialogues: English Studies in India*. Delhi: Aakar.

Tasildar, Ravindra Baburao (2019). *English Studies in Indian Universities: The Present Scenario*. Newcastle upon Tyne: Cambridge Scholars.

INTRODUCTION

The retirement of Professor GJV Prasad from the Centre for English Studies (earlier named Centre for Linguistics and English) in November 2020, after 41 years of teaching at the Jawaharlal Nehru University (JNU), New Delhi, amidst the distressing Covid-19 pandemic, gave his former and current students a rare and motivating occasion to connect digitally and rethink respective journeys with him as well as the discipline of English studies. As notes were compared across generations of students through memory books, Zoom farewells, YouTube tributes, Facebook–Instagram posts and in-person meetings, the editors of this volume coalesced around the idea of this Festschrift as a means of honouring GJV as a memorable and beloved teacher.

GJV, as he is fondly called, started his teaching career in JNU at the turn of the 1980s when JNU was barely a decade old. As a teacher, he wore many hats. Arriving as a novelist and poet, he began by teaching proficiency in English language before transitioning to teaching literature; first drama, then poetry, the novel, Indian writing in English and other courses. In a country like India, this was perhaps an apt trajectory because anyone seeking to teach English literature has to sooner or later reckon with teaching the language as well. The discipline and Indian English literature itself are still fraught with constant tensions between language and literature. It is a given that there are enormous asymmetries in English language proficiency among students in any classroom and more so in JNU with its unique deprivation points' admission policy aimed to admit students from diverse and deprived backgrounds from across India. So, even while English studies has remained an aspirational discipline to gain entry into the corridors of power

DOI: 10.4324/9781003399926-1

and culture, the journeys of both English literature and English language in India have progressively been of democratization and anti-elitism, and GJV has been an integral part of those journeys.

In the 1980s, English literary studies were still coming to terms with English writings in India. In 1962, KR Srinivasa Iyengar took the first comprehensive stock of *Indian Writing in English* in his expansive book of the same name. But he was still wondering whether 'Indo-Anglian' literature, as it was called then, should be evaluated as 'a minor tributary of English literature' or as another tributary of Indian literature (Iyengar, 1985: 5). By 1965, linguist Braj B Kachru began emphasizing the *Indianness* of Indian English (Kachru, 1965). In the early 1970s, Meenakshi Mukherjee, another stalwart, made a compelling case for evaluating 'Indo-Anglian' novels not as a part of the wider tradition of the English novel, but independently, as a 'branch of Indian fiction'.[1] In 1982, MK Naik was still grappling with a suitable nomenclature and used 'Indian English Literature' instead, emphasizing unity with Indian literature across many languages as well as an Indian sensibility.[2]

The decades of the 1980s and 1990s were poised for great upheavals in the discipline of English literary studies in India. The focus of English studies started shifting away from Anglo-American literature and liberal humanism in both course content and pedagogic approach. The twin impulses of postcolonial theory and feminism generated heated debates within the academia. One of the first important interventions was Gauri Viswanathan's *Masks of Conquest: Literary Study and British Rule in India* (1989). Soon, there were other crucial contributions in the form of edited and authored volumes and collections proposing concrete changes in course content, syllabi and theoretical paradigms – Rajeswari Sunder Rajan (ed.) *The Lie of the Land: English Literary Studies in India* (1991); Svati Joshi (ed.) *Rethinking English: Essays in Literature, Language, History* (1991); GN Devy, *After Amnesia: Tradition and Change in Literary Criticism* (1992) and *In Another Tongue: Essays on Indian English Literature* (1995); Kapil Kapoor and RS Gupta (ed.) *English in India* (1991) and *Language, Linguistics and Literature: The Indian Perspective* (1994); Susie Tharu (ed.) *Subject to Change: Teaching of Literature in the Nineties* (1998). As will be discussed in a section evaluating contemporary course content, the reaches of these debates were perhaps confined to the more metropolitan universities.

The nomenclature for Indian English writing also evolved after several revisions (each turn emphasizing a different focus) – initially fraudulently called Anglo-Indian literature, then Indo-Anglian literature emphasizing the Indianness of English literature with Anglian orientation, Indo-English literature focusing on the uniqueness of language as well as emphasizing the base in English, Indian writing in English with Indian being its cornerstone, Indian English writing that was more accommodative of ancestry and sensibility than nationality or location, the hyphenated Indian English writing denoting a register of language irrespective of location or nationality and anglophone literature indicative of English language literatures within the wider body of world literatures. The nomenclature for literature in other Indian languages also weathered changes, variably labelled vernacular literature, employed mainly to qualify not quite fully developed colonial languages; literature in Indian languages used often to demarcate Indian-origin languages from English, regional language literature, that ran into a wall with increasing migration and geographical spread, and *bhasha* literature, as coined or re-coined by GN Devy, to accept English as one of India's own languages but to still distinguish it from other languages. These labels were indicative of the evolving positions on the significance and relation of Indian writing in English and *bhasha* literature.

The publication of Salman Rushdie's *Midnight's Children* in 1981 established international affinities across the anglophone and Western world in a dramatic fashion. Rushdie followed this up in 1983 with an essay that was much discussed in India, '"Commonwealth Literature" Does Not Exist', where he termed it a 'phantom category' that served to obscure, divide, ghettoize and hierarchize literatures written in English language with the presumption that literature somehow has to be an expression of nationality and tradition, and hence authentic.[3] This 'authenticity' debate about Indian English literature continued well beyond the turn of the century involving Meenakshi Mukherjee, Amit Chaudhuri, Vikram Chandra, Rajeshwari Sunder Rajan and others amidst fraught relations between English and other Indian language literatures from India. After Rushdie's infamous observation about the lesser importance of literature in other official languages of India compared to English in 1997, VS Naipaul's dismissive insinuations about *bhasha* writers during his address to the grandiose opening of the 2002 ICCR Conference inaugurated by the then Prime Minister of India, titled *At Home in the World*, only added more fuel to fire (Saccidānandan et. all, 2005). Such admonitions perhaps had a positive spin-off by spurring frantic translation activities in India.

More recently the authenticity debate 2.0 has acquired an English-versus-English dimension, or the new-versus-the-old English-speaking middle classes in India, with popular and commercially successful writers like Chetan Bhagat arguing that 'I want to tell the "English types" what India is all about. They don't own the language and my question to them is, will you not give someone a voice just because you don't like their accent'.[4] Since the beginning of the new century, Dalit intellectuals like Kancha Illiah and Chandra Bhan Prasad have also been staking claims to greater access to the English language for pursuing social justice in India, arguing that the politics of mother-tongue education has been a great deception engineered by the ruling classes and upper castes upon the oppressed castes to deprive them of English-medium education and hence access to resources and power (Illiah 2005, Prasad 2001). The past decade has also witnessed many regional political parties that were earlier opposed to English-medium education, modifying their positions to more nuanced ones.

The role and status of the English language have undergone changes in the post-globalization era. The context, scholars argue, has shifted from multilingual to metro-lingual wherein 'people of different and mixed backgrounds use, play with and negotiate identities through language. The focus is not so much on language systems as on languages as emergent from contexts of interaction'.[5] Teachers are also well aware of the changing terrain of the *bhashas* in India. While there are still a substantial number of students who struggle with the English language, it has become practically impossible to get students who can speak consistently in their mother tongues without a spattering of English. So, the penetration of the English language into the *bhashas* has increased manifold in recent times. In popular culture, the all-India popularity of a 2011 film song like 'Why This Kolaveri Di' in Tanglish (a mixture of Tamil and English) perhaps best exemplified the growing trend wherein the inadequacies of the umbrella term 'Indian English' paved the way for Hinglish, Tanglish, Kanglish, Tenglish, etc., denoting the admixture of English with Hindi, Tamil, Kannada and Telugu, etc., respectively. Linguist Suzette Haden Elgin has termed such usage 'panglish' (Elgin, 2004).

Similarly, the umbrella term 'Indian English literature' has also given way to disability literature, gender and sexuality studies, literature from the Northeast, Dalit literature, partition literature, children's literature, etc. In the post-globalization period, course content for undergraduate studies in English literature has exploded into a frantic reckoning with diversity, departing from an earlier notion of depth and history of BritLit. Today, our courses are formed from a wide range of literature and genres – British, American, European, World, African, Latin American, Classical, Popular, Translation, Indian English – as well as a wide range of issues – gender, caste, tribe, race, nation, colonialism/post-colonialism, diaspora, etc. Independent courses are variably organized around genre, period, location, style, theme, language, etc. Even while many literary canons have been dismantled, others have been re-configured, with texts often lending themselves to different interpretations of the application of literary theory. Theory, while often being a cementing factor, also remains contentious in India; with prevalent pedagogies across as well as within departments, ranging from approaches rooted in pre-theory, theory and post-theory, as also a desire for more home-grown thought. Moreover, since it is difficult to teach all courses and issues at the undergraduate level, syllabi are divided into core/compulsory and an ever-growing list of elective courses leaving many wondering if the whole amounts to greater than the sum of the parts. The result is often a cornucopia of course offerings which include the 'residual' as well as the 'emergent', to borrow Raymond Williams' terms, wherein it may be difficult either to assess the overall landscape of English literary studies in India today or to see a clear direction for it. The everyday realities of our contexts of globalization, caste, patriarchy, religious fundamentalism and post-truth force us to confront the question of whether we are adequately addressing the needs and challenges of today.

Increasingly, there is also a digital divide that confronts the discipline of English studies, never more than during the Covid-19 pandemic, when digital education has become the order of the day. A growing number of students are feeling left out even as others are engaging in voracious online reading, which is often rapid, open-ended, multi-sequential, unfinished, intertextual and fragmentary (Landow, 1992). The unwieldy and disorganized web archive is fast becoming integral to contemporary educational practices. Teachers in the classroom are no longer the central source of knowledge for students. In such a context, it is impossible to either dismiss or offer unqualified endorsement of the web archive. How do we conceive of better ways to aid our students in working along with the anarchy of the web and yet develop critical thinking that is organized, methodological and coherent? Moreover, what do we do for students who do not have equal access to the web?

As has been stressed in this introduction, the 1990s were a tumultuous time for 'English' studies in India, with many departments and academics questioning the basis of the very ground on which they stood and the landscape of English studies changing radically with new ideas and frameworks. These theoretical frameworks formed the context for discussions of pedagogical practices in the classroom; Susie Tharu talks of 'alienation' as a dominant motif in this thinking in this context – alienation from the context of teaching/reading, alienation from the texts, students alienated from the teachers and classroom concerns and the practice alienated from the theory. Ania Loomba takes it further while discussing the experiences of teaching Shakespeare in JNU as well as of trying to practice a particular kind of pedagogy and approach – one of questioning, of critical inquiry and of democratization of the classroom, in every possible way. Loomba raises the idea that students found it easier to say what they thought of Georgette Heyer rather than Macbeth. One of the aspects of GJV's classes that initially took most students by surprise was precisely this democratization of texts – you could discuss Heyer or Christie in literally the same breath as Plath or Shakespeare, and it would be discussed with equal seriousness. You could even discuss mainstream Hindi cinema (Bollywood) and not have it treated as a dirty little secret.

Amidst these unfolding changes and questions, GJV's pedagogic approach was uniquely poised to accommodate these different nodes within the classroom and for research. Any commentary or description of GJV's academic career would be seriously lacking without discussing his classroom teaching and methodologies in some detail. Instead of placing the teacher on a pedestal, with a largely one-way communication from the teacher to students, GJV, after a few introductory lectures, would allow students to bring in their own interests, perspectives and interpretations into his seminar courses. The 1990s were also a time when different critical and pedagogical approaches to overcoming the 'alienation' and 'elitism' of the English literature classroom were being debated and written about. There have been several notable seminars and publications on this very subject; however, there are those who teach/write and those who learn – one of the most under-rated aspects of sitting in a class taught by GJV in JNU in the 1990s was how gently but precisely you were made aware of the un/conscious privileges of class and cultural capital you assumed. Even the most strident leftist Marxist students speaking from high pedestals of theory and political thought would be pulled short – not by a sarcastic comment or rebuke but by a quiet exposure of privilege.

It was at this time that the 'silencing' of students from less privileged sociolinguistic backgrounds was noticed and commented – the idea of speaking a deracinated and flattened English was debunked, and literally every single voice was sought to be heard – GJV's classes put all this theory into practice. The so-called vernacular languages or *bhashas* of India – the languages many students spoke at home – were slowly being given some importance in the English studies classroom. Perhaps it was 'JNU', perhaps it was GJV's self-claimed status as an 'outsider', *In Delhi without a Visa* as his first collection of poetry was titled, that all languages were allowed, indeed celebrated, in the 'English' classroom. The very course titles – Literature in English other than British – were a marker of the non-anglocentric and non-anglophonic environment we lived in.

Reframing the canon – JNU of course gave the faculty and students a dream location, where there were no 'syllabi' and no canonical lists written in stone. The courses were simply given 'placeholder' names – Drama I, Drama II, The Novel I and so on. In the poetry class, the canon was not even acknowledged – it was debunked by students being encouraged to select anything for presentations, including rock lyrics and pop songs. These were subject to the same intense academic scrutiny that Plath or Yeats or Tagore would receive, and as a bonus, we could discuss the difference between 'poetry' and 'rhyming'. The texts chosen for study, it can be argued, reflected the choice of the faculty member – the 'teacher' – in this case, the students were 'taught' that they had as much choice and right to exercise that choice as anybody else. The only consultation they had with the 'teacher' was sometimes the availability of texts. Students learnt many things in these courses other than academic theory and analysis – we learnt about our own proclivities as academics – how many of us selected texts that were 'easy' or had a large amount of secondary material to enable us to not really think independently and how many selected texts for abstract or shock value. The advantages of choosing texts that had hefty critical support quickly disappeared in the classroom, subject to intense questioning and cross-examination by fellow students who had equal access to secondary material, while the benefits of presenting an individual (I won't say 'original') point of view meant that you could have an honest and surprisingly smooth discussion in class.

Since students were already trained in approaches to literature during their undergraduate education before joining the English Studies Centre of JNU in a course on poetry for instance, students were encouraged to bring linguistic and generic diversity into class. Pop and rock song lyrics, limericks, folk and ritual songs, canonical and non-canonical poets of multiple languages from across the world or India could be discussed without judgement. Theory could speak to non-theory, personal interpretations could strike conversations with social justice, and so on. With GJV's gentle moderation, debates remained vibrant and interesting without descending into bitterness. During his classes and engagement with research scholars, GJV accomplished what was not easy – canons were demolished and reconstructed, diverse methodologies were able to speak to each other, and generations of students were able to find their voice, confidence and literary niches. The fact that his classes continued with voluntary participation of students far exceeding the designated hours speaks volumes about his method.

In his own career, GJV has been a creative writer of novels and poetry, an academic expert on drama, a translator, the writer of a book on food and published critically evaluative volumes on Vikram Seth, Amitav Ghosh, John Osborne and Samuel Beckett apart from translating and writing his own poetry and novels. GJV Prasad started his higher education like many other young people then and now. He quit Engineering to better his writing skills in the English Department at the University of Delhi. The time of serious introspection and self-questioning for those involved in studying and teaching English in India began in the 1970s, as the aftermath of the language agitations (anti-English in the North and anti-Hindi in the South), the Naxalite movement and the general atmosphere post-Emergency.

'Searching for relevance', in his own words, GJV looked for Indian writers in English and came to the grim realization that he passed on to students many decades later: 'good Indian English writing' did not emerge from Indians living/writing in India! Although stalwarts like CD Narasimhaiah and Srinivasa Iyengar had ensured that by the 1990s Indian writing in English was part of most syllabi in Indian universities, unlike the well-funded American and Canadian programmes, Indian English courses and teachers did not get much financial support to run seminars or do research.

Joining JNU as a part-time teacher in late 1979, GJV found himself in a very different setting from his initial training at Delhi University. Apart from being much smaller and more focused on postgraduate teaching, the Centre for Linguistics and English (CLE), as it was then known, took language teaching very seriously unlike most (if not all) other English departments. The MA English programme that was revived in CLE in the 1980s was also unique, emphasizing on non-British literature, especially Indian writing.

The 1990s were a heady decade for those interested in Indian writing in English, and GJV's own bent towards creative writing and poetry resulted in several publications. Displaying a broad range that was equally matched with depth in critical thinking, GJV published on Amitav Ghosh, Indian English poetry, postcolonial theory, Tamil fiction, translation theory and, of course, drama and theatre. Alongside his research he taught a large number of courses on British and non-British drama, novels, poetry and English in India, inspiring and supervising generations of scholars who started their careers arguing and debating endlessly in GJV's classroom.

GJV's particular interest in translation worked at both the theoretical and practical level – aware of the multiple cultural minefields of translation, he wrote on the form and the process and published his own translations. Continuing to translate Tamil writing apart from writing his own novels and poetry, GJV has always been ahead of the curve; he was working on literature other than British before mainstream departments were being funded to teach them, working on translations and translation theory before *bhashas* and indigenous writings became buzzwords. Inspired by his personal classroom experience he has worked on the Northeast, Dalit writing and Disability Studies, before they were 'canonized' and included in graduate and postgraduate programmes.

While English literature programmes continue to be one of the most sought after degrees in contemporary India, the curricula for these programmes themselves have represented contestation over the last several decades. In this respect, there are two parallel approaches to the discipline. 'English' as a discipline is taught in most Indian universities, but the titles of the programmes remain ambiguous. The title can imply the programme of study being the study of 'English Literature' or of the 'English Language'. Little has changed over the last three decades. Writing in 1995, Harish Trivedi noted that

> an English teacher's first and often last job in India is … to reduce the most creative and the most inventive use of English ever to a paraphrase at the level of fairly elementary ESL (English as a Second Language).[6]

Populating such classrooms would be students who have thus far been schooled in non-English mediums of education and who were subjects of the pedagogic method of 'learning English language through literature'. At the other end is the study of 'Literature' as an entry point to learning about a culture – as inaugurated by the Macaulayan project or about critical approaches to literature and culture. Interested in this second approach are students whose primary interests lie not in learning English as the language of power. They are ones who may have various degrees of interest in learning literary texts. Writing in 2019, Somdev Banik almost echoes Trivedi when he notes that majority of Indian universities 'are in semi-urban areas and small towns in different states to cater to students, majority of whom come from families with almost no literary or basic education background'. So 'English' classrooms in India comprise 'broadly of two categories of students – the anglicised English-medium educated from privileged backgrounds and the ... vernacular-medium educated from socially backward backgrounds'.[7] Banik further locates a distinction between approaches to degrees in English between metro and non-metro universities. 'Many students in the small-town universities', he writes, 'take this course for it endows them with a social recognition and height' as well as opening avenues to job opportunities where proficiency in the English language is a prerequisite. Thus, Trivedi and Banik, writing years apart, note a distance between the approaches to 'English' degrees from the viewpoints of language and literature learning. Both of them note the dilemma of the framers of syllabi as they have to cater to these divergent motives for 'English' education in contemporary Indian universities.

But beneath this apparent similarity between the two points of time lies another reality that is vastly different. In an article on the growth of Indian universities, Pankaj Jalote notes the exponential growth of the number of universities and degree-granting institutions in India since the year 2000. While in the early decades of independence India saw the creation of several institutions of higher education – notably the Indian Institutes of Technology (IITs), University of Hyderabad, Jawaharlal Nehru University, Jadavpur University and All India Institute of Medical Sciences (AIIMS) – most of these institutions were located in the metropolitan cities of India. In 1980, there were less than 200 degree-granting institutions in India.[8] The growth was linear at a rate of 'about 5 to 6 universities every year'. Between 2000 and 2015, however, this expanded from 240 in 2000 to over 750 in 2015, with about 35 new universities being added each year. This growth was multifaceted. Besides the numeric growth, higher education in India has grown geographically, expanding its scope to smaller towns and districts across India. Further, the deepening of affirmative action through successive legislations in this period brought into the fold of higher education first-generation learners who were the first graduates, postgraduates or doctorates in their families. Another area in which higher education expanded in India has been through involvement of the private sector. According to the

All India Report on Higher Education 2019–20 (AISHE), private un-aided colleges now constitute 65.2% of all colleges in the country. In certain states like Andhra Pradesh, this proportion is as high as 81%.[9] The applicability of policies of affirmative action, however, has not been extended by most private educational institutions.[10] This massive expansion in higher education needed to be supported by an increased recruitment of teachers who emerged from those who completed their postgraduate degrees from the institutions in the metropolitan cities, thus allowing these institutions to have an associated role in deciding and managing the academic structures of the emerging institutions. Though there is no reliable statistical record on what proportion of the degrees granted was in the domain of 'English', the AISHE noted that the total enrolment of the Arts courses among all undergraduate courses is 32.68% distributed among all 'Arts' disciplines.[11] Given the social position of 'English' recounted earlier, it is safe to assume that the subject would be a significant proportion of the Arts courses counted under the survey.

Besides being an integral participant in this story of expansion of higher education, the departments of English in various institutions have also been involved in a crucial task of remaking themselves in a process that came to be identified as the 'crisis in English studies in India'. According to Rajeswari Sunder Rajan, this 'crisis' commenced 'in the 1980s as a flurry of conferences organised by English departments and edited volumes arising from them, which began to articulate questions about the relevance of English studies' in India.[12] In what is now a well-documented shift in English literary studies in India, at the epicentre of this crisis is the discourse of decolonizing English literature curricula from a 'BritLit'-centric course to one that encompasses a much wider literary experience ranging from literatures in English in other English-speaking countries, former colonies as well as English translations of works written in various languages across the world, particularly in the Indian languages. Along with the agenda of questioning the colonial basis for the study of English literature in India, the efforts of change also sought to reframe the canon by including in the syllabi works by women and authors from under-represented identities. Moreover, this progressive vision of the curricula was to be informed by a study of critical theory that allowed students to approach these works as well as those of the hitherto dominant canon through pedagogical perspectives that led to feminist readings or readings that were critical of colonial race relations or dominant caste perspectives.[13] However, the task of reconfiguring the syllabi was not a task easily accomplished. For, alteration of syllabi was very often accompanied by questions of turf – or whether it would lead to a change in competencies? Were some people likely to lose their jobs? Such changes are invariably closely linked with publishing interests – whose text would fall out of demand or who would prepare and publish the new texts that would now be demanded?[14] Moreover, given that there has always been a market for oversimplified guidebooks or *kunjis* for the vast sections of students who are motivated greatly by examination preparedness, and the utility value of degrees, there has existed a nexus between syllabus framing and the bazaar for the *kunjis*.[15] And beyond the market forces, liberal or progressive efforts to alter syllabi are prone to suspicion and ire from conservative impulses among administrators and public opinion. Hence, there have always existed counter-currents that have aided and hindered syllabus restructuring. Banik notes that the loci of efforts to bring in progressive changes to English literature syllabi in the extended sphere of universities in non-metro locations in India, usually come from faculty who have been trained in the universities in the metro cities, prior to the year 2000 – 'many faculty members in non-metro universities are themselves products of elite universities having experienced "authentic and universal English teaching-learning" there and are eager to reproduce a similar teaching-learning experience at the local level'.[16] This divergent set of motivations and contexts of English literature pedagogy in the metro and non-metro locations has had a significant impact in the process of reframing of English literature syllabi in India.

In the 1995 essay quoted earlier, Harish Trivedi had suggested a strategy for easing out English literature as 'master literature'. He termed it as a 'Panchadhatu' (five elements) model.[17] The five elements are (1) literature written in English in England; (2) literature written in English in English-speaking countries other than England; (3) literature written in various languages across the world other than English, but available in English translation; (4) literature in an Indian language that is prevalent in the region where the particular university is located, such literature being studied not in translation but in the original; and (5) the study of classical literature in the original. While proposing this model, Trivedi acknowledges that some of these elements – particularly the fifth – may 'prove to be more unfamiliar and ambitious still' but opines that access to classical literature is 'an essential and indispensable preparation for the reading of modern literatures which have grown out of particular classical literatures'. Trivedi's model of a concentric widening of the circle of literature for study in 'English literature' classrooms is but one model for reconfiguring English literature syllabi in India. Various commentators, particularly those noted above, have called for the inclusion of more literature by women and other under-represented sections of the population.

Given this background of the great expansion of higher education on the one hand and a concerted effort to expand the scope of English literary studies in India on the other since the 1980s, it is time for us to once again ask the questions: 'is English literature still the master literature' for English literary studies? What are the new areas which now populate the syllabi for English literature programmes – what is the spread? In order to answer these questions we undertook a quantitative study of 12 top-ranking institutions in India according to the QS World University Ranking 2020 and 2021 – considering only those universities that have a graduation or post-graduation programme in English available on their institutional websites.[18] Alongside this, we also mapped the question papers of the National Eligibility Test for Lecturership overseen by the University Grants Commission, popularly known as the UGC-NET. These examinations are conducted twice a year, and we have analyzed the question papers for the examinations that were held between 2004 and 2020. The UGC-NET in English is a qualifying examination for anyone with a master's degree who wishes to apply for the position of an Assistant Professor in an institution that receives aid from or is fully funded by the University Grants Commission on behalf of the Indian government. Various state governments in India conduct State-Level Eligibility Tests (SLET) for Lecturership, but these examinations are close approximations of the UGC-NET. Given that the NET examinations form the gateway to an academic career, they act as a de facto arbiter of curricula. For the purpose of this study, we accessed the electronic files of the syllabi and extracted the titles of the various courses and the names of the authors included for study under each of them. We then extracted the date of birth, citizenship and gender of each of the authors from the Wikidata database. Unfortunately, Wikidata does not record any intersectional data on specific identities or groups that particular authors emerge from. To discover inter-sectionality of various authors as represented in the syllabi, we relied on the titles of the various courses under which the university curricula have housed the works. It should be noted that there were several courses, especially in the categories of English Language Teaching, Linguistics and Language Studies or Academic Writing that did not prescribe the study of specific literary or critical works. In such cases, only the course titles were included as part of the dataset. We further classified the various place names – both contemporary and historical into larger groups, viz. (1) United Kingdom (UK), (2) Australia, Canada and Ireland, (3) United States of America (USA), (4) Rest of Europe, (5) India and (6) Asia, Africa and Latin America. This classification was guided by the debates on extension of the scope of English literary studies beyond the 'BritLit' canon. The mapping also considered the gender and period of activity of the said authors. It should be noted that certain universities like Pondicherry University and Jadavpur University do not specify complete syllabi for their elective courses on their websites, providing either the title of the course only or at best an indicative course outline.

Figures 0.1 (a) and (b) visualize the distribution of the authors of works prescribed in the syllabi followed by the various universities. The distribution is divided between core and elective courses. Also included in the chart for comparison is the distribution of authors for the UGC-NET question papers for the year 2019–2020. The figures clearly demonstrate a stark

(a)

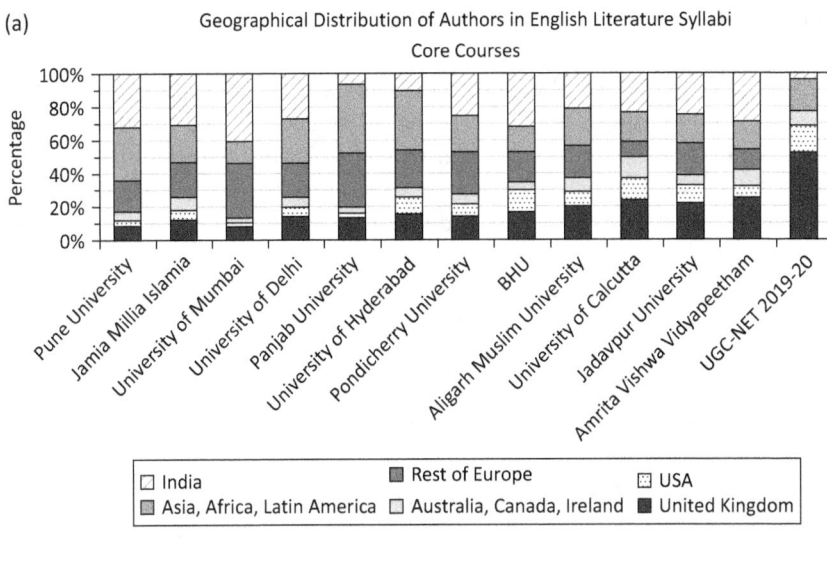

(b)

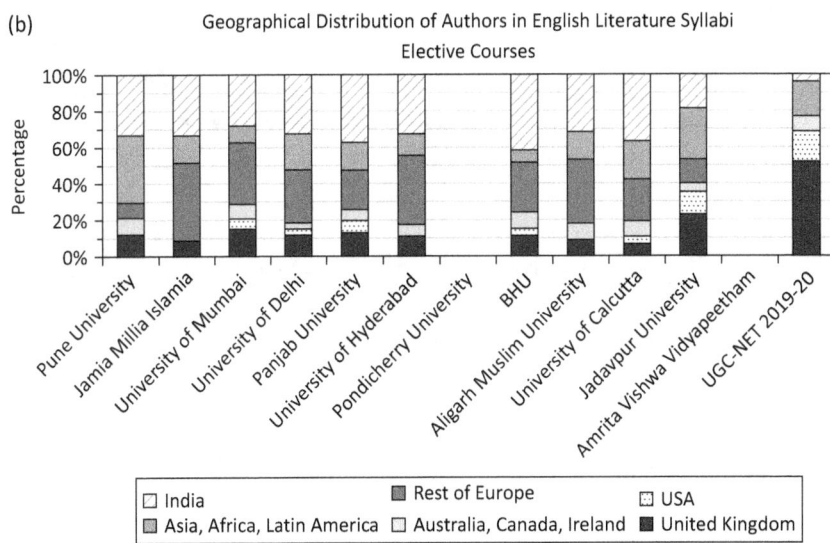

FIGURE 0.1   (a) Geographical Distribution of Authors in English Literature Syllabi: Core Courses; (b) Geographical Distribution of Authors in English Literature Syllabi: Elective Courses

difference between the UGC-NET examination and the syllabi of the universities included in the study. While 51.89% of the questions in the UGC-NET concern authors identified with the 'United Kingdom' place category, this category accounts for an average of only 14.76% in the university syllabi.

If one includes the collective figure of the place categories – the UK, the USA, Australia, Canada, Ireland and the Rest of Europe – the corresponding figures are 76.33% for the UGC-NET and 48% for the university syllabi. For authors broadly labelled within the category of 'India', the shares are a mere 3.88% for the UGC-NET compared to 29.16% for the universities. Thus, we find that there exists a non-trivial difference between the contents of the UGC-NET, which seeks to certify faculty for the English literature classrooms in India and the top Indian universities that produce graduates in English.

Now let us look at the time distribution of authors in the two contrasting datasets. Figure 0.2(a) shows the distribution of authors identified in UGC-NET questions between 2004 and 2020, according to the periods of their activity and the place categories. Figure 0.2(b) maps a similar distribution for authors whose works have been prescribed for study in the universities

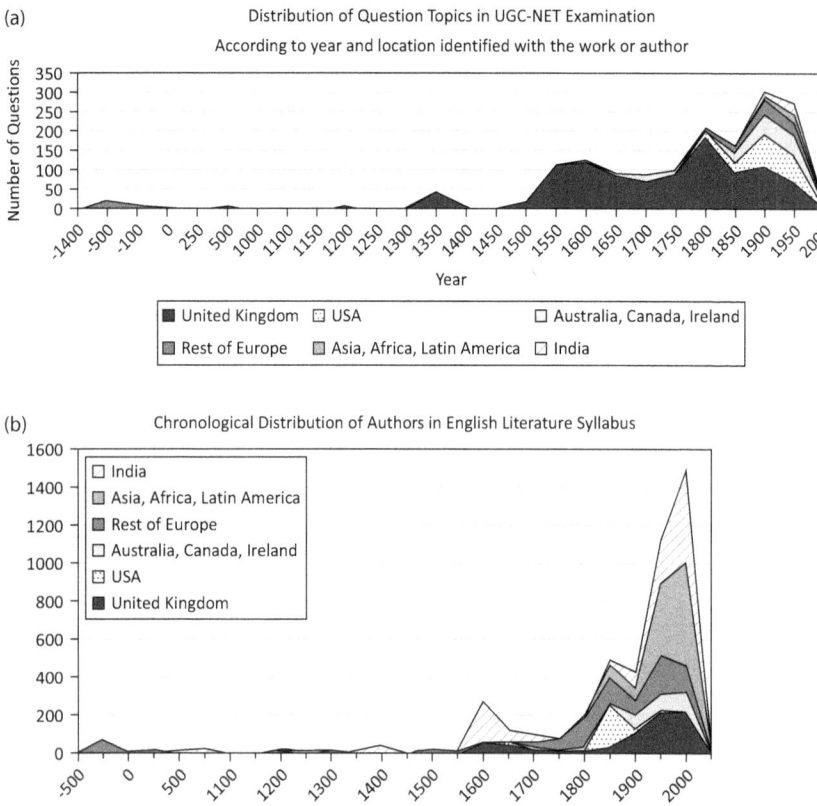

FIGURE 0.2 (a) Distribution of Question Topics in UGC-NET Examination (according to Year and Location Identified with the Work or Author); (b) Chronological Distribution of Authors in English Literature Syllabus

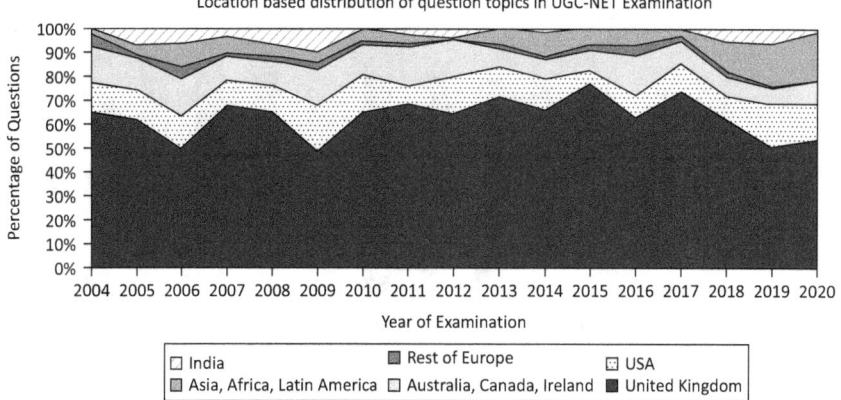

FIGURE 0.3   Location-Based Distribution of Question Topics in UGC-NET Examination

under study. The UGC-NET chart demonstrates that though the UGC-NET has sought to test candidates on their knowledge of non-British authors as well, this inclusion has only considered authors who have operated in the last 150 years. Thus, the examination still attributes to literature produced in Britain the status of 'master literature', the knowledge of which it sees as fundamental to trace a tradition of literary practice. By contrast, the 12 universities under study trace for their students an extended and diverse tradition of literary practice. The exception being the literary tradition of the 'Asia, Africa, Latin America' space category, where a bulk of the authors belong to the twentieth century.

Thus, we find that the UGC-NET has resisted the trend to redefine English literary studies as a field that extends beyond the 'BritLit' canon and be more inclusive of non-British works and indeed more works from India and the Global South. But a closer look would show that the UGC-NET's distribution of authors and works has not been static. Figure 0.3 presents a stacked area chart that shows the distribution of authors identified with various place categories across the years – data being available only for the years 2004–2020. The chart shows that though the dominance of 'United Kingdom' in the share of question topics has remained unchallenged, its extent has varied in the range of 50%–75%. In recent years, however, the UGC-NET has sought to increase testing candidates for their knowledge of works by American and European authors.

On the issue of the gender of the authors in question, however, there is a greater agreement between the UGC-NET and the university syllabi (Figure 0.4). While 89.84% of the authors identified in the UGC-NET dataset

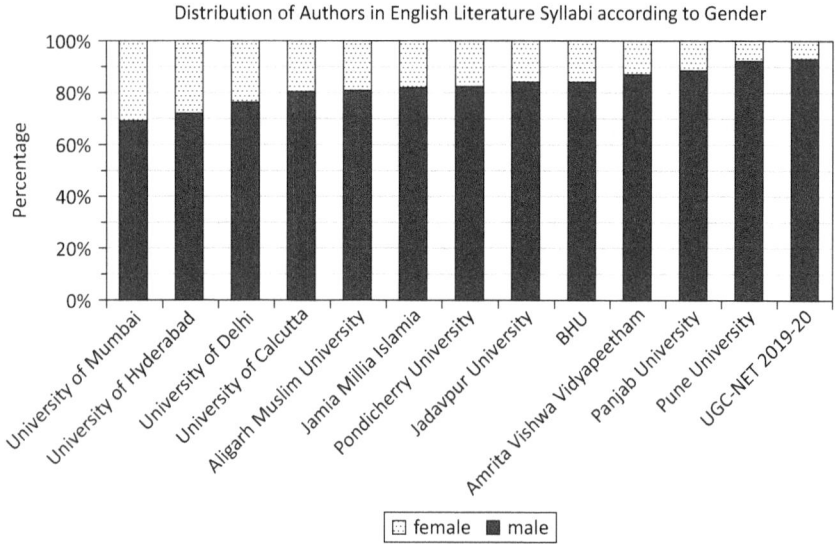

FIGURE 0.4 Distribution of Authors in English Literature Syllabi according to Gender

are male, the corresponding share for the university syllabi is 80.62%. There is, of course, a degree of variation among the universities in this regard with the University of Mumbai having the highest share (31.25%) of texts authored by women.

A return to Figures 0.1(a) and (b) will show that there exists a similar tension among these 12 top-ranked universities with regard to the geographical distribution of authors. Let us take the University of Hyderabad as an example. The Department of English, University of Hyderabad, offers a Master of Arts programme in English. The current study included the syllabus for this programme as it existed in the year 2020. The core courses for this programme, the prescribed texts by authors identified as belonging to the place category 'India', amounted to 10.10% of the total texts. By contrast, the corresponding share of such authors in the elective courses is 32.21%. The figures for the MA programme in English offered by Panjab University, Chandigarh, are 6.45% for core courses and 37.06% for elective courses. Thus, we find that the impulse for expanding the scope of English literary studies achieves greater propensity in the design of elective courses. Core courses approximate closer to the UGC-NET pattern of questioning. Clearly, the scholars and administrators who deliberate on the framing of syllabi are affected by the ground rules set by the UGC-NET. It needs to be noted that the universities that we have included in this study are from the larger cities of the country. The UGC-NET maintains the balance of forces between the 'metro' and 'non-metro' institutions and between the 'English-type' and 'non-English-type' students. The effect of the UGC-NET on curriculum in 'non-metro' locations can be the theme of another study.

As has already been pointed out, it is difficult to take stock of the landscape of English literary studies in India today amidst the creative chaos of the new and emergent and the residual structures of the classical canons. This collection of chapters from scholars who are outstanding voices in the field as well as sharing a deep and affectionate network with GJV Prasad attempts to do that. With essays ranging from Covid-19 to corporate imperialism, from Kashmiri literature to Henry James, we hope that this collection will not only mark our gratitude and respect for GJV but also be of some value to the area of literary studies in English in India.

An invaluable contribution to this collection, M Asaduddin's review of how the histories of Indian literature have been written, 'Rethinking and Resituating Histories of Indian Literature(s)', maps the specific problems of historiography in the multilingual society that is India. The easier connections between language and literature or nation and literature don't work quite so well here, and Asaduddin shows the pitfalls of undertaking this project in our social and political milieu. Taking into account the politics of selection itself, this chapter looks at the genealogies of history writing in India, drawing attention specifically to the gaps, erasures and silences. Departing from the conventional practice of tracing literary histories within one language, Asaduddin looks at 'language clusters', translations and inter-literary conditions, bringing a fresh perspective on regional relations and interactions without privileging 'unity' over diversity and cultural specificity. Drawing attention to the often-ignored connections between ideology and historiography, this chapter reminds us of the effects of deliberately excluding Urdu and Persian literatures from histories and formations of 'Indian' literature.

This volume was conceived and put together during the Covid-19 pandemic. In the first of two chapters that look at literary and scholarly responses to a pandemic-like crisis, Rukmini Bhaya Nair retreats into spaces of three literary texts that centre around large health and humanitarian crises from across the centuries. In her chapter, 'Coronavirus Spacesuits: Or, Hard Times As Launching Pads for Literary Travel', Nair argues that located strongly within their own histories, these texts can serve as guiding lights for the psychological, moral and social survival strategies of the human species and the human spirit in times of challenges that threaten civilization. Nair bases her study on Giovanni Boccaccio's *The Decameron* (1353), Knut Hamsun's *Hunger* (1890) and Albert Camus's *The Plague* (1947). The chapter ends with Nair's experience of having to change track in the middle of a semester's coursework, interrupted by Covid-19 – the opportunity allowing the class to study Camus's text to contemplate the position of the individual who was suddenly plunged into isolation and social distancing in the early days of the Covid-19 pandemic.

History repeats itself through pandemics. The bubonic plague of the 1890s and 1900s and the 1918–1919 Spanish flu are notable evidence that brings in the resonance of the colonial past. While history provides stern lessons, it also opens up, from a postcolonial perspective, the 'trauma of colonialism' and colonial policies. In her chapter, 'The Pandemic and the Postcolonial', Meena T Pillai interrogates how Covid-19 as a 'history of the present' has profoundly influenced the meaning of the postcolonial as a 'political, cultural, and social collective'. By doing so, she argues that 'conventional Western-centric colonial hierarchies' have been challenged while simultaneously 'reinforcing the neo-imperial agenda of the contemporary capital'. As she teases out the complex interplay between politics and the ambiguity/uncertainty of the prevailing pandemic, Pillai writes,

> the latest pandemic has been instrumental in mooting the idea that public health is a global issue, thus in a sense destabilising, however slightly, the neo-colonial slant to public health and well-being, and its patronising lingo when referring to developing or once colonized nations.

An example of India being requested for medicines and its vaccine diplomacy is explained as an indicator of a significant turn or paradigm shift where the past flow of Western knowledge and medicine from the dominant centre to the less-dominant periphery is reversed and no longer 'a colonial tool for installing power and subjugating colonised population'. That said, Covid-19 has equally exposed how the virus, while having crossed borders with impudence, is defined largely by policy actions within the national territory exerting inordinate power and surveillance of a vast population. The author concludes by observing that while the pandemic has emphatically reversed colonialist hierarchies, it has allowed for a re-emergence of Orientalist discourses, especially in the postcolonial states in Asia, characterized with deep-seated racism, inefficiency and irresponsibility and expressed in the nomenclature like the 'Chinese virus' or the 'Wuhan virus'. A fitting end line, 'The post in the postcolonial will remain suspended in a supreme state of exception', leaves us with much to think about.

Mala Pandurang takes us on a personal journey in her chapter 'From "Commonwealth" to "Global South": Engaging with African Literature in Indian Literary Studies'. This deeply personal account demonstrates the linkages between our individual contexts, institutions of academia, the importance of a body like the Indian Association for Commonwealth Literature and Language Studies (IACLALS) and our scholarly perspectives and growth. Pandurang traces the changes in curricula in postgraduate English departments as they slowly (and perhaps superficially) included 'newer national canons' of India, North America and Australia influenced by the radical scholarship of Svati Joshi, Rajeshwari Sunder Rajan, Bill Ashcroft, Gauri Vishwanathan and others. Outlining in rich detail how African literature was introduced and framed by Euro-American paradigms of availability, translatability and award-ability, Pandurang's chapter lays out the opportunities, challenges and ideals of studying African literature from a unique on-the-ground perspective. This piece is an illuminating insight into the challenges, contexts and conditions of syllabus building in Indian universities.

In 'The State of the Stage: An Interview with Mahesh Dattani', Angelie Multani asks a series of key questions regarding Indian English Theatre in general and Dattani's works in particular. The conversation gives the reader a clear idea about the range of dramatic forms now available, the issues taken up by playwrights in recent times and the changes in Indian English Theatre. Questions related to virtual performances, the role of art forms in ushering change in the fabric of society, the undervaluing of, drama and the underlining of its importance, theatre spaces, the academia, and theatre are all answered by Dattani through his personal experience and observations as a practising playwright.

'Performing the Dalit: A Reading of Dalit Plays' by B Mangalam examines the way in which Dalit literature and literary discourse have evolved in India and the potential of such literature and discourse in interrogating structures of power. In particular, the chapter chalks out the role of Dalit theatre, which additionally uses all the paraphernalia of performance to create a space for dialogue with the oppressed, not just from amongst the Dalits but from other groups marginalized by caste, race, gender, and sexuality. Through a close analysis of the plays of Premanand Gajvee and KA Gunasekaran, Mangalam, enables the reader 'to understand the dynamics of power, performance, and resistance in Marathi, Malayalam and Tamil Dalit theatre'. The two playwrights evidence through their plays the fact that Dalit performances are essentially those of resistance to 'casteist assertions in the domain of ideas, culture, electoral politics as well as against the unleashing of violence and marginalisation in academic and corporate work spaces'. Woven into the chapter is the history of the emergence and growth of Dalit literature in different Indian languages as well as its institutionalization as a discipline within educational institutions. This chapter is a meaningful insight into Dalit discourse, dynamics of theatre and a valuable contribution to the understanding of Dalit literary history.

The chapter, '"Interpreting Euripides" *Medea* in the Contemporary Indian Context', by Anuradha Marwah is an outcome of a play written by Marwah, in Hindustani as an adaptation of a classical Greek play, *Medea*, by Euripides. Performed by Pandies' Theatre with the original intention of bringing the classics to the layman, the play had over 15 shows and toured in Delhi and Rajasthan. Marwah joined the tour and was a part of the team from the inception through to the staging. The demand for the play to be staged on extremely varied platforms and its serving different purposes underscores the fact that though the original *Medea*, by *Euripides* is a classical Greek play, it can be meaningful even in the twenty-first century to audiences in India, urban or rural, young or old, academic or not. However, it is by no means an 'easy' play to interpret and perform, and Marwah's chapter traces the history of the staging of the play and the conflictual reception by a divided audience. There were those (feminists of the suffrage movement in England) for whom the play was almost iconic and thus a favourite, and there were those who vehemently opposed such archetyping. Besides these responses to its staging, Marwah talks about how challenging it is to represent *Medea* in a sympathetic manner. The chapter maps the way in which Marwah's adaptation spoke to the different audiences in India for whom it was performed and how each of these audiences made a play, much removed in time and culture, its own.

Keki N Daruwalla in his chapter, 'Poetry, Plague and Locusts: About Writing Sonnets on the Black Death', draws the backdrop of several pandemic situations that have plagued human civilization before he moves to sharing his own sonnets on the Black Death pandemic. He gives examples of the ways in which literature and litterateurs have dealt with pandemic situations – whether it be in the Bible, Petrarch or Shakespeare. He shares his own experience as a poet and how difficult it might be for a poet to express his thoughts through poetry on something like a pandemic. He also relates how he would choose which form of poetry to write if he chooses to write on the Black Death. Living during the Covid-19-induced pandemic in India and the locusts' invasion, he decided to write on the Black Death pandemic.

Udaya Kumar's 'Translation and Variation: Literary Studies, Reading Practices, and the Vernacular' is an incisive study into the variations of the meaning of translation. He elaborates through his experience of translating the works of Sree Narayana Guru from Malayalam to English, how translation does not mean a transfer merely from one language to another. It also involves transference from oral to the written, from performative to the academic. He aptly points out the processes of translation involved in the production of a text within the same language. That said, translation from a vernacular to the language of the colonizers has its own set of challenges – with the different registers from the 'physical and informal' and 'the ordinary and the everyday' to the 'impersonality' and 'reasoned argumentation' of the academic discourse in English, as just one instance of change that is needed. In explaining how linguistic variations work within the same language, he discusses the undeniable aspect of caste, the 'oral-formulaic', the importance of the mnemonic exercise, the vernacular element and the effects of the local and regional cultures. Significantly, Udaya Kumar explores translation not as a mere linguistic but also as a cultural activity.

Santosh K Sareen in his chapter, 'Of Dreamtime and Dream-Tracks: Revisiting Australian Indigenous Identity Construction with Reference to Select Poems by Oodgeroo Noonuccal and Kevin Gilbert', analyzes the poems by the authors mentioned in the title. Santosh Sareen shows how land, nature, the authors' aboriginal identities and their battle to etch a plural multi-ethnic Australia, free from the 'White' dominance in all things social and cultural, are achieved by the poets through their constant struggle to establish their indigenous identities. Sareen draws parallels between Indian Hindu beliefs and the Australian aboriginal belief in ancestry and rootedness, concepts of 'motherland' and their unfailing bond with their native culture.

In her chapter, 'An Equal Music', CS Lakshmi briefly outlines her relationship with Prof GJV Prasad as a fellow Tamil who later translated her fiction into English. Importantly, CS Lakshmi shares some of her own views from her early writings and lectures about translation. She strongly reacts to the way footnotes have to be included in the English translations of works from Indian regional languages. 'To that extent, a hundred per cent translation from one language to another is impossible. Some Tamil words would fall flat in English, their depth of meaning lost when taken out of the cultural context from which they spring'. CS Lakshmi mentions about the politics of translation, the hierarchy between the author, the translator and the target language reader. She also mentions that the translator must have the humility to translate the text as a whole and not from the translator's perspective. She touches upon issues of translation when translating between two Indian languages. A tone of dissatisfaction can be traced in her writing, about the position allotted to the author of a text in the field of translation – to the extent of feeling like a 'circus monkey on exhibit'. Her displeasure about the secondary position allotted to the author of an Indian language text vis-à-vis the translator seems to have been put to rest after her experience of working with Prof GJV Prasad, when he accepted her offer to translate her work of fiction. Ambai's paper is a personal note about her views on translation as both a process and the relationship between the author and translator.

Somdatta Mandal addresses the problems of translation, the process of transformation or 'growth' that a text undergoes in translation in her chapter, 'Translation, Interpretation, and Transcreation: Texts and Contexts in the Indian Scenario'. She does this with reference to four categories. The first is when the authors themselves translate their own works, which is discussed in this chapter with reference to Tagore's translation of his *Gitanjali* and the criticism it received. She also mentions Qurratulain Hyder and Alka Saraogi's translations of their own novels as cases in point. The second category that Mandal cites is when a work is translated by someone close to the author as in the case of Joginder Paul's novella in Urdu – *Sleepwalkers* – that was translated into English where one of the translators was his own daughter. The third category is where she considers several translations of the same text – in this case Saadat Hasan Manto's story 'Toba Tek Singh' and Jibananda Das's poem 'Banalata Sen'. The final fourth category is of adaptation of texts into films – Mahasweta Devi's *Hazaar Churasir Ma* and 'Rudaali' and Tagore's *Ghare Baire*. Mandal, by referring to theorists of translation like Walter Benjamin and Susan Sontag, and with reference to some important texts, has analyzed the process of translation and transcreation to address the question of who is an 'ideal' translator. Through her study, she has raised important issues of translation about 'negotiation', transcreation, problems of translating from one language to another and the problems of translating between different mediums.

Radha Chakravarty's 'Translating South Asia: Women and Radical Textuality' is about the important aspect of translating women's writings. With reference to several examples, she chalks out the various ways in which writings by women from South Asia address various issues that are local, indigenous and specific to culture. By translating such texts, a comprehensive view of the challenges that these writings pose to the dominant patriarchal and restrictive nationalist discourses can be achieved and that in turn can posit an alternative discourse to the Western notions of radical feminist texts. While discussing texts from South Asia – written specifically by women, and their translations – Chakravarty mentions women's writings and the intersectionalities of gender with caste, class, ethnicity, etc. The importance of anthologies which collect writings of women of several generations, the role of publishing houses and market forces are also discussed. Through translation of writings by women, Chakravarty visualizes how this would lead to the acceptance of 'otherness' of women of different nationalities and ethnicities and that in turn may affect a change in the lives of women, representing a bond among these diverse groups of women through their similar experiences of discrimination and oppression, while also comparing their differences in experience. She also mentions translations of works that could help form the 'discourses of the queer' from South Asia. She speaks about translation as 'textual metamorphoses and translingual mutability' and mentions language and power. Chakravarty's chapter does well to include all aspects of both translations and the importance and issues of translating women's 'radical' writing from South Asia.

Tabish Khair's chapter, 'Are the Ghosts in Henry James's *The Turn of the Screw* Real?', takes a 'classic' text, Henry James's *The Turn of the Screw*, and interrogates it as a text ultimately not about fantasy or the marvellous or the uncanny, but as one that emphasizes the importance of literature as literature. In reading or teaching literature, too often we get swayed by the theory of the day – we tend to reduce the text to the current theoretical frameworks or make it 'transparent' or an echo chamber to validate contemporary political concerns. Khair reminds us that literature is not just about language but also about the relationship between language and reality and our own response to it. Reading imaginatively and sensitively will always lead to a unique experience, adding up to much more than the sum of the syntax and semantics.

Meenakshi Bharat's 'Marginalization and Dispossession in the Kashmiri Novel: A Look at Mirza Waheed's *The Collaborator* is a rich if saddening reading of the Kashmiri novel. Bharat discusses the peculiar situation of Kashmiris denied the expected sense of national identity that borders are supposed to grant; in the battles between India and Pakistan, the Kashmiri is erased. Unable to fully claim or be claimed by either side, the Kashmiri is literally caught in between, overwhelmed by loss, ambivalence and liminality. Rejecting both sides of the border, Kashmiris realized the desire for being simply Kashmiri and the call for Azadi rings out in the English writing from Kashmir through the 1990s expressing the malaise and anger at dispossession and marginalization. In this thought-provoking chapter, Bharat shows us that borderlands do indeed inspire creativity, even if it is a bitter fruit. Her reading of *The Collaborator* brings us a novel about the quintessential Kashmiri, riven by liminality, by 'not-belonging', the 'in betweeness' that characterizes the ordinary Kashmiri of the 1990s.

The only 're-print' in this collection, Jisha Menon's chapter 'Calling Local/Talking Global: The Cosmopolitics of the Call Centre Industry', brings together performance arts theory, postcolonial frameworks and a critique of globalization to examine the effects of neo-imperialism and global capital on local cultures and identities. A theatre and performance studies scholar by training, Menon examines four dramatic performances that represent encounters between differently situated labourers and consumers and the interface between nationalism and globalization/cosmopolitanism. Looking at the specificities of the IT/BPO industry's materialist practices, Menon highlights the ways in which global capital functions and disrupts local social and cultural ways of living. This chapter reminds us that despite its apparent contemporaneity, globalization is very much part of the continuities of empire and capitalism.

KB Veio Pou and Achingliu Kamei in their chapter 'An Emerging Literary Tradition: An Overview of Writings in English from the Northeast', true to its title, adhere to discussing the various themes and issues in the writings being produced from the seven states in Northeast India. Beginning their chapter with an introduction to the region, its constituent states and the kinds of literary production from the area, the authors are acutely aware of, and make evident throughout their chapter, the 'marginalized' position these states are relegated to. The chapter deals with the major themes of the literature produced from this region – the political content of the writings, the quest for identity that most often leads them to their cultural roots, the identity crisis expressed in the writings of the region, adapting the oral tradition of storytelling in the written narrative. Ecological issues and nature are identified as strong elements in these stories that are narrated by and for people who belong to a region that is still so beautifully decorated by nature. While being neglected by the Centre – politically, socially and even in the area of Indian English writing – the Northeast has evolved into a region with its distinct character as well as an ever-growing parallel body of literature that is distinctly its own. Veio Pou and Achingliu Kamei's chapter works as a good introduction for the uninitiated to the rich world of literature that is produced from the Northeast regions of India.

This unique multi-genre compilation is inspired by GJV's own forays in the course of his career. The collection includes contributions on the state of literary studies in India, drama, poetry, fiction, translation and language. We as editors are grateful to all the contributors for readily agreeing to be a part of this volume and being patient as the volume took shape.

Editors

Notes

1 Meenakshi Mukherjee, *The Twice Born Fiction*, Pencraft International, Delhi, 1971; Preface. p. 33.
2 M. K. Naik, *A History of Indian English Literature,* Sahitya Akademi, 1982, 2004, p. 5.
3 Salman Rushdie, '"Commonwealth Literature" Does Not Exist', in *Imaginary Homelands*, Vintage Books, London, 2010, p. 67.
4 News18, 2014.
5 Alastair Pennycook and Emi Otsuji, *Metrolingualism: Language in the City*, Routledge, London & New York, 2015, p. 3.
6 Harish Trivedi, *Colonial Transactions: English Literature and India*, Manchester University Press, 1995, p. 233.
7 Somdev Banik, 'Teaching English Literature/Language: Perspectives from a Non-metro University', in Banibrata Mahanta and Rajesh Babu Sharma (Eds.), *English Studies in India: Contemporary and Evolving Paradigms*, Springer, Singapore, 2019, pp. 167–74.
8 Pankaj Jalote, 'Evolution of Research Universities in India', *Higher Education in India* (blog), 12 April 2021 at https://jalote.wordpress.com/2021/04/12/evolution-of-research-universities-inindia/ [accessed 25 December 2021].
9 *All India Survey on Higher Education 2019–20*, p. 31.
10 'Private Institutions to Come under Reservation Ambit, Govt Prepares to Bring in Bill', *The Print*, 2019 <https://theprint.in/india/> [accessed 13 February 2022].
11 *All India Survey on Higher Education 2019–20*, no. 9, pp. 14–15.
12 Rajeswari Sunder Rajan, 'English Literary Studies, Women's Studies and Feminism in India', *Economic and Political Weekly*, 43, no. 43 (2008), p. 67.
13 For more on the reframing of English literary studies in India, see C. D. Narasimhaiah, *English Studies in India: Widening Horizons*, Pencraft International, 2002; C. D. Narasimhaiah, *Moving Frontiers of English Studies*

in India, S. Chand, 1977; Gauri Viswanathan, *Masks of Conquest: Literary Study and British Rule in India, Twenty-Fifth Anniversary Edition*, Columbia University Press, 2014.
Gauri Viswanathan, 'The Beginnings of English Literary Study in British India', *Oxford Literary Review* 9, no. 1 (1987), pp. 2–26. Rajeswari Sunder Rajan, *The Lie of the Land: English Literary Studies in India*, Oxford University Press, 1992. Susie J. Tharu, *Subject to Change: Teaching Literature in the Nineties*, Orient Blackswan, 1998. M. Manuel and Ayyappappanikkar, eds., *English and India: Essays Presented to Professor Samuel Mathai on His Seventieth Birthday*, Macmillan, 1978.

14 Rajeswari Sunder Rajan, 'After "Orientalism": Colonialism and English Literary Studies in India', *Social Scientist* 14, no. 7 (1986), pp. 23–35. https://doi.org/10.2307/. p. 29.

15 Ania Loomba, 'Criticism and Pedagogy in the Indian Classroom', in Svati Joshi (Ed.), *Rethinking English: Essays in Literature, Language, History*, Trianka, 1991.

16 Somdev Banik, 'Teaching English Literature/Language: Perspectives from a Non-Metro University', in Banibrata Mahanta and Rajesh Babu Sharma (Eds.), *English Studies in India: Contemporary and Evolving Paradigms*, Springer, Singapore, 2019, p. 168, 167–74.

17 Harish Trivedi, no. 6, pp. 229–51.

18 These English programmes are the ones offered by Aligarh Muslim University (Bachelor of Arts and Master of Arts), Banaras Hindu University (BA and MA), Jadavpur University, Kolkata (BA and MA), Jamia Millia Islamia, New Delhi (BA and MA), Panjab University, Chandigarh (BA and MA), Pondicherry University (MA), Pune University (BA and MA), University of Calcutta (BA and MA), University of Delhi (BA and MA), University of Mumbai (BA and MA) and Amrita Vishwa Vidyapeetham (BA).

References

'All India Survey on Higher Education 2019–20', Ministry of Education, Department of Higher Education, Government of India, 2020. https://www.education.gov.in/.

Anand, Siriyavan. 'Interview with Chandra Bhan Prasad', 6 March 2001. DOI: http://www.ambedkar.org/chandrabhan/interview.htm.

Banik, Somdev. 'Teaching English Literature/Language: Perspectives from a Non-Metro University', in Banibrata Mahanta and Rajesh Babu Sharma (Eds.), *English Studies in India: Contemporary and Evolving Paradigms*, Springer, Singapore, 2019, pp. 167–74.

Ilaiah, Kancha. 'Walking on Two Legs', *Deccan Herald*, 25 August 2005. DOI: http://archive.deccanherald.com/Deccanherald/aug252005/editpage1622462005824.asp.

Iyengar, K. R. Srinivasa. *Indian Writing in English*, Sterling Publishers, New Delhi, 1985.

Jalote, Pankaj. 'Evolution of Research Universities in India', *Higher Education in India* (blog), 12 April 2021. https://jalote.wordpress.com/2021/04/12/evolution-of-research-universities-inindia/ [25 December 2021].

Joshi, Svati. *Rethinking English: Essays in Literature, Language, History*, Trianka, New Delhi, 1991.

Kachru, Braj B. 'The Indianness in Indian English', *Word*, 21 (3), 1965, pp. 391–410. DOI: 10.1080/00437956.1965.11435436

Landow, George P. *Hypertext: The Convergence of Contemporary Critical Theory and Technology*, The John Hopkins University Press, Baltimore and London, 1992.

Loomba, Ania. 'Criticism and Pedagogy in the Indian Classroom', in Svati Joshi (Ed.), *Rethinking English: Essays in Literature, Language, History*, Trianka, New Delhi, 1991.

Manuel, M., and M. Ayyappappanikkar (Eds). *English and India: Essays Presented to Professor Samuel Mathai on His Seventieth Birthday*, Macmillan, Madras, 1978.

Mukherjee, Meenakshi. *The Twice Born Fiction*, Pencraft International, Delhi, 1971, 2010.

Naik, M. K. *A History of Indian English Literature*, Sahitya Akademi, New Delhi, 1982, 2004.

Narasimhaiah, C. D. *English Studies in India: Widening Horizons*, Pencraft International, 2002.

Narasimhaiah, C. D. *Moving Frontiers of English Studies in India*, S. Chand & Co., New Delhi, 1977.

Pennycook, Alastair, and Emi Otsuji. *Metrolingualism: Language in the City*, Routledge, London & New York, 2015.

Rajan, Rajeswari Sunder. 'After "Orientalism": Colonialism and English Literary Studies in India', *Social Scientist*, 14 (7), 1986, pp. 23–35.

Rajan, Rajeswari Sunder. 'English Literary Studies, Women's Studies and Feminism in India', *Economic and Political Weekly*, 43 (43), 2008, pp. 66–71.

Rushdie, Salman. '"Commonwealth Literature" Does Not Exist', in *Imaginary Homelands*, Vintage Books, London, 2010, p. 67.

Tharu, Susie J. *Subject to Change: Teaching Literature in the Nineties*, Orient Blackswan, New Delhi, 1998.

The ICCR Conference was hosted by the then Prime Minister Atal Bihari Vajpayee. See discussions in Saccidānandan et al Eds., *At Home in the World*, Indian Council for Cultural Relations, New Delhi, 2005, and Rashmi Sadana, *English Heart, Hindi Heartland: The Political Life of Literature in India*, University of California Press, Berkeley, Los Angeles, London, 2012.

Trivedi, Harish. *Colonial Transactions: English Literature and India*, Manchester University Press, Manchester and New York, 1995.

Venkatesan, V. 'The Dalit Cause', *Frontline*, 19 (3), 2–15 February 2002. http://www.frontline.in/navigation/?type=static&page=flonnet&rdurl=fl1903/19030920.htm.

Viswanathan, Gauri. 'The Beginnings of English Literary Study in British India', *Oxford Literary Review*, 9 (1), 1987, pp. 2–26.

Viswanathan, Gauri. *Masks of Conquest: Literary Study and British Rule in India, Twenty-Fifth Anniversary Edition*, Columbia University Press, New York, 2014.

'We Have Always Spoken Panglish', SciFi.com, 2004 (Panglish appears in *Native Tongue*).

SUB-THEME I

Literary Studies in India

1

RETHINKING AND RESITUATING HISTORIES OF INDIAN LITERATURE(S)

M. Asaduddin

Literary historiography is a genre that is very much a work in progress in India, as in much of the world. We have a plethora of models before us, though none seems entirely satisfactory. Perhaps it is in the nature of the genre itself that militates against any definitive framework. Histories of literature have been written from different frameworks/perspectives in different historical moments. If we take a cursory look at the better-known histories of English literature, often prescribed in Indian classrooms, from Hudson, through Compton Rickett, Ifor Evans, Legouis and Cazamian[1] and David Daiches to the Routledge *History of Literature in English*[2] (Ronald Carter and John McRae), we will find that each one of them has followed a different framework and that students/scholars of literature should be ill-advised to depend solely on any one of them. If such is the variety of framework for a literature produced in a monolingual country, one can only imagine the challenges of writing histories of literatures in a multilingual country like India, where language boundaries and geographies are porous and intersectional, sharing common myths and literary conventions. The language–literature equation or literature–nation equation that served as the bases for European or Eurocentric literary histories do not simply work in multilingual societies like India.

A substantial corpus of scholarship has been accumulated in recent times around the concept of literary historiography, which has become a genre by itself. From Hippolyte Taine to Rene Wellek, from Hayden White, Paul Ricoeur to Stephen Greenblatt, from Suniti Kumar Chatterjee, Sujit Mukerjee and Sisir Kumar Das to G.N. Devy, we have a wide range of views on the scope, significance and methods of literary historiography that have

DOI: 10.4324/9781003399926-3

enriched our understanding of the genre. Without going into the difference between history of literature and literary history and the difference in their approaches, one foregrounding 'history' and the other 'literary', one using multiple contexts for greater illumination and the other attempting to be context-free stressing literature's autotelic status, my endeavour in this chapter would be to point to the beginnings of this genre, its growth and challenges, and then some areas of silences, gaps and inadequate representation in the context of histories of different literatures in India.

The Idea of the 'Literary' in Literary History

Literary histories, directly or indirectly, engage with the question of writings that constitute literature. Even if we keep its oral manifestations out of reckoning, for the sake of convenience, the question remains as to the attributes or traits of literary writings, and how far back do we go in tracing the lineages of such a tradition. Opinions will differ on the idea of what is 'literary'. Even the aesthetics will be arguably different for such categories as Dalit literature or Black literature. The literary historian inevitably works through a process of selection whereby some texts are preferred over others depending on the historian's idea of literariness. In other words, a process of canon-making is already involved in the process of selection. Literary historians are often cited as authorities on texts, authors and periods. The evaluative criteria the literary historian adopts will depend on the historical moment, the prevalent climate of opinions and his own, often ideological, preferences. In other words, the process of selection is not an innocent one. The selection of literary texts/events and even historical epochs has remained the dominant mode of representation. Moreover, since the idea of 'literariness' is ever-evolving, and literary works are constantly re-evaluated in the light of insights from new domains of learning and interpretation, a latter-day literary historian might find the earlier histories faulty, inadequate and unrepresentative. If one looks at the histories of literature pertaining to different Indian languages, one finds vast areas of silences and erasures.[3] It is the duty of contemporary literary historians to address these areas of silences and erasures so that the readers are offered a balanced perspective and an appropriate vantage point from where they can have a long view of the growth and development of a particular literature.

Literary History in India: Beginnings

As with general history, literary history writing in India, too, has multiple genealogies. Whether it is Vansabali in Sanskrit, the Tazkira tradition in Persian and Urdu, the Kissa and Janamsakhi traditions in Punjabi, Burunji in Asamiya or charit in several Indian languages, each tradition had its specific social and cultural circumstances within which it prospered and left traces for later historians to pick threads to connect the past with later developments. These early texts dealt with biographical details of writers (or rulers/saints) and a listing of works, sometimes in narrative and sometimes in descriptive forms. Not strong on historicity[4] in terms of the accuracy of dates and events, and largely impressionistic or hagiographic in their orientation, they, nevertheless, contained blueprints of more sophisticated accounts later. Moreover, it is not as if these traditions grew and developed in total isolation from or independent of each other. For example, the Tazkira tradition had greatly influenced Punjabi,[5] Sindhi, and quite possibly other literary histories. However, though we see the currency of such traditions built around specific languages of India, there was no endeavour to write or conceptualize the history of 'Indian literature' as a single entity. This effort first came from the West. Albrecht Weber, a friend of Max Mueller, known to be the first scholar to attempt it, equated the history of Indian literature with that of Sanskrit (German 1852/English translation 1880). Maurice Winternitz who came later with his three-volume history of Indian literature (Vol I, 1907 in German/English translation 1926) also mainly concentrated on Sanskrit. The French orientalist J.H. Garcin de Tassy expanded the scope of Indian literature beyond Sanskrit in his three-volume *Histoire de la littérature hindoui et hindoustani* (1839–1871) which, unfortunately, has not yet been translated into English, Urdu or Hindi in its entirety. Then we have George Abraham Grierson's *The Modern Vernacular Literature of Hindustan*, first published in 1888. The latter two titles contain formulations and assertions, not always entirely correct, which extended the scope of Indian literature to embrace literary expressions in the Indo-Gangetic plane. Literary historians in India refer to the above pioneers[6] of the genre from the West either to reinforce their arguments or mark their points of departure. They were the first to introduce the concept of 'Hindustani' or 'Indian' literature, though the contours of that literature remained limited, fuzzy and problematic. When Indians began to write their own histories of literature, they concentrated on specific languages, rather than the generic 'Indian' literature, which always offered challenges of an unimaginable magnitude. Hans Harder is right when he says,

> The bulk of literary histories that are to be found in India, and that are on the whole produced with unabating frequency, are not histories of Indian literature, but histories of literature in one specific language, usually written either in that very language or in English

(Harder 14)

Much before Harder, Sujit Mukherjee, too, flagged this issue in his monograph, *Towards a Literary History of India*:

Most of our histories of regional literatures are no more than descriptive accounts of literary works and their authors in these languages, with demonstrably greater emphasis on the historical aspect of the enterprise than on the literary. Of course, our traditions of literary criticism themselves are not fully evolved and this continues to be a great handicap in the general area of literary research, whether in theory or in history or in criticism.

(Mukherjee 1975: 9)

What Mukherjee says about the state of literary criticism in India has changed much in the intervening period of nearly half a century. Our literary histories ought to come abreast with the trends and developments that have taken place during this period.

Inter-literary Lineages

One way to make greater sense of the growth and development of Indian literature over different time periods is to think about them in terms of language clusters, i.e., neighbouring languages that are close to each other in their formal and thematic features and literary conventions. One may think of clusters like Bengali-Odia-Assamese-Manipuri or Urdu-Hindi-Panj abi-Dogri-Sindhi-Kashmiri, etc. How the development of this literature takes place can be seen more comprehensively and in greater depth within the clusters. S.K. Das has explained this in detail in the section 'Pro-phane and Metaphane' of his monumental work, *A History of Indian Literature*, Vol. 8 (Das, 44–46). In a multilingual country, the dominant language in a region or a cluster will influence (even hegemonize) less developed literatures and languages. This has to be acknowledged as a fact of life. For example, for a considerable period in the late nineteenth and early twentieth centuries, Calcutta functioned as the clearing house for the new knowledge systems that came from the West and travelled eastward through the mediation of Bangla. Calcutta was the educational hub for the first generation of Assamese intellectuals and writers where they were exposed to Western ideas and modernism. Even though the imposition of Bangla on undivided Assam by the British did not last too long, the influence of Bangla language and literature on Asamiya was considerable. There were prolific translations of Bangla literature into Asamiya that enriched its literature and literary traditions. Even works of European and world literature sometimes came into Asamiya through the mediation of Bangla. In other words, many classics of world literature were translated not from the original but from their Bangla versions. This trend continues even today. A minor literature enriching itself through translation from and imitation of a major literature is a common phenomenon. A similar relationship existed between Bangla and Odia too.

So, the literary histories of these modern Indian literatures are intertwined with each other. The shared lineages make it almost impossible to evaluate specific language literatures as totally insular and independent and make it obligatory that the interdependent nature of these histories be paid sufficient attention. The shared social and cultural histories in the neighbouring languages make it desirable that the inter-literary conditions be investigated. Das talks about unity of 'thoughts and ideas', despite differences in scripts and languages, and invites our attention to 'a common core of metaphors and symbols, myths and legends, conventions and norms that has evolved during the last thousand years and despite all diversities, linguistic and non-linguistic, the literatures produced in different languages tend to converge' (Das, 9). A clear idea about these areas of convergence will help us identify elements of commonality animating literary endeavours in different Indian languages and present them in a coherent framework.

What should be stressed, however, is the fact that over-emphasis on 'unity' often tends to blur elements of diversity and cultural specificity, as it happened in India immediately after independence. If one looks at the literary histories sponsored by the Sahitya Akademi (the National Academy of Letters), one finds that the authors of these histories, in their eagerness to present a unified picture of unity of Indian culture, tended to ignore minor/alternative/subaltern voices, what is known more popularly as the 'second tradition'. These histories need be updated, offering a fuller account of literary expressions of all classes, particularly the marginalized sections of the Indian society.

Multilingualism and Literary History

Closely allied with inter-literariness is the phenomenon of multilingualism and multiculturalism in India. Literary histories written by Westerners that often acted as models for Indian historians were written largely from monolingual cultures. In India, at any point in time, we have had a large number of writers who have been bilingual or tri-lingual. This is a phenomenon not fully accounted for in the historiography of literary histories. Literary histories written in India have yet to develop a methodology to accommodate multilingual works by the same writer. For example, if Kiran Nagarkar wrote ambidextrously in Marathi and English, Manoj Das in Odia and English, and Premchand wrote in both Hindi and Urdu, the methodology in our history writing should be capacious enough to accommodate this bi/multilinguality. To quote Devy:

Indian literature has in it the peculiar phenomenon of bilingual writers. The number of bilingual writers in India is so large, and the longevity of this practice is so substantial, that bilingual literature is more a norm than an exception in India. Considering these major differences in literary practices in India and Western countries, it is obvious that the concept of a single dominant literary tradition, a single and fairly well-defined literary canon and historical criticism couched in a unidirectional philology will not prove adequate to interpret the literary history of India.

(Devy: Meta 400)

Despite linguistic reorganization of the states in India, the linguistic and political boundaries cannot always be mapped onto each other. There may be regions within the same state that share the literary cultures and traditions of a neighbouring state. Such literary contiguity exists on state borders and other contact zones. Let me illustrate it by means of an example. Though located in Assam, the Barak Valley, consisting of three districts, has close to 80% Bangla-speaking population. Historically, the main inspiration and influence for the stream of Bangla literature in the Barak Valley came from Calcutta and mainstream Bangla literature, but it had a tone and temper of its own because of its location within Assam and away from West Bengal.[7] Histories of Bangla literature would not spare a page or even a paragraph for the literature produced in this region, and histories of Asamiya literature have much less reason to do so. Bangla literature produced in Tripura, too, given its geographical location and local influences, has this tenuous and tension-ridden relationship with mainstream Bangla literature produced in West Bengal. Indeed, there are such remote, neglected and unhoused literary pockets pertaining to several Indian languages.[8] Our histories of literature must develop a model to negotiate such spots of marginality and erasures. These are the challenges in a complex multilingual country like ours, and it would require extreme sensitivity to navigate the local, the regional and the mainstream within the same language.

Literary History and Translation

The role of translation in the growth and development of any literature is seminal but is never fully accounted for. Translation often provides models for new genres and helps in the emergence of new traditions and new writings. Literature in translation enriches target literatures by introducing new models and themes, even worldviews, and plays a seminal role in developing/changing literary taste. The notions of World Literature or Comparative Literature would not exist or would have no relevance without the availability of literature in translation. Devy says, 'In the Indian literary tradition, translation has had a place of crucial importance since most literary traditions in modern Indian languages originate in some pioneering work of translation'.[9] Fictional literature in India, in its early phase, developed through translation of European novels, and then through extensive translation of Bankim

Chandra Chatterjee, Sarat Chandra Chatterjee and Rabindranath Tagore in different Indian languages. At one phase in its development, Hindi literature was dominated by translation, mostly of Bangla works, so much so that it was designated as *anuvadjeebi sahitya* (literature that feeds on translation). Premchand lamented the preponderance of translation to the detriment of creative literature in Hindi. In his essay 'Upanyas' published in *Samalochak* (January 1925), he offers a counter-view on translation in his effort to provide a balanced perspective:

> (At one time) European detective novels were translated and published in Hindi because they were popular. Once that phase was over it was expected that original novels would be composed in Hindi but the tide of Bangla novels overwhelmed us and it is still on. Whatever novels in Bangla - good or bad – are being translated without any discrimination. I have no objection against enriching the treasure of your own literature with the jewels of some other literature ... However, is a literature worth anything if it has nothing to call its own but only translations?[10]

Apart from Hindi, translation from Bangla also dominated Odia, Assamese and Manipuri literatures in the early stages of their development. The same paradigm would be seen to operate in different other language clusters in India. Yet, when one reads histories of literatures in different Indian languages, one hardly sees this phenomenon treated with some coherence, let alone profundity. The vast corpus of literature in translation has been treated, if at all, as non-canonical or as some branch of para-literature. Granted that there are difficulties in classifying and slotting works of translation, that the question whether literature in translation belongs to the history of the source language or the target language or makes a different category altogether is not yet settled, but when Translation Studies has made significant strides in the last couple of decades, literary historians must make adequate room for discussing the role of translated literature in fostering growth and innovation in different Indian literatures.

Grounds for Comparison: A Question of Methodology

Literary historians trained in Western epistemology applied Western epochs, texts and authors as the benchmark of standard and canonization. If Grierson in his *Modern Vernacular* has compared the age of the Bhakti movement with the Augustan[11] Age in England and Tulsidas with Milton, we see the same tendency in Garcin de Tassy who often refers to genres in French literature which, for him, constitute models and benchmarks for determining the standard. Histories of literature of Indian languages written in English by Indians which have an international audience in mind, almost invariably, apply the same method. An extreme example of this proclivity can be seen in Muhammad Sadiq's monumental *History of Urdu Literature*[12] where one of the avowed purposes of the author seems to exhibit his wide acquaintance with European literature. The following passage from his book will be self-explanatory:

> Akbar (Ilahabadi) has not the geniality of Dickens or Fielding. He stands between the two extremes – not an Aristophanes, or a Cervantes, or a Rabelais, much less a Dickens or a Meredith, but a cross between Thackeray and Swift.
>
> *(Sadiq 403–404)*

Ralph Russell, a latter-day historian of Urdu literature, castigates Sadiq for his unfair method of comparison, always to the disadvantage of Urdu literature, in an essay appropriately titled 'How Not to Write the History of Urdu Literature'.[13] He extended his critique to include the earlier two historians of Urdu literature in English, i.e., Rambabu Saxena[14] and T. Graham Bailey[15] who too exhibit the same tendency of comparing some genres/writers of Urdu literature with those of English quite simplistically. Russell's pointed critique of the above remark by Sadiq underlines the fatuity and irrelevance of such comparisons where the contexts and parameters of evaluations are vastly different:

> The words (Sadiq's) tell us nothing relevant except that Akbar is lacking in geniality for Dr Sadiq does not tell us what his 'two extremes' are, or what qualities are in his view exemplified by the authors in his impressive list, or what he thinks a 'cross' between the last two produces. This constant parading of Western parallels and (more often) contrasts (invariably to the detriment of Urdu) is not merely annoying; it suggests at every step the relevance of comparisons which are in fact not relevant at all. It is rather as though one were to write a history of the English novel proclaiming at every page that Dickens cannot compare with Tolstoy or Gaskell with Dostoevsky.
>
> *(Russell, 32)*

I have presented this quotation in full because our literary histories are littered with such irrelevant comparisons. It is not my intention to dismiss all comparisons as irrelevant. Indeed, in literature we often take recourse to comparisons for the sake of clarity, understanding and emphasis. What is required is that we should be fully aware of the grounds of comparison and whether they are relevant to the contexts/situations to which they are applied. Another fact that seems evident is that for histories of literature of different Indian languages written in English, the intended audience encompasses both national and international readership, and the methodology adopted by historians is often oriented towards that. Literary historians need not fall to the temptation of ingratiating themselves to an international audience by adopting a methodology that is questionable.

Literary History and Ideology

Ideological biases, whether political or communal, intervene in significant ways in determining the point of view of the historian. In India, it started with Grierson, if not earlier. With all his vast scholarship, pretensions and occasional humility, he determinedly pursued the agenda of not only marginalizing Urdu language and its literature but its total erasure in *Modern Vernacular Literature of India*.[16] This seems more glaring when we remember that Garcin de Tassy had already published his *Histoire* several decades earlier where he paid equal attention to Hindi and Urdu literary expressions, using more capacious and inclusive terms such as 'Hindui' and 'Hindustani'. Even Suniti Kumar Chatterjee, the famed linguist whose career straddled India's colonial and postcolonial periods and whose opinions often mattered in formulating language policies, conflates Hindustani with Hindi literature.[17] The contribution of Muslim writers in different types of Indian literature is either ignored or simply glossed over. Muslims are grudgingly mentioned, let alone properly represented. Sudipta Kaviraj[18] and Torsten Tschacher[19] showed how it happened in Bangla and Tamil literatures, respectively. Navina Gupta[20] points out how Acharya Ramcharan Shukla, in his foundational work, *Hindi Sahitya ka Itihas*, constantly emphasizes Sanskritic elements and undervalues Perso-Urdu tradition in tracing the development of Hindi literature. Gupta quotes Krishna Kumar to underscore the damaging impact of such communal bias:

> By denying the literary works written in the mixed Hindi-Urdu tradition a valid place and status in Hindi's literary history, he performed a decisive symbolic act in shaping the cultural identity of college-educated men and women for generations. The identity Shukla gave to the Hindi heritage was a distinct Hindu identity.[21]

In the literary history of several Indian literatures, the Muslim interregnum in Indian history is designated as the 'age of darkness' (tamaha yug) when all creativity stopped because of the deleterious effect of 'foreign' invasions. So, there was/is a deliberate attempt by literary historians, some of them men of vast erudition and credibility, to 'purge' the foreign elements that, in their way of thinking, contaminated the 'pure' Hindu tradition.[22] Nothing is further from the truth. Both Sisir Kumar Das and Ganesh Devy – contemporary Indian literary historians with impeccable scholarly credentials– have pointed out how Persian and other Islamic languages facilitated the growth of indigenous languages. In this context, the following remark by Devy is revelatory:

> The emergence of *bhasha* literatures coincided with, even if it was not entirely caused by, a succession of Islamic rule in India. The Islamic rulers – Arab, Turks, Mughals – brought with them new cultural concerns to India, and provided these currents legitimacy through liberal political patronage. The languages – Arabic and Persian, mainly, and Urdu which developed indigenously under their influence – brought new modes of writing poetry and music. This intimate contact with Islamic cultures created for the *bhasha* literatures new possibilities of continuous development.
>
> *(Devy, 1995: 9)*

It is amply documented that translations from Perso-Arabic literature into Indian languages not only enriched literatures in different Indian languages but their generic repertoire as well. If one takes a rough count of the Perso-Arabic vocabulary, idioms and proverbs in any Indian language, one realizes the depth of this literary-cultural encounter. Persian literature was cultivated by both Muslims and Hindus[23] during the Mughal period continuing up to the early phase of British colonialism, and almost all the languages of India bear the deep imprint of this linguistic and literary encounter. This reprehensible communalism of the wise and the cognoscenti needs to be called out and corrected. Literary histories which are supposed to give a truthful account of the literary activities of an entire people need not be contaminated with the bias and prejudices of a few.

Periodization

In the scholarship corpus of literary historiography, the linear chronological model is often frowned upon, because of its limitations without suggesting an alternative model that is easily intelligible and pragmatic. There is always an element of reductiveness in naming a period after a dominant theme or a literary or political figure or using dynastic or communal markers like 'Mughal' or 'British' or 'Hindu'. They are usually used as shorthands to indicate either a dominant pattern or historical or communal markers. As Sisir Kumar Das says, 'All periodizations are arbitrary, and yet insisted upon more for convenience than for any other reason' (Das, 17). It cannot be denied that often literary efflorescence does happen because of the conducive circumstances existing during a period, like political patronage, prosperity in the country/region or the birth of a great genius, and to that extent, naming the period accordingly indirectly signals the condition of production of literature at the time. Conversely, literary productions could get stifled because of oppressive political regimes, repressive laws and several other reasons, leading to lean periods in the growth of literature. However, concepts of literary periods drawn from Western literary histories sometimes seem problematic and lack conceptual clarity. For example, three periods that are almost ubiquitous in literary histories in India are the Renaissance, the Romantic period and the Modern period, named after the scheme in histories of European literatures. The concepts of 'renaissance', 'romantic' and 'modernity', as they are used by literary historians in India, are often vague and differ substantially, on the one hand, from its European versions and, on the other, among Indian languages themselves. Debates about these labels are rife and not settled.[24] New literary histories written should contribute to these debates to underline the essentially provisional nature of these labels. Moreover, what should be kept in mind is that no period in literature is self-contained and so should not be studied in isolation. It marks either a continuation of, or a rupture from, trends and tendencies of the preceding period, and texts written in the two periods are often compared or contrasted to explore continuities/discontinues in the tradition.

Major Absences

Major absences in literary histories in India lie in the realms of popular literature, children's literature, literature from below and literature in cyberspace. Both popular literature and children's literature have been prolific in Indian languages, but literary historians did not consider them worthy of their attention. With their slow insertion/inclusion in the academia, it is expected that literary historians will now pay attention to these two domains that have been rich in creativity. Dalit literature has made quite a splash in the last two decades, and tribal literature is following suit. Debates about the need for a different aesthetic for such literatures from below have generated valuable insights in the field. A Dalit literary historiography will have a different understanding of literary traditions. This historiography must account for the differences and particularities that exist within Dalit literature in different Indian languages. A considerable amount of literature is now being produced in the cyberspace, which is also giving birth to new genres suited to different platforms. Literary historians can no longer afford to be elitist and ignore these absences and must find ways and means to accommodate them in their narratives.

The above discussion is intended to draw attention to the challenges that literary historians face/will face in their attempt to give the fullest account of the literary activities in Indian languages. Sensitivity to the inadequacies in earlier histories in matters of perspectives, method and coverage will certainly lead to the writings of more balanced and comprehensive histories. I would still argue that no single history, however capacious, can either accommodate or treat all that needs to be accommodated. What we need to do, as is being done in several languages, is to have a chain of histories written from different perspectives, offering a wide variety of theoretical and historical models. More specifically, we can have two broad models – one that concentrates on individual languages and literary traditions and the second that encompasses several or all Indian languages and literary traditions as a whole. A third model could be genre-specific, i.e., to see the development of a particular genre such as poetry or novel across languages. The second and third models will be far more challenging and complex that will resist any temporal framework, as literature, languages and literary cultures in India followed an extremely uneven trajectory, growing and developing at different historical periods and following specific routes of impact, influences, resurgence and decline. Challenging but rewarding, because that will truly represent the richness and depth of Indian literary cultures in their entirety.

Notes

1 The first substantial history of English literature written by two French scholars, providing a much-needed perspective from outsiders who were not born into the language. Many of the histories of Indian literature are also written by foreign scholars who were not insiders to the languages/literatures. Sujit Mukherjee in his *Towards a Literary History of India* makes a distinction between these two kinds of literary historians providing perspectives that are complementary to each other.
2 It took almost two centuries for the perspective to shift from the history of 'English literature' to 'Literature in English' encompassing several countries of the world producing substantial works of literature in English.
3 It is good news that Orient Blackswan has a projected series called 'Critical Histories of Indian Literatures', aimed at correcting the anomalies of earlier literary histories in Indian languages, and addresses areas unattended or glossed over by earlier histories. The volumes on Marathi and Kannada are complete. The volumes in other languages are in different stages of completion.
4 Though Sheldon Pollock argues that contrary to the popular belief of its indifference to history, the Sanskrit literary tradition provided reasonably accurate historical survey of earlier works at the beginning of each work; I did not find this to be true in case of the *tazkiras*. Even the most important of them, i.e., *Ab-e hayaat* provides dates, if at all, in approximate terms, and these dates are not verified or verifiable. Garcin de Tassy in the Preface to his *Histoire de la literature hindouie et Hindustani*, says, 'Unfortunately, these *tazkira* are written in a very unsatisfactory manner. Often only the name of the poet concerned is mentioned, together with a few extracts from his verse as specimens of his talent. Even in the more extensive notes, their date of birth is almost never mentioned. Their date of death and details of their private lives are very rarely mentioned'. Sujit Mukerjee and Gita Krishnakutty, "Prefaces to Garcin de Tassy's History: Introductory Note", *Indian Literature*, 27 (3), May–June, 1984, pp. 90–91. Shamsur Rahman Faruqi's comment that no two historians of Urdu literature agree on the date of birth of a writer or publication date of a work is not entirely facetious. It has a grain of truth in it. In fact, one of the difficulties for scholars conducting research

in Indian literatures as a whole is to establish accuracy of dates with reasonable certainty.

5 Christopher Shackle in his 'Making Punjabi Literary History' (*Sikh Religion, Culture and Ethnicity*, 2001) shows how Muhammad Husain Azad's *Ab-e Hayat* was used as a model by early Punjabi literary historiographers.

6 Out of these four, Garcin de Tassy is the one least referred to because his three-volume *Histoire* is not available in English translation. Scholars looking for an introduction to his works may consult the following in English: Sujit Mukerjee and Gita Krishnakutty, no. 22; S. Kamal Abdali, "Some Comments on de Tassy's *Les Auteurs Hindoustanis et Leurs Ouvrages d'Apr`es les Biographies Originales*", *Annual of Urdu Studies*, University of Wisconsin, Madison, USA, No.28, 2013.

7 I have attempted to deal with the complex and messy way literatures have developed in India's Northeast and how no histories of literature can capture or account for this complexity in my article,"Canon Formation and Literatures from India's Northeast: Some Reflections", in K.M. Baharul Islam (Ed.), *Literature from Northeast India: Beyond the Centre-Periphery Debate*, Routledge, 2022.

8 In his essay, 'Multiple Literary Cultures in Telugu: Court, Temple, and Public', in *Literary Cultures in History*, Velcheru Narayana Rao points out how the literary geography of Telugu cannot be equated with the political boundaries of contemporary Andhra Pradesh. As he demonstrates, Telugu literature was produced in several areas outside the boundaries of modern Andhra and that writers have conceived differing notions of Andhra at different historical epochs. Further, even though Telugu had a vast spread, it was not the only language of importance, and significant literatures have been produced in other languages as well within the same territory.

9 G.N. Devy, "Literary History and Translation: An Indian View", *Meta* 42 (2), 1997, p.395.

10 Quoted by Avadesh Kumar Singh in Avadesh Kumar Singh and Sanjay Mukherjee (Eds.), *Critical Discourse and Colonialism*, Creative Books, New Delhi, 2005, p. 76.

11 Ira Sharma stresses the significance of such appellations: 'When Grierson calls the literary epoch of the sixteenth and seventeenth centuries the "Augustan Age of Hindustani literature" he therefore not only applies an evaluative term, he also establishes a direct connection between Hindi literature and "classical" paragons of European literature: the classics. Hindi literature becomes, through the employment of this term, incorporated into a system of world literature or "classics" of general acclaim'. "George Abraham Grierson's Literary Hindustan", in Hans Harder (Ed.), *Literature and Nationalist Ideology*, Social Science Press, New Delhi, 2010, p.187.

12 Muhammad Sadiq, *History of Urdu Literature*, Oxford University Press, 1964.

13 'How Not to Write the History of Urdu Literature', in Ralph Russell, *How Not to Write the History of Urdu Literature and Other Essays on Urdu and Islam*, OUP, New Delhi, 1999, pp.29-41.

14 Rambabu Saxena, *A History of Urdu Literature*, Ram Narayan Lal, Allahabad, 1927.

15 T. Graham Bailey, *A History of Urdu Literature*, YMCA Press, Calcutta, 1932.

16 Ira Sharma in her article, 'George Abraham Grierson's Literary Hindustan', examines Grierson's communal bias: 'By banishing Urdu from this account, Grierson excludes from his literary Hindustan a whole field of the literary vernacular culture of northern India. Given the strong presence of poets from Avadh and especially Lucknow in Grierson's work, the neglect of the pivotal role of Urdu culture in this city is even more striking. Furthermore, Grierson decides

to use the Devanagari script throughout his work, even for those texts that had originally been written "in the Persian character", like Malik Muhammad Jayasi's Padmavat', Ira Sharma, no. 29, p.197.

17 The opening paragraph of Ira Sharma's article reads as follows: 'On 28 March 1928, Suniti Kumar Chatterjee writes to George Abraham Grierson: "Is there any likelihood of a second edition of your 'Vernacular Literature of Hindustan' being taken in hand? [...] The work is a fundamental one for the History of *Hindi* literature, and there is still some demand for it." ... Grierson produces—through his very selection, presentation and authorial comments—a historiographical framework, and also demarcates for the first time a literary space for north Indian vernacular writings, establishing in his discourse geographically determinable centres and peripheries within a region called "Hindustan"' (my emphasis), Hans Harder (Ed.), no. 29, pp.176–77.

18 Sudipta Kaviraj, "The Two Histories of Literary Culture in Bengal", in Sheldon Pollock (Ed.), *Literary Cultures in History: Constructions from South Asia*, University of California Press, Berkeley and Los Angeles, 2003.

19 "Drowning in the Ocean of Tamil: Islamic Texts and the Historiography of Tamil Literature", in Hans Harder (Ed.), no. 29.

20 Navina Gupta, "The Politics of Exclusion? The Place of Muslims, Urdu and Its Literature, in Ramchandra Shukla's *Hindi sahitya ka itihas*", as cited in Hans Harder, no. 29.

21 Krishna Kumar, *Political Agenda of Education: A Study of Colonialist and Nationalist Ideas*, Sage Publications, New Delhi, 1991.

22 In the context of Marathi literature, Milind Wakankar has shown how V.K. Rajwade, the great Mahrashtrian historiographer, in his critical edition of *Dhyaneswari*, had undertaken the project of rescuing the 'unmiscegenated and urbane' Marathi culture before it was corrupted by Arabo-Muslim/Persianate influences. For a detailed account, see "System and History in Rajwade's *Grammar* for the *Dnyaneswari*", in Raziuddin Aqil and Partha Chatterjee (Eds.), *History in the Vernacular*, Permanent Black, Ranikhet Cantt, 2008, pp.248–291.

23 Rabindranath Tagore in his autobiography *Jiban Smriti* (1912) mentions how he whiled away many long summer afternoons reading the story of *Gul-e Bakawali*, a popular story from Persian literature. His father Maharshi Devendranath was steeped in Persian poetry, particularly Rumi, Hafiz and Sa'di. Vivekananda and Raja Ram Mohun Roy were well-versed in Persian. Many Hindus from the *Kayasth* caste in North India were great scholars of Persian and held important posts in Mughal administration. Harivansh Rai Bachchan, the famed Hindi poet and father of Amitabh Bachchan, in the first volume of his Hindi autobiography *Kya Bhoolun Kya Yaad Karoon* (1969), describes in detail how he was given his first lesson in *Khaliqbari*, the Urdu-Persian Reader. The following extract from Rupert Snell's English translation of Bachchan's autobiography illustrates the place of Persian-Urdu in early schooling in some parts of northern India less than a hundred years ago: 'It was through my elder cousins and sisters that I picked up the fundamentals of the Hindi script. My mother had already taught me the Urdu letters. Before my regular education began there was a little ceremony at home: the family priest made me write Shri Ganeshay namah (Salutation to Lord Ganesh) on one side of a writing board, and the Maulvi Sahib made me write Bismillah ir Rahman ir Rahim (In the name of Allah the kind and merciful) on the other side, after which both received a rupee from my hand. That was the last I saw of the purohit, but the Maulvi Sahib used to come to teach every day.... Teaching in those days was done by rote. For a whole year, I was made to repeat nothing but the *Khaliqbari*, which I recited blindly: eventually the constant repeating dinned

the style and the structure into my head. I was thrilled when I finally got to the end of the text....Then the maulvi Sahib immediately started me on *Karima* of which I still remember several lines by heart...' (Bachchan, 78–80). It will not be far-fetched to assume that this early acquaintance with Urdu and Persian led him to translate Omar Khaiyaam's *Rubaiyaat* and absorb and assimilate it to his poetic sensibility so intensely as to create his own *Madhushala* (1935). Kazi Nazrul Islam, the Bengali poet, created the genre of ghazal in Bangla, having been influenced by Urdu-Persian traditions. Moreover, though a Muslim, he also composed *Shyama Sangeet*, songs devoted to the Goddess Kali, demonstrating conclusively (there are very many such instances in several literatures of India, if not all) the fact that Indian literatures were never insular on the basis of religion or any other sectarian considerations. Instances of prejudices or bigotry were exceptions rather than the rule and need to be called out for what they were.

24 In a brilliant book, *The Textures of Time: Writing History in South India1600–1800* (Permanent Black, Ranikhet Cantt, 2002), the authors Velcheru Narayana Rao, David Shulman and Sanjay Subrahmanyam stress the elasticity of processes of reading and interpretation that militate against reductive readings of texts making them adhere to a purported 'spirit of the age'. Similarly, Vasudha Dalmia and Stuart Blackburn in their book, *India's Literary History: Essays on the Nineteenth Century* (Permanent Black, Ranikhet Cantt, 2004), discuss alternate practices of literary historiography and critique static notions of 'tradition' and 'modernity'.

References

Avadesh KumarSingh and SanjayMukherjee (Eds.), *Critical Discourse and Colonialism*, Creative Books, New Delhi, 2005.

G. N.Devy, *After Amnesia: Tradition and Change in Indian Literary Criticism*, Orient Longman, Bombay, 1995.

G. N.Devy, "Literary History and Translation: An Indian View", *Meta*, 42 (2), 1997, p. 395.

George Abraham Grierson, *The Modern Vernacular Literature of Hindustan*, Asiatic Society, Calcutta, 1889.

Hans Harder (Ed.), *Literature and Nationalist Ideology*, Social Science Press, New Delhi, 2010.

Harivansh Rai Bachchan, *Kya Bhulun Kya Yaad Karoon*, Rajpal and Sons, Delhi, 1969, The first volume of his four-volume autobiography.

Harivansh Rai Bachchan, *In the Afternoon of Time: An Autobiography*, Translated by Rupert Snell, Viking Penguin India, New Delhi, 1998.

J. H. Garcin de Tassy, *Histoire de la littérature hindoui et hindoustani*, 3 volumes, Adolf Labitte, Paris, 1839–1871.

K. M. Baharul Islam (Ed.), *Literature from Northeast India: Beyond the Centre-Periphery Debate*, Routledge, London, 2022.

Krishna Kumar, *Political Agenda of Education. A Study of Colonialist and Nationalist Ideas*, Sage Publications, New Delhi, 1991.

Muhammad Sadiq, *History of Urdu Literature*, Oxford University Press, Delhi, 1964.

Ralph Russell, *How Not to Write the History of Urdu Literature and Other Essays on Urdu and Islam*, OUP, New Delhi, 1999, pp. 29–41.

Rambabu Saxena, *A History of Urdu Literature*, Ram Narayan Lal, Allahabad, 1927.

Raziuddin Aquil and Partha Chatterjee (Eds.), *History in the Vernacular*, Permanent Black, Ranikhet Cantt, 2008, pp. 248–291.

Sheldon Pollock (Ed.), *Literary Cultures in History: Constructions from South Asia*, University of California Press, Berkeley and Los Angeles, 2003.

Sisir Kumar Das, *A History of Indian Literature*, Vol. 8, Sahitya Akademi, New Delhi, 1991.

Sujit Mukherjee, *Towards a Literary History of India*, Indian Institute of Advance Study, Simla, 1975.

Sujit Mukherjee and Gita Krishnakutty, "Prefaces to Garcin de Tassy's History: Introductory Note", *Indian Literature*, 27 (3), May–June, 1984, pp. 83–97.

T. Graham Bailey, *A History of Urdu Literature*, YMCA Press, Calcutta, 1932.

Vasudha Dalmia and Stuart Blackburn, *India's Literary History: Essays on the Nineteenth Century*, Permanent Black, Ranikhet Cantt, 2004.

Velcheru Narayana Rao, David Shulman and Sanjay Subrahmanyam, *The Textures of Time: Writing History in South India 1600–1800*, Permanent Black, Ranikhet Cantt, 2002.

2

CORONAVIRUS SPACESUITS

Or, Hard Times as Launching Pads for Literary Travel

Rukmini Bhaya Nair

Introduction

Hard times call for hard choices. Why, after all, should one seek to ferret out, of all things, the secrets of literary texts at a time of crisis such as the world is now experiencing? Why should one write essays for festschrifts? Do these not constitute particularly egregious examples of fiddling while Rome or Ranchi burns? This chapter argues otherwise. It suggests that literature that has survived the vicissitudes of time also invariably encodes a basic set of algorithms for species survival, *especially* during difficult times. That is what makes it invaluable; that is why it is emblematic, in John Milton's prescient words, of 'reason itself'.

Here, in this volume, for a colleague who has helped generations of Indian students to voyage intrepidly towards their literary futures, I want to focus on three master texts that embody the narrative impulse to persuade communities out of the emotional fatalism and despair that can beset them during calamitous times. They are Giovanni Boccaccio's *The Decameron* (2003), Knut Hamsun's *Hunger* (2008) and Albert Camus's *The Plague* (2010). Without much in the way of explicit theoretical framing or a postcolonial defence of why I have chosen such a lineage of patriarchal 'Western' texts to analyze, I want to argue that world texts, however embedded in the snobberies and pieties of their history, serve as global immunity shields against individual and social mental breakdowns when the going gets really rough. Regardless of their contingent cultural origins, they are critical messaging devices from distant spheres and their core message is simple: Extreme risk is an essential part of the human cognitive environment. Dangers can come

DOI: 10.4324/9781003399926-4

at us anytime from wars and viruses, from out-of-control technologies, from inner devastation or from outer space. Crises in narrative help us to imagine coping strategies against these myriad dangers.

It is true, of course, that one can go about one's quotidian life without ever having read a novel or listened to Raag Yaman Kalyani or stared in open-mouthed wonder at a Kahlo painting. One would surely still survive in a physical sense, but one's capacity to anticipate that unexpected jolt to the nerves, to experience life's intangible thrills and small rewards, to empathize with one's radical others, would be so severely diminished that one would be rendered virtually comatose. We would risk losing that vital part of the human psyche specifically designed to insure against hopelessness and hazard: namely, the narrative belief in a future where countless worlds must be imagined into existence – at least one of which we would want to live in, whose enchantments draw us in. To me, that is a good enough reason to don our coronavirus masks and open wide our post-coronavirus eyes with the first of our textual logbooks.

The Decameron

What textual wonders might we encounter if we voyaged back in time to the 'Great Plague' of 1348 and looked for messages from that remote age to our present world of 2020, more than six and half centuries later, when Covid-19 holds sway?

To begin with, a true story: 12 ships dock in the Italian port of Messina in 1347. The sailors who man them are all either dead on arrival or very gravely ill, covered in the oozing, pus-filled black boils that gave the greatest pandemic of the Middle Ages its lasting moniker: the 'Black Death'. This was the bubonic plague which was to wipe out a third of the population of Europe, or more than 20 million people, in less than a decade. How, we might ask, was 'social distancing' practised then, almost 700 years ago, and how different is the situation today?

A couple of historical coincidences concerning a world narrative of disease transmission and spread could be germane at this point. In 2011, an international group of scientists (Bos et al.) published a paper in the journal *Nature* that traced the genetic route of *Yersinia pestis*, the bacterium that caused the pandemic of bubonic plague in the Middle Ages. Their conclusion then, as now, was that the infection originated in China or someplace nearby. It moved variously via the Silk Road and other land trade routes, until sea traders brought it to the docks of Europe. Then, as now, the first major epicentre in Europe was Italy. Then, as now, the recombinant transmission was animal to human: rats were the proximate cause then, as is the bat or, perhaps, the pangolin, today. Travel routes were the pre-eminent vectors then, as now. Fear, apprehension and hope were the dominant emotions then, as now. What will befall us, the most common question – and isolation the most common preventive strategy.

Medically, it is true that some large differences must be conceded: the infection in the case of the bubonic plague was caused by a bacterium while it is a virus, the *SARS-CoV-2*, to be accurate, that can precipitate the deadly symptoms of respiratory and organ failure in today's patients. For this reason, most comparisons made so far have been, appropriately enough, with the 'Spanish Flu' pandemic between 1916 and 1920.

Yet, in terms of social symptomology, just as revealing could be the long-term impact of the Black Death, which hit Europe in times of relative peace, a century after the bloody fervour of the Crusades had peaked, just as the coronavirus has now gone global in peacetime. To this day, as we know, the Great Plague remains stamped in world memory through the ubiquitous children's rhyme 'Ringa roses' – where the 'roses' refer to the buboes on the bodies of plague victims and the innocuous ending 'all fall down' indicates mass death – although we should note that many credible historians of the medieval period think this a false etymology. False or not, that nursery rhyme remains a lasting literary contribution to the myths of the period. It also turns out that, almost immediately after the Black Death made its dramatic entry into Italy, Boccaccio, an established literary name, began to record the story of the isolationist measures that the elite society of his time took to combat the awful crisis that had so unexpectedly overcome them.

Boccaccio's descriptions of the distress caused by the plague are graphic. He writes of the 'multitude of corpses', of graveyards so full that 'vast trenches' had to be dug 'wherein those who came after were laid by the hundred and being heaped up therein by layers, as goods are stowed aboard ship' and of whole families thrown pell-mell into the streets each day. Conditions were so 'piteous', especially among the 'common people' that:

> what more can be said save that ... so great was the cruelty of heaven (and in part, peradventure, that of men) that, between March and the following July, what with the virulence of that pestiferous sickness and the number of sick folk ill tended or forsaken in their need, through the fearfulness of those who were whole, it is believed for certain that upward of a hundred thousand human beings perished within the walls of the city of Florence, which, peradventure, before the advent of that death-dealing calamity, had not been accounted to hold so many

Another coincidence: the arc of the infection. Boccaccio specifically mentions the period March to July of the following year. Which is precisely where we are now with the coronavirus. Note, too, the reference to the teeming populations of cities. Here, too, Boccaccio's observations are acute: 'fearfulness' and the capacity for 'cruelty' among the unaffected population;

the high death toll in the city of Florence where 'upward of 100,000 perished' when no one even guessed the city held so many! Our cities from Milan to Mumbai have over a hundred times the medieval densities; on the other hand, the coronavirus is far less fatal than the plague – but the bottom line still is 'lockdown'.

The Decameron is the tale of ten aristocrats, young, well bred and well read, who barricade themselves in a villa in order to avoid the grim fates they have witnessed. Call it self-quarantine, if you will – and then recall the advice of governments and experts today: severely limit your travel trajectories, stay put at home, avoid physical contact with possibly infected individuals, try not to stress out. The imperatives of social behaviour in the Middle Ages, it appears, were not dissimilar to ours.

True, we know immeasurably more about medication, drugs and genetic epidemiology today. Global cooperation of the sort that organizations like WHO so swiftly call on would have been unthinkable then. The Great Plague, after all, preceded the births of Shakespeare and Galileo in 1564 by more than 200 years and continued sporadically well into their time, and beyond, to the Indian city of Surat in the late 20th century. Back in 1348, though, modernity and its rationalist, 'scientific' view of natural laws was barely a glimmer in the eyes of even great humanists such as Dante or Boccaccio; and democratic norms were unimaginable. But turn to human nature and its anxieties and we find in *The Decameron* a universal text.

What seems to have remained stubbornly unaltered down the centuries is the generic role that narratives – 'a hundred stories or fables or parables or histories or whatever you'd like to style them' says Boccaccio cheerfully – play in coming to terms with the stress generated by the vengeful and 'devilish' unknown. All that the characters in *The Decameron* do is hang out, telling stories and singing songs. Together, however, they cooperatively create a durable tapestry of hope.

Most modern interpretations of *The Decameron*, such as Pier Paolo Pasolini's famous 1971 film based on the book, have highlighted the bawdy concupiscence, the persistent lust and lechery on display in these stories. But it does not take a Freud to surmise that the obsession with the body in *The Decameron* at a time when the mutable human body is under terrifying siege makes robust psychological sense. These stories form immunity cordons. They ring-fence the young people marooned in their Italian villa against desperation.

One of the striking features of *The Decameron* is that its cast of characters is so young and, rather surprisingly, mostly female, consisting of seven women (Boccaccio specifically mentions that their ages range between 18 and 28), and only three men. Why? Well, for one thing it is clear throughout the text that Boccaccio thinks women are more naturally talkative and empathetic. Indeed, at the end of his book, he credits his female neighbour with complimenting his 'tongue' as 'the best and sweetest in the world' although some, by implication male critics, are of the opinion that the selfsame tongue is quite 'venomous'.

More fundamentally, Boccaccio's underlying philosophy appears to be that it is not so much the sagacity of old age that is required in times of unprecedented crisis but a buoyant belief in the future such as that comes naturally to the young. Today, we'd say that the evolutionary will to survive and mate for the good of species, and to lead a good life, *la dolce vita*, is a primal instinct in the young – in today's millennials, for example. In this respect, we could argue that the coronavirus metaphorically follows the pattern set by Boccaccio. It spares the young. The young are certainly 'not invincible' when confronting an unpredictable virus or bacterium, as the present Director of the WHO has acutely cautioned. Should they believe they are, though, the Director of the National Institute of Allergy and Infectious Diseases in the US, Dr. Antony Fauci (himself, by coincidence, of Italian origin) adds a wise ethical footnote: the young, as much as any, owe a debt to the rest of the species not to act irresponsibly and selfishly. It is here that the message of *The Decameron* resonates.

Boccaccio, I would argue, offers us a microcosm of an early humanist world in the making. Though embedded in the local and inevitably mired in the prejudices of the time, its vision is astonishingly non-polarizing and inclusive. For example, the trope of the Jew as the iconic 'other' is prominent. But Boccaccio's Jews are not evil or worthy targets of hate; they are rational agents capable of changing their views and becoming 'Christians' when confronted with unpalatable facts. Simultaneously, the Christian clergy are roundly condemned for their hypocrisy and venality, as are the 'pickmen' who collect and dump the dead for money; Boccaccio calls them 'bloodsuckers'. Today, such leeches could well include the very highly placed, such as, let's say, present-day politicians charged with acting in the interests of the people who seek instead to profit from the calamity.

On display in *The Decameron* is the entire range of human folly: deceit, duplicity and dread violence. In one typically melodramatic story, a father cuts out his daughter's lover's heart and offers it to her in a silver dish, whereupon she pours poison into the bloody bowl and consumes the gory potion, killing herself instantly. The point is that these harrowing instances of 'man's inhumanity to man' only throw into luminous relief the innate goodness and generosity of ordinary folk. In this sense, Boccaccio intelligently recognizes that nature, in essence, is non-hierarchical, even if culture chooses to privilege some over others.

If the adage is that death is the great leveller, infectious diseases surely come a close second. *The Decameron* begins with the pious declaration: 'A kindly thing it is to have compassion for the afflicted' and then proceeds to examine, with no small degree of irony, the forms and genealogy of such empathy. It ends with deep, self-reflexive humility: 'I confess that the things of this world have no stability and are still on the change and so it may have befallen on my tongue'. In other words, no judgment is infallible, and even one's most cherished beliefs are subject to correction. Part of this humility may be due to the demands of literary convention but part of it seems to stem from genuine conviction. Boccaccio was deeply aware of the instability of his world and, consequently, his words. Admit it, as Boccaccio bravely did – or not – we are perhaps just as uncertain about the 21st-century twists and turns in the continuing story of Covid-19. That is why reading the medieval *The Decameron* in the modern corona hotspots of New York and New Delhi (a bit like *Reading Lolita in Tehran* during the years of the Islamic Revolution of the 1980s) could be just the social prophylactic against the desolation, depression and despair that we need in these troubled times.

The Global Text of *Hunger*

If *The Decameron* was about attractive young aristocrats dealing with the mental stress of the Great Plague by exchanging stories and making music, Knut Hamsun's starkly titled novel *Hunger* was half a millennium down the road about another kind of breakdown also witnessed in our own Covid-19-stricken times. This is the impact that the economic crisis engendered by such an event can have on the most precariously placed in any society. Hamsun received the Nobel Prize for Literature in 1920, about a century ago, and his best-known work to this day remains *Hunger*, an alarmingly accurate study of the physical and mental distress caused by extreme poverty in a Norwegian town sardonically named Christiania, towards the end of the 19th century. As Hamsun saw it, hunger broke the back of rational thought; it destroyed the body in a manner that the soul could not tolerate, leading to 'immoral' actions such as theft, corruption and enraged destruction of property.

Reading *Hunger*, like reading *The Decameron*, teaches us that great literature, like the most potent of viruses, does not recognize national boundaries. The harrowing scenes in recent Indian media of daily wage earners, informal workers and migrant labour wanting to return at all costs to their villages, reduced as they are to living in the unbearable conditions imposed on them without warning by the stringent lockdown measures in our cities, remind us that the text of hunger is – and always has been – global. It is no accident that the Director of the UN Food Programme has just warned of a 'hunger pandemic' also looming in 2020 that could kill as many as 300,000 *every day* for the next few months, in addition to the Covid-19 toll, unless quick action was taken. And in India, the irony of farmers agitating across the country because broken supply chains, complicated procurement laws and unstable markets have left them bereft at the very moment when they have borne the burden of feeding the entire country has not escaped anyone's notice. As Covid-19 moved from the metropolises of Mumbai and Delhi out into a rural hinterland where medical help is scarce or non-existent, we see with the sure fatefulness of a Greek tragedy that it is the poor in our far-flung village localities who will finally be hit hardest by this 'global' pandemic.

So, if the world today collectively seeks to effect an enormous paradigm shift from the familiar competitive model of 'the survival of the fittest' to the compassionate one of 'the survival of the weakest' – the poor, the sick and the old – the deep probes of the human sciences could in fact prove invaluable in this endeavour, since a post-coronavirus situation, like a post-truth one, will actually depend on a sophisticated skill set that can separate fake data from the real and derive qualitative empathy from quantitative graphs. Arguably then, Indians have as much to learn, in terms of our shared humanity, from Hamsun's dark and complex portrayal of hunger as Norwegians from, say, Premchand's descriptions of utter destitution in 'Kafan' or *Godaan*. And at this point I offer, as I did with *The Decameron*, a single extended passage from Hamsun's text:

> The pains of hunger were unbearable and never let me alone. I swallowed spit over and over to take the edge off, and I felt it did some good. I had had very little to eat generally for several weeks, even before this current trouble, and my strength now was falling off noticeably. Whenever I had been lucky and scraped up five kroner by some maneuver or other, the money never managed to last long enough to get me back on my feet before a new famine fell on me.
>
> How could it be that nothing ever turned up for me! Didn't I have the same right to life as anybody else, Pascha, the rarebook seller, for example, or Hennechen, the steamship clerk? And didn't I have shoulders like a giant and two strong arms for work, and hadn't I in fact tried to get a job chopping wood on Møller Street to earn my bread? Was I lazy? Hadn't I applied for jobs … and worked night and day like a madman? And hadn't I lived like a miser, eaten bread and milk when I was rich, bread when I wasn't, and gone hungry when I had nothing? Did I live in a hotel, did I have a suite of rooms on the second floor? I lived in a shack, a loft, in a tinsmith's shop deserted by both God and man since last winter because snow came in.

Substitute the word 'snow', and you will recognize the unsentimental accuracy of this description in 21st-century India. For all the well-intentioned talk of 'we are in this together', we hear so frequently in these Covid-19 times, a novel like *Hunger* forces us to remember that while every society in the world struggles with the demeaning facts of inequality, in every case it is invariably those citizens whose rights, even in the best of times, come last, who are the first to suffer when disaster hits. They may have done nothing in the least criminal, but they are the ones most likely to be 'criminalized' for breaking the rules. Disasters throw into sharp relief the fissures that already exist within cultures: between those at the edge of poverty lines and those at the pinnacles of the social order. But is it not perverse to select a novel from Norway, of all places, to make this point?

Norway, after all, is one of the richest countries in the world and ranks first on several global indices, such as the Human Development Index (HDI), the Index of Public Integrity (IPI) as well as the Democracy Index (DI). In contrast, India stands at an unconscionable 102 on a list of 117 countries on the 2019 Global Hunger Index (GHI). This is not, however, an attempt at self-flagellation; it is simply to observe that, at first glance, there seem to be few points of comparison between these two vastly different countries. For starters, India's size and diversity imply that its tryst with democracy and development has to be incommensurable with Norway's, which has a population of under six million.

Yet, the fact is that hunger and farmland poverty were a grim reality in Norway not all that long ago, leaving an indelible mark on the psyche of the nation. Hamsun's novel *Hunger* is a literary manifestation of that scar.

At a time when the pandemic appeared to have presented India with disturbing choices between 'lives and livelihoods', between deaths from hunger and deaths from an infectious disease, my suggestion is that we can maybe learn more than meets the eye from the unlikely juxtaposition of the Indian and Norwegian scenarios through the lens of Hamsun's iconic novel *Hunger*. Posing the dilemmas of human vulnerability in terms of a face-off between 'nature' (the course of a pandemic) and 'nurture' (the economics of making available goods and services to people at large) immediately comes under a critical scanner when we do this. This is because vulnerabilities vary. Norway was once a conservative and relatively stressed country; it is now a very wealthy one, partly because of its large reserve of oil deposits but, equally, it is rich because it has a highly progressive democracy and an educated electorate. The huge hit that oil prices have taken during the present crisis might affect Norway's economy, but we can safely bet that its longstanding social investments will stand it in good stead. And ironically, Norway still imports basic items such as cereals, whereas India possesses huge buffer stocks of grains that, for some unfathomable reason, it has as yet failed to distribute freely and without question to its hungry – and increasingly angry – population.

But can fictional texts possibly contribute to a debate on such basic social questions? I believe that they do so by revealing a fundamental flaw in most top-down policy recommendations concerning the amelioration of distress. In our straightjacketed bureaucratic imaginations, the poor are often conceptualized as mere bodies. These 'masses' must be fed, clothed and kept healthy, but their individuality is less than important in a developing society.

This is a cardinal error. *All* humans, including the children most likely to suffer the lifelong effects of malnutrition, are perpetual thinking machines, fuelled by endless desires, intentions and emotions (see Nair 2003, 2020a). It is exactly these mental resources that give the 'common man' the uncommon resilience to resist the good advice of 'the authorities' and proceed on long marches without any support from the state, risking death along the way.

Disciplines like literature, philosophy and psychology are crucial because they typically view civilization and its discontents in terms of insubordinate minds rather than just as passive bodies – they show that minds are idea factories that can produce either horror or healing, fake news or true insight (see Nair 2009, 2011a, 2018). Consider a last chilling illustration: both Knut Hamsun and the infamous Anders Behring Breivik, who shot dead 77 people in Oslo and Utoya in 2011, were Norwegians with explicit Nazi and fascist sympathies. Both were subjected to significant cruelty as children, leading to psychological problems in adulthood. Despite being born 120 years apart, both were obsessed with Christendom, subscribed to cultural nationalism and celebrated nativist 'son of the soil' ideologies. It is the differences, though, that are crucial.

Every page of *Hunger* offers a compellingly honest, excruciatingly self-aware text that transcends its author's faux beliefs. Breivik's e-compilation *2083: A Declaration of European Independence*, in contrast, presents a shallow and silly 'manifesto' where one is hard put to find a single original observation. Breivik believed Muslims were being encouraged to immigrate to Norway because of the government's liberal policies. Hence, supporters of that view deserved to die! In Hamsun's fiction, one can literally hear the birdsong amid the silences; genuine empathy pervades his narratives. But in Breivik's global social media echo chamber, all you hear is endless chatter. Empathy is crowded out. This could be why Breivik was oblivious to a stunning social detail that I feel sure Hamsun would have noticed.

Indian newspapers back in 2011 reported that Breivik 'was wearing a uniform with an embroidered insignia at the time of his arrest. The insignia, ordered online by Breivik for his militant outfit Justiciar Knight, was embroidered by Mohammad Aslam Ansari'. So absorbed was the Muslim baiter Breivik with his own narcissistic image that it appears he could not care less that its backend producer happened to be a Muslim weaver from the holy Hindu city of Varanasi! In an interview published on 26 July 2011, the newspaper *The Hindu* noted a further irony. It reported that not only was Ansari horrified when informed of the identity of his buyer, his hopes of a financial boost through his rich Norwegian contact were completely dashed.

I am back to square one, doing jobs on my family loom for others. Generally, we are paid Rs. 150 a metre, of which half goes to the weaver who is working on the loom. It is too meager to meet even our daily needs.

If the coronavirus crisis has brought one truth home to us, it is that going 'back to square one' is not an option. Independent India has managed to wipe out the famines of the colonial period and eradicate dread diseases like smallpox. Visionary leaders such as Gandhi also developed the fast or 'hunger strike' as a highly effective political tool. Now post-coronavirus, India must find the same willpower to eliminate hunger and strengthen its rickety healthcare system. This goal is eminently achievable – but only if India simultaneously undertakes the cognitive challenge of training its youthful, mobile-savvy citizenry, such as the students we attempt to school at local Delhi institutions like JNU, IIT or Jamia, say, to distinguish between the real voices of Ansari and Hamsun and the false ventriloquisms of a Breivik. For this to happen, we must absolutely lift the prolonged lockdowns to which our education systems have been subject over the years (see Nair, 2017, 2022).

The hunger for knowledge or 'epistemic hunger' has been an evolutionary constant in human societies (see Nair 2003, 2011b, 2014). Like viruses, like food hunger, it has lived within humans for millennia. Each of these forces shares in the neurochemical design of human warning systems. What we need today is a deeper understanding of the phenomenology of these intimate enemies. The nameless narrator in *Hunger* in fact invents a whole new word for his hunger experiences: *Kuboaa*. This word, as it first enters the character's consciousness, could signify anything: *padlock* or *sunrise* or even *God*. It is precisely this destabilization of normative semantics that presages coronavirus times. As the narrator comments: 'My thoughts took amazing leaps as I tried to establish the meaning of my new word'. Few would deny that our shaken world is now ready – even hungry – for precisely such 'amazing leaps' of thought.

The Plague

If ever there is a space where 'amazing leaps' of thought can coexist with soul-killing boredom, an Indian classroom surely constitutes that ambiguous space of interpretation and interaction. This last section of my chapter simply comprises a sort of tacit 'teacher-to-teacher' communication. I share here, without much comment, part of a question paper from a recent course 'hybrid' I taught at IIT Delhi, with GJV and other colleagues in the field of 'literary studies in India'. Why do I do so? Well, this was a course on 'Modern Fiction' or more cryptically, in characteristic IIT fashion, HUL238, intended for undergraduate students in engineering, some doing a 'humanities' course for the very first time, while others were veterans who'd soldiered their way through several such courses.

Some among this large class of 120 or so students even admitted to 'loving literature', and thus, beginning with Virginia Woolf's classic 1919 essay on 'Modern Fiction', we enthusiastically chomped our way through theoretical perspectives from Marxism to Symbolism to New Historicism. We had already discussed Joyce and Kafka and were relentlessly moving towards Rushdie and Roy when we were interrupted by the coronavirus lockdown. And so, mid-semester, HUL238 suddenly morphed into a protean hybrid: face-to-face in its early avatar and entirely virtual in its later one. Such a dramatic move to an 'online' mode also inevitably brought in its wake a host of issues ranging from problems of logistics to controlling plagiarism to a certain degree of haunting alienation – but these are matters for longer term discussions as the world now lurches towards the unknown dangers and seductions of 'virtual learning' (see Nair 2015, 2019, 2020b, 2021).

The point is that Covid-19 acted as a *force majeure*. It decreed that we should make space on HUL238 for a text that would not necessarily have attracted our attention in more 'normal' times. This was Albert Camus's *The Plague*. First published in 1947, a year that recalls a tryst with destiny for every Indian, this novel offers a splendid illustration of the basic thesis with which I began. Literary texts comprise rescue squads at times of crisis; they enable that life-sustaining move from states of stunned inaction and hurt to those of startling self-recognition and psychological healing.

Some questions I asked specifically on *The Plague* in HUL238 follow. I regret very much that I cannot include my students' answers here, both for reasons of space and because I have not had the chance to seek their permission. But questions of any variety are always a good starting point for discussion, so here goes:

HUL238 'MODERN FICTION' MAJOR EXAMINATION SEMESTER II 2019–2020
Question I–IV. On *The Plague* by Albert Camus:

Ii. SUBALTERNISM: *The Plague* is set in the ordinary 'modern' French colonial city of Oran on the Algerian coast. The main characters are all French. Why do you think there is such a noticeable absence of African 'locals' in the novel? Can you find them, for example, among the patients that Dr. Rieux cares for or among the congregation to whom the priest Paneloux preaches or anywhere else? If so, how are they represented? Does the concept of the 'subaltern' from postcolonial theory explain this absence? How?

Or:

Iib. All the main characters in the book are male; the women are subsidiary. Could we argue that the women characters in this novel are a type of 'subaltern'?

II. NARRATIVE POSITIONING: The third person narrator in *The Plague* reveals his identity toward the end and becomes a first-person narrator. Why do you think Camus makes this unusual stylistic move in the novel?

III. EMBODIMENT: 'New Historicism' emphasizes the body as a textual site for the representation of great conflict as well as unusual insight. Select any **two** or **three** representations of the body (human, animal) in *The Plague* that illustrate, in your opinion, its historical, as well as universal, significance.

IV. THE RELEVANCE OF FICTION: Do you think reading the novel *The Plague* at a fraught time when the Coronavirus is spreading throughout the world has special implications? Choose any **two** or **three** scenes from the novel that you believe have parallels in the present, and explain how you think these scenes help us understand our own predicaments better.

V. Read the long passage below carefully and then answer the four questions below in not more than **150** words each. You may write less, of course.

Next day, by dint of a persistence that many thought ill-advised, Rieux persuaded the authorities to convene a health committee at the Prefect's office … The Prefect greeted them amiably enough, but one could see his nerves were on edge. "Let's make a start, gentlemen," he said. "Need I review the situation?" Richard thought that wasn't necessary. He and his colleagues were acquainted with the facts. The only question was what measures should be adopted. "The question," old Castel cut in almost rudely, "is to know whether it's plague or not." Two or three of the doctors present protested. The others seemed to hesitate…

Rieux, who had said nothing so far, was asked for his opinion. "We are dealing," he said, "with a fever of a typhoidal nature, accompanied by vomiting and buboes. I have incised these buboes and had the pus analyzed; our laboratory analyst believes he has identified the plague bacillus. But I am bound to add that there are specific modifications that don't quite tally with the classical description of the plague bacillus." Richard pointed out that this justified a policy of wait-and-see; anyhow, it would be wise to await the statistical report on the series of analyses that had been going on for several days.

"When a microbe," Rieux said, "after a short intermission can quadruple in three days' time the volume of the spleen, can swell the mesenteric ganglia to the size of an orange and give them the consistency of gruel, a policy of wait-and-see is, to say the least of it, unwise. The foci of infection are steadily extending. Judging by the rapidity with which the disease is spreading, it may well, unless we can stop it, kill off half the town before two months are out.

That being so, it has small importance whether you call it plague or some rare kind of fever. The important thing is to prevent its killing off half the population of this town." Richard said it was a mistake to paint too gloomy a picture, and, moreover, the disease hadn't been proved to be contagious; indeed, relatives of his patients, living under the same roof, had escaped it. "But others have died," Rieux observed. "It doesn't matter to me," Rieux said, "how you phrase it. My point is that we should not act as if there were no likelihood that half the population would be wiped out; for then it would be." Followed by scowls and protestations, Rieux left the committee-room.

Some minutes later, as he was driving down a back street redolent of fried fish and urine, a woman screaming in agony, her groin dripping blood, stretched out her arms toward him. (1960, 46–49)

*The above is a shorter version of the passage from The Plague that the IIT students were actually asked to analyze.

Vi. Discuss **four** features of Dr. Rieux's character as it emerges from this passage, supporting your analysis with quotations from the text.

Vii. Describe the differences between the **three** points of view that are represented by: a. The Prefect; b. Castel and c. Richard. Then say with whose perspective you most **disagree** with and why.

Viii. a.   Three out of the four characters in this scene are doctors. How do you know this from their utterances? Provide one example for each character from the text.

b.   Which **one** is not a doctor and what is his role in the meeting?

c.   Who do you think has the **most** medical expertise? Pick **four** phrases from the text that support your hypothesis.

d.   Why do you think Dr. Rieux is followed by 'scowls and protestations' as he leaves?

Viv. What do you think is the significance of the passage ending with the **last two lines** which apparently have very little to do the meeting at the Prefect's office? What larger message do you think Camus is trying to convey to his readers through this image?

VI. **CRISIS AND TRAUMA:** The sociolinguist William Labov has argued that any story has the following six parts: **Abstract, Orientation, Complicating Action** or **Crisis, Resolution, Evaluation** and **Coda.** In class, we discussed Labov's position that by far the most important of these parts was the **Crisis.** On this question, you have to compare the crisis in Kafka's *Metamorphoses* with the crisis in Camus's *The Plague.* Spell out **two** ways in which these crises are **similar**; and **two ways** that they are **different.** Briefly discuss your views on how the **crises** in **both** texts relate to the other structural parts of a story.

Or

Vb. On your Minor I question paper, you had to write a short dialogue between a Marxist and an Absurdist critic discussing their divergent views on Kafka's *Metamorphosis*. This time you have to write a short fictional dialogue between God, the coronavirus and a human being (e.g. a doctor, an economist, a 'common man' or even yourself), arguing about the traumatizing matters of life and death raised by the present global crisis and its possible future consequences.

Or

Vc. How do you think reading fiction and telling stories helps understand the dilemmas and crisis of modernity – in particular the present coronavirus crisis? You can illustrate your answer both with reference to fictional texts and non-fictional anecdotes and facts. This question is a free-ranging, speculative one and, for once, I am not setting any boundaries for it. **END OF PAPER – GOOD LUCK!**

My question paper, I note, ends by conventionally wishing my students good luck. As I end this quasi-academic paper, though, it strikes me that 'a little bit of luck' is not just what students need in exams; it may be what all of us yearn for in hard times. Literary texts from *The Decameron* to *Dui Bigha Jomi* (Tagore, 2004) form, in this regard, a very precious part of our species inheritance not of loss (see Desai, 2006) but of sheer luck as we now attempt to negotiate our post-coronavirus, post-truth and even perhaps our post-human futures.

Acknowledgements

I would like to thank *The Hindu* in which parts of this chapter appeared in 2020; I am grateful to all my students on HUL238, as well as my Teaching Assistants, Susan Haris and Sevali Hukku, for their many insights.

References

Boccaccio, Giovanni, *Decameron*, Penguin Classics, London, 2003 (first published circa 1353).

Bos, K., Schuenemann, V., and Golding, G., (2011) in *Nature* **478**, 506–510.

Camus, Albert, *The Plague*, Penguin Essentials, London, 2010 (first published 1947).

Desai, Kiran, *The Inheritance of Loss,* Hamish Hamilton, London, 2006.

Hamsun, Knut, *Hunger,* Farrar, Straus and Giroux, New York, 2008 (first published 1890).

Nair, Rukmini Bhaya, *Narrative Gravity: Conversation, Cognition, Culture,* Routledge, London and New York, 2003.

Nair, Rukmini Bhaya, *Poetry in a Time of Terror: Essays in the Postcolonial Preternatural,* Oxford University Press, New Delhi and New York, 2009.

Nair, Rukmini Bhaya, "The Nature of Narrative: Schemes, Genes, Memes, Dreams and Screams!", in A. W. Geertz and J. S. Jensen (Eds.), *Religious Narrative,*

Cognition and Culture: Image and Word in the Mind of Narrative, Equinox Series in Religion, Cognition and Culture, London, 2011a, pp. 117–146.

Nair, Rukmini Bhaya, "Thinking Out the Story Box: Creative Writing and Narrative Culture in South Asia", in *Text,* **10**, 2011b, pp. 1–22.

Nair, Rukmini Bhaya, "Narrative as a Mode of Explanation: Evolution & Emergence", in Michael Lissack and Andrew Garber (Eds.), *Modes of Explanation: Affordances for Action and Prediction,* Palgrave Macmillan, New York, 2014, pp. 140–154.

Nair, Rukmini Bhaya, "Virtue, Virtuosity and the Virtual: Experiments in the Contemporary Indian English Novel", in Ulka Anjaria (Ed.), *The History of the Indian Novel in English,* Cambridge University Press, Cambridge, 2015, pp. 251–266.

Nair, Rukmini Bhaya, "Imaginaries of Ignorance: Five Ideas of the University in the 21st Century", in Mrinal Miri (Ed.), *The Place of the Humanities in the Indian University,* Routledge, London, 2017, pp. 140–175.

Nair, Rukmini Bhaya, "Intending to Mean, Pretending to Be: Reflections on the Limits on Genre", in R. Page, B. Busse, and N. Nørgaard (Eds.), *Rethinking Language, Text And Context: Interdisciplinary Research In Stylistics,* Routledge, London, 2018, pp. 147–163.

Nair, Rukmini Bhaya, "Epithymetics: The Psychology of Desire", in G. Misra (Ed.), *Annual Review of Indian Psychology,* Volume 1 'Cognitive and Affective Processes', Oxford University Press, supported by the Indian Council of Social Sciences Research (ICSSR), Oxford and New Delhi, 2019, pp. 204–270.

Nair, Rukmini Bhaya, "Figuring it Out: Old Modes and New Codes for Multimodality, Technology and Creative Performativity in 21st Century India", in Hidalgo L. Downing and Mujic B. Kraljevic (Eds.), *Performing Metaphorical Creativity,* John Benjamins, Amsterdam, 2020a, pp. 311–342.

Nair, Rukmini Bhaya, and Peter deSouza (Eds.), *Keywords for India: A Conceptual Lexicon for the 21st Century,* Bloomsbury, London, 2020b.

Nair, Rukmini Bhaya, "'Do You Believe in God, Doctor?' The Atheism of Fiction & the Fiction of Atheism", in *Sophia: International Journal of Philosophy and Traditions,* Special Issue on Living Without God: Multicultural Spectrums, Springer Nature, Amsterdam, 2021, https://link.springer.com/article/10.1007/s11841-021-00888-8.

Nair, Rukmini Bhaya, "Postcolonial Pragmatics", in J. A. Ostman and J. Verschueren (Eds.), *The Handbook of Pragmatics,* John Benjamins, Amsterdam & Philadelphia, 2022, pp. 35–77, https://benjamins.com/catalog/hop.24.pos2.

Tagore, Rabindranath, "Dui Bigha Jomi", in *Katha o Kahini,* Visva-Bharati Press, Kolkata, 2004 (first published in 1899).

3

THE PANDEMIC AND THE POSTCOLONIAL

Meena T. Pillai

How does the Covid-19 pandemic force a paradigm shift in the way social identities are imagined by the various processes of colonization and Western dominion? As the virus went on a rampage in many once colonizing nations, did it also create a rupture in the epistemic history of the postcolonial? What kind of shifts can be seen in the subjective meaning of being postcolonial, not as a historical referent but more as a political, cultural and social collective that is in a state of perpetual negotiation with a shared legacy of colonial domination? How do the discourses around the virus unsettle the very idea of cultural hegemony and oppression, put into place by various master narratives of colonialism, both amongst people living their lives in once colonized and once colonizing countries? Moreover, within the affective and material economies of neo-imperial and neo-liberal capital, how does the virus destabilize the subordinating discourses around health and hygiene both prior to and since formal decolonization? Has the continuing validation of the historical necessity of colonization and its imperial logic in discourses around modernity and modernization, especially those surrounding modern medicine and its scientific and moral authority over what was perceived to be 'pestilence-stricken multitudes' in need of lessons in sanitation and hygiene, begun to be questioned during the time of the coronavirus?

This chapter thus seeks to look at the pandemic through the idea of the postcolonial, situating both within a 'history of the present'. By identifying certain key strands in contemporary negotiations — discursive as well as material — of the pandemic, the chapter seeks to demonstrate that the responses to the pandemic have problematized the genealogy of (post)coloniality by virtue of the contradictory currents it has enabled: on the one

DOI: 10.4324/9781003399926-5

hand, it has upset the conventional West-centric colonial hierarchies. On the other hand, this has both coexisted with reinforcements of conventional orientalist discourses and reinforced the neo-imperial agenda of the contemporary capital.

The Empire under Quarantine

While colonial discourses invested the British colonial masters with a medical authority that was allegedly wanting in the (again) allegedly 'irrational' natives, postcolonial re-evaluations of the colonial state's (mis)handling of epidemics have questioned the validity of such claims. This section outlines this questioning and then goes on to propose that the current pandemic has brought about a reversal of the vestigial (neo-)imperialist hierarchies.

The British Empire's handling of the Spanish flu epidemic in India in 1918 is now considered as an instance of the facile nature of the claims of the infallibility of the colonial medical authority. The colonial administrators continued to evince a high sense of confidence in their engagements with curbing the magnitude of the disease, even though it is estimated that nearly seven million Indian lives were claimed by the pandemic. It is deeply ironic that "the self-styled purveyors of European science and medicine proved unable to grasp the significance, or even the dimensions, of the single greatest medical crisis of modern times" (Tomkins, 75). A global history of pandemics shares an uneasy relation with the history of Western imperialism, both of which are precariously seeped in superior claims of Western science and medicine, so crucial to the civilizing logic of colonialism. It has been argued that epidemics in the past had created conditions favourable to the consolidation of imperial or government rule. Therefore, whenever the status quo was questioned, empires which based their claims of occupation and settlement in part on the superiority of European civilization were forced by an obligation to this moral imaginary to secure the safety of their subjects, finding that their power to keep the disease in check was inextricably tied to their credibility as purveyors of European culture and rational government (MacLeod and Lewis, 10–11). In fact, it has been pointed out that oftentimes the colonial administrators constructed a veritable mythology of the epidemic experience, dipping into a crafted storehouse of images that showed "the European community selflessly united to minister to its stricken subjects" (Tomkins, 73). They also accused indigenous people, alternatively for fleeing or congregating, while condemning their "'superstitious' rejection of drugs, which they themselves knew to be useless" (Tomkins, 78). Such claims, however, need to be critiqued from multiple points of view. There are many records of how pandemics left people in colonial India to fend for themselves. Harishankar Parsai has recorded in his *GardishKe Din*, how in 1937–1938, when another episode of the plague struck India, it marked the most dismal time of his life and how in the dead silence of the night, the family would take to chanting bhajans to keep the fear away, because there was nothing much else they could do. "The plague raged in our small rural town, and most people had abandoned their homes and fled to live in huts in the jungle. Our family hadn't. Ma was terribly sick. We couldn't take her to the jungle" (Parsai 158). He further notes:

> In our desolate neighbourhood, enveloped in silence, only our house showed any trace of life. The nights were dark and their only light was a tiny candle in our home. And I was scared of candles. Even the town's stray dogs had disappeared. In the overwhelming stillness of those nights, even our own voices frightened us.
>
> *(quoted in Rai)*

He has written that to describe the terror, uncertainty and despair amidst which his family lived would require many many pages.

In Nirala's memoir *KulliBhat* (translated *A Life Misspent*), written in 1938, he described a Ganges swollen with corpses from the Spanish flu. He writes:

> This was the strangest time in my life … My family disappeared in the blink of an eye. All our sharecroppers and labourers died, the four who worked for my cousin, as well as the two who worked for me. My cousin's eldest son was fifteen years old, my young daughter a year old. In whichever direction I turned, I saw darkness.
>
> *(quoted in Spinney)*

It has been pointed out that in other parts of their colonies too, the British colonial administration failed to make a more fundamental and enduring response to a disease that killed millions of its subjects within a matter of weeks, which, looking back today, is "the epidemic's most striking revelation" (Tomkins, 78).

In the British African colonies during the time of the influenza pandemic of 1918–1919, it has been argued that despite having knowledge of the outbreak and in spite of the claims to greater scientific expertise, the Colonial Office failed in both warning its dependencies and in practical dealings to curb the severity of the outbreak.

> Moreover, in their eagerness to employ "scientific" European remedies vis-a-vis local "superstition," British administrators often indulged in highly unscientific practices. Even though medical science was claimed the victor over African obscurantism during this influenza epidemic, the only true victor was the virus itself. Hence, a blinkered and prejudiced

ideal of European medical superiority, when put into practice, belied its "scientific" basis.

(Tomkins, 64)

The Spanish flu epidemic caused much damage to India's reputation, and the country was viewed as an unlikely party in providing key scientific insights into the spread of the disease.

Indeed, in the global narrative India was viewed almost as collateral damage, a transit station in the wayward peregrinations of a global disease. Besides, India, the most populous society on the planet, was notorious for its poverty and famines: deaths there, even in their millions, were to many outside observers, unsurprising. To read the medical literature of the period is to feel that India's twelve million dead had rapidly become a mere appendage to a more compelling Western story of disease and public health.

(Arnold, 190)

However, it has been argued that not much evidence has been left of the fact that 12 million people died which seems a compelling evidence to draw the conclusion that,

British India was an unmodern society ruled over by an unmodern state, chaotic in form and conduct, unknowing or uncaring about mass mortality or perhaps, after decades of pestilence and famine, impervious to the suffering of its subjects. Appointing enquiry commissions, compiling statistics and reports, applying science to social need – this is surely what modern states do when faced with a crisis of such momentous proportions. Seen thus, India's colonial government in 1918–19 might seem not to have fulfilled its modern responsibilities.

(Arnold, 186)

Many like Ira Klein have pointed out that the huge casualty of the Spanish flu pandemic was the result also of a protracted cycle of mass suffering and mortality which reinforced and accentuated a long-established pattern of death and disease, arguing that,

British attempts to modernize India were themselves partly to blame for this "woeful" saga: by disrupting natural lines of drainage and creating swamps where none had existed before, irrigation canals and railway embankments facilitated the spread of malaria; British rule, along with railways, the opening of the Suez Canal and the new steamship routes, exposed India to outside epidemics in a manner not previously possible;

while at the same time the inherent insufficiencies of colonial medicine and public health failed to check or reverse this fatal trend. But in the context of the 1918–19 influenza epidemic is an argument about botched modernisation and "tatterdemalion" health services sufficient to account for what happened to India and its apparent historical neglect?

(Arnold, 186–187)

The Indian state's management of the pandemic during the Covid-19 outbreak in India poses an interesting contrast in terms of the postcolonial subject positions it has enabled. Public health as a political practice gains new relevance here, as the biopolitical act of governance over populations through modern medicine, technology, surveillance, etc. gains a strange legitimacy in the postcolonial state, even when the structures of monitoring and control might not have been significantly altered from the colonial period. The shift in focus from the colonial elite to the national elite might not greatly impinge upon the modalities of function of the biopolitical apparatus. The biggest lockdown in the world was effected in India on 25 March 2020, with a staggering 1.3 billion people forced to stay at home completely, many of whom had no roof over their heads to call the spaces they inhabited a home, with millions hungry and clueless on how to survive, and more than 12 million pushed into extreme poverty. Yet, a survey result published in the *Times of India* on 23 April 2020 claimed that 93.5% of the people who participated felt that the Indian government had handled the crisis very effectively. The paradigm shift from colonial to postcolonial has to a large extent contributed to the loss of imperial significations around discourses of medicine and its history of hegemonic dominance and control over colonized populations. This does not however mean that colonial mindsets in the perception and use of medicine were completely buried. Race as a visible category/tool of medical distinctiveness or utility might have lost its validity, but class, caste and gender persisted as its variant axes. This, on the one hand, created new forms of exploitation and, on the other, passive and captive markets where vast communities and bodies within the politic find it easy to surrender themselves to the aura of the postcolonial state, imbuing its practices with unique yet contingent identity effects, and thus bringing to bear upon it a sensitivity crafted out of a certain kind of ideological desire. Medicine, as a mediated social practice, becomes embedded within a need for both validation and representation. On 23 August 2020, PTI reported that the Indian Council of Medical Research (ICMR) was in the process of developing an online vaccine portal which will provide information related to Covid-19 vaccine development in India and abroad. The Union Health Minister Dr. Harsh Vardhan was reported saying that India would get a vaccine against the novel coronavirus by the end of the year.

Three COVID-19 vaccine candidates, including two indigenous ones, are in different phases of development in India. The phase-one human clinical trials of the two indigenous COVID-19 vaccine candidates, one developed by Bharat Biotech in collaboration with ICMR and the other by Zydus Cadila Ltd, have been completed and the trials have moved to phase-two, ICMR Director General Dr. Balram Bhargava had said recently.

("India Could Get")

It is interesting to note that the citizens of many erstwhile colonies, and in that sense postcolonial subjects, take an evident pride in governments managing the pandemic better than in the West. It was reported that most people were proud of how India managed the coronavirus crisis, placing the country at the third spot amongst 23 nations.

An overwhelming 87 per cent of Indians felt that their country has managed the crisis well ... "With an index score of 59, India is tied for third place with the United Arab Emirates amongst 23 countries in the study," the survey pointed out.

It said that more than half of Indians rated their national leaders favourably amid the crisis, with 69 per cent satisfied with their top national political leaders.

According to the survey, 45 per cent of Indians felt business leaders responded well in the COVID-19 crisis, above the global average and placing India in the top five. Moving forward, it said one of the top things Indians want most post-crisis is better pandemic technology for contact tracing in future crises. With an index score of 85, China tops the list with the most citizens rating its performance favourably across all four indicators, followed by Vietnam in second with an index score of 77.

("Most People")

Such discourses are often situated within a certain political reflexivity of resisting medicine's overtly hegemonic historiography and within new modalities of staging it in the context of the new pandemic. While it has gained wide acceptance that the postcolonial state may have *actually* managed the crisis better than the colonial government, the argument made here pertains to the lived experience of postcolonial subjects which gains analytical salience by virtue of their role in shaping the contemporary public cultures.

Furthermore, the latest pandemic has been instrumental in mooting the idea that public health is a global issue, thus in a sense destabilizing, however slightly, the neo-colonial slant to public health and well-being, and its patronizing lingo when referring to developing or once colonized nations.

The understanding that the so-called developed nations had efficient public health systems in contrast to low-income nations received a setback as some of the global economic giants came crumbling down under the pandemic and their public healthcare systems drew severe criticism from all quarters. The world came to know that the United States, for example, one of the high-income countries in the world, did not have universal health coverage. Interestingly, countries that best managed the pandemic were not developed countries from the West like the US, the UK, France, Italy or Spain but small East Asian states and territories along with China and Japan. Countries like South Korea have surged far ahead of the historical 'first world' in pandemic control and management, with President Moon declaring South Korea to be "the undisputed 'No.1' epidemic response country leading the world." Through collective mobilization and government-subsidized efforts, South Korea along with China "demonstrated a highly nationalist and politicized model of pandemic containment, linking a country's pandemic response to its global status and to the ruling party's political agenda" (Yi and Lee, 6).

The pandemic has thus also problematized the idea of the 'third world', unsettling some of the deep-seated colonial prejudices that constitute the fulcrum of the imperial logic and civilizing mission. It has been argued that international health issues often tended to be addressed in the context of colonialism,

> where the practical and ideological needs of the colonizing power governed the ideology of public health. Initially, assuring the health of European soldiers, traders and settlers in hostile climates was the priority, and strategies of avoidance and separation the preferred methods. In time, the focus shifted to the health of indigenous populations, primarily as a means of ensuring the availability of a pool of productive labour. In either case, "public health" served the interests of colonial powers.
>
> *(King 765)*

And yet, the recent pandemic has universalized 'isolation', 'distancing', and 'separation', cutting narratives around epidemics and public health adrift from their unholy liaisons with colonial economic and ideological interests. The colonial strategy of pinning down infectious diseases to 'unhealthy', 'infected', non-Western populations and locations, though significantly whipped up by people such as the American President, did not hold currency for long as many Western countries including the US and Italy topped the charts in infections and death, with many non-Western nations sealing off their borders and not permitting traffic with these countries. Thus, there was a reverse notion of segregation and sanitary cordons with developed countries being perceived as sources of contamination.

One can see a paradigm shift of perception that is also marked by "anxieties and solutions, envisioning a world in which the security of territorial borders has faded, to be replaced by one in which vast networks are not only conduits of infection but also prophylactic tools" (King, 773). The following report regarding a 'request' for medicines from India is an indicator of this shift where the earlier ideology of Western medicine and the supposed flow of medical knowledge and resources from the centre to the peripheries, a colonial tool for installing power and subjugating colonized populations, takes a different turn.

US President Donald Trump has said that he has requested Prime Minister Narendra Modi to release the amount of hydroxychloroquine ordered by the United States after India banned the drugs for exports the previous month. Trump said that he spoke to Prime Minister Modi on Saturday morning and made a request to release hydroxychloroquine for the US. "I called Prime Minister Modi of India this morning. They make large amounts of Hydroxychloroquine. India is giving it a serious consideration", Trump said at his daily news conference at the White House on Saturday. India's Directorate General of Foreign Trade on 25 March banned the export of hydroxychloroquine but said that certain shipments on humanitarian grounds may be allowed on a case-by-case basis ("Trump Requests").

The erasure of different epistemological and ideological practices in the interest of centring the practice of Western medicine, as also in foregrounding the logic of colonial civilizing missions, which also resulted in the demonizing of alternate practices and modes of healing, has also come increasingly under scrutiny. While the claims to the salience of ancient Indian forms of knowledge are often a discredited discursive strategy, one cannot completely dismiss all alternatives to Western medicine as being 'fraudulent'. It is in this context that one should read the claims of the efficacy of an Ayurvedic drug in curing Covid-19. The news reports regarding Indian Institute of Technology (IIT) Delhi's collaborative project with a Japanese institute are instructive because the quoted news bytes underline the need to scientifically test the possibility of this approach rather than assuming a priori that it will be effective. Moreover, the report acknowledges that the process may take time and also includes a note of caution. D. Sundar of IIT Delhi said that although these are easily available and affordable, one has to be cautious about the content of bioactive ingredients. While Caffeic Acid Phenethyl Ester (CAPE) is a major component of propolis, its amount and stability are critical factors that could be managed by generating its complex with cyclodextrins ("Aswagandha can be effective"). Such discourses should be differentiated from less nuanced claims of alternative epistemologies. A case in point would be a news report that reads thus:

A group of eminent Indian-American scientists and doctors met with the Indian Ambassador to the US, Taranjit Singh Sandhu, to discuss joint Indian and US trials of Ayurveda formulations for Covid-19. Researchers argue that these medicines have a remarkable record in treating various diseases including Covid-19. They believe that clinical trials are needed to "get rid of all the doubts" around its effectiveness. Huge networks of institutional engagements have finally brought scientific communities between the two countries together in the fight against the novel coronavirus.

("US Joins India")

While this report goes on to feature a comment by the Indian Ambassador which references the IIT Delhi initiative discussed above, the healthy caution voiced in the earlier article is absent in the latter. The phrase "get rid of all the doubts" implies that any questioning of the alternative approach is unwarranted. Nevertheless, this also means an overreach from the postcolonial to the neo-colonial, where indigenous systems of medicine and knowledge are often co-opted into neo-liberal frameworks of market-oriented research, to be packaged, produced and circulated through a global flow of commodified goods within a free market economy. As has been argued, especially in the context of Anthony Giddens's reminder of new alliances within the networking impulses of Western modernity,

This postcolonial imaginary is characterized not so much by the overt export of medical theories (though this does doubtlessly occur as a matter of course), but rather by the integration of localities into the global circulation of information and commodities.

(King, 783)

To push that argument further, the multinationalization of indigenous medical epistemologies and health practices explicates the rather problematic and complex intertwining of the colonial, postcolonial and neo-colonial in a vast commodity, capital, information and communication network. Thus, while the history of unholy liaisons between Western medicine and imperialism has been unsettled by newer kinds of political economies of global healthcare, this has also created new centres of corporate power where market economies often make the postcolonial welfare state seem redundant. The US President's threat of 'retaliation' against India in the event of hydroxychloroquine not being exported, which India had banned 'without an exception', and the lifting of that ban give vital clues on fear of trade embargoes today.

However, at another level, the flow of goods and ideas is also a reminder of the flow of identities and bodies, especially so during the pandemic, giving crucial indicators to the need to resist the essentialisms, so integral to resurgent nationalisms of both hegemonic superpowers in the Global North and that of postcolonial developing nations in the Global South.

Survival of the Hegemony

The responses to the pandemic in the postcolonial world have been characterized not only by ruptures with the colonial epistemologies but also by problematic continuities. In other words, the postcolonial states have drawn on repressive state mechanisms established during the colonial era in their efforts in combating the pandemic, thereby adding on to the repression of the non-elite. The Spanish influenza, considered to be one of the worst pandemics in the modern age, is estimated to have killed nearly 39.3 million (Patterson and Pyle, 1991) worldwide. The flu, which killed 13.88 million in India's British-ruled districts, was brought from the West through ships carrying the troops returning from the First World War. When the Bubonic Plague struck parts of the Bombay Presidency in British India in 1896, it spread rapidly with almost 1900 reported deaths per week during the peak span. What constitutes modern India, Pakistan and Bangladesh were then under the rule of the Queen and British Parliament. In 1897, the imperial government created an Epidemic Diseases Act enacted by the British Parliament to curb the spread of the plague. It is extremely significant that this Act continues to be the mainstay of the postcolonial nation's fight against the Covid-19 pandemic. What is also interesting is the Act itself, which betrays a constant preoccupation with the 'power' to surveil, govern and regulate individual and social bodies.

> Power to take special measures and prescribe regulations as to dangerous epidemic disease — (1) When at any time the [State Government] is satisfied that [the State] or any part thereof is visited by, or threatened with, an outbreak of any dangerous epidemic disease, the [State Government], if [it] thinks that the ordinary provisions of the law for the time being in force are insufficient for the purpose, may take, or require or empower any person to take, such measures and, by public notice, prescribe such temporary regulations to be observed by the public or by any person or class of persons as [it] shall deem necessary to prevent the outbreak of such disease or the spread thereof, and may determine in what manner and by whom any expenses incurred (including compensation if any) shall be defrayed.
>
> *(The Epidemics Diseases Act 1897)*

One can see how the postcolonial nation too is scripted in the same narrative that more than a hundred years ago helped imperial powers use pandemics as states of exception to govern whole populations. As pointed out by Agamben in the context of Covid-19, "manifest here is the growing tendency to use the state of exception as a normal governing paradigm. The executive decree (decretolegge), approved by the government 'for reasons of hygiene and public safety,' produces a real militarization" (Agamben). Epidemic management thus becomes a point of convergence for the biopolitics of the colonial empire and the postcolonial state, a common political rationality for exerting more power and surveillance for the administration of populations. Regulating lives and livelihoods through the dispersed networks of biopower during the time of the Covid-19 pandemic in fact functioned much more efficiently though oppressively in many of the more 'disciplinary' societies of Asia like China, Korea and, to a certain extent, India, where surveillance and curtailment of personal freedom were much more rigorously implemented than in the 'liberal' West.

One important point not to be missed is how the pandemic exposed the systemic inequalities and structures of oppression and exploitation that continue into the postcolonial state. The precarity in the lives of millions of Indian agricultural and migrant labourers revealed itself during the lockdown, when the middle and upper classes enjoyed the luxury of 'work from home' while vast sections of the Indian populace struggled with poverty, hunger and ignorance, the ire of the state surveillance systems, police atrocities, and broken food and transport systems (Sengupta and Jha, 2020; Ghosh). However, having said this to illustrate how the shift from the colonial to the postcolonial need not translate into alleviation in the conditions of 'bare life' that the most marginalized face during a pandemic, it is to be added that this has also been happening all around the world in differing magnitudes. It has been reported that in just the past six months, more than 22 million American jobs have been lost, and many people are not earning enough to get by (Nova). To think that the most dominant colonizing power less than eight decades ago is haunted by food poverty today might seem like a travesty of history. It has been pointed out that there is another pandemic stalking Britain – hunger, because people have been deprived of the most basic security by deliberate policy (Harris).

Pandey Bechan Sharma's short story *Vibhatsa* described the dehumanization that the Spanish flu brought to the poor people of India, who realized only at the point of death that the corpses they counted included them too. In Master Bhagwan Das's poignant short story 'Plague Ki Chudail', one sees the withering away of humanity and inhuman acts of callousness that epidemics can instil in the human heart. Such stories could be placed in juxtaposition with the long walk the migrant labourers in India undertook during the times of the coronavirus when within a postcolonial nation, its most marginalized citizens were reminded of the failed promise of democracy that is often the legacy of the oppressed in once colonized nations where new forms of collusion of caste, class and capital induce neo-colonial agendas surface most pronouncedly during the time of crisis. If India had been co-opted into a capitalistic economy as a colony by British imperial agendas, the resultant postcolonial nation cannot be entirely innocent of the quagmires of exploitation, the cesspools of oppression that large sections of its population find themselves in as a result of the slow erosion of the postcolonial welfare state under the onslaught of neo-liberal imperatives, as also state market collusions. As Gandhi had pointed out, "to make India like England and America is to find some races and places on the earth for exploitation" (quoted in Prasad, 192).

In closing this discussion, it is vital to briefly dwell on the most evident way in which the Covid era has enabled the continuities of colonialist discourses: the reversals of colonialist hierarchies discussed in the previous section notwithstanding, there has also been a resurgence of orientalist discourses, triggered by the fact that the virus is believed to have first appeared in China. This has led to the resurgence of the orientalist stereotypes of the pestilence-stricken multitudes of the East and irresponsible Orientals. One telling instance would be the US President Donald Trump's controversial words during a press conference held on 11 May 2020. The President's claim that "America leads the world in testing" provoked a query from Weijia Jiang, an Asian-American reporter, as to the appropriacy of the President seeing testing as a sphere of competition while several Americans are losing their lives. Trump's reply was, "Well, they are losing their lives everywhere in the world. Maybe that is a question you should ask China. Don't ask me. Ask China that question. When you ask China that question you may get a very unusual answer". This reply was, justifiably, seen as being racist, and Jiang immediately queried as to why he was addressing that statement to her (Smith). Trump's statement as well as Jiang's retort should be read in the context of the escalation of racist violence against Asian-Americans after the outbreak of Covid-19 (see Tavernise and Oppel Jr.). Trump's claim regarding America's effective testing has been disputed (Smith), and it is an instance of American exceptionalism. Given the United States' stature in the contemporary world order, it is an instance of neo-imperialist discourse. A challenge to that discourse was countered by a statement that was prejudicial to both the marginalized sections of the American society as well as the Chinese, who as a whole were being tarred as being irresponsible and malicious.

An instance from contemporary India complicates this scenario further. A survey conducted between 6 March and 3 April by Manoj Kewalramani of the Takshashila Institution found that 67% of the respondents considered China responsible for the spread of the pandemic. While the majority of these respondents (48.7%) blamed China for what they perceived as its failure to stop illegal wildlife trade and contain the early outbreak, and "lying to the world", the rest (18.2%) believed that China had knowingly engaged in biological warfare (Kewalramani). The responses to the Covid-19 pandemic thus form a significant instance of everyday racism in postcolonial India.

Conclusion

Exploring the pandemic by pitching it in the tenuous terrain of the postcolonial and its rather contingent engagements with the colonial and neo-colonial helps trace a genealogy of 'modern' medicine as a biopolitical strategy, especially in the management and control of risky bodies. Both the race of risk and the risk in race are thus biopolitical in a Foucauldian sense. However, as all that is 'living', and all domains of life come directly under the scanner of political power, and as newer kinds of biometrics surveil, monitor and control bodies during a pandemic that has intensified biopower as never before in history, the 'post' in the postcolonial will remain suspended in a supreme state of exception.

References

Agamben, Giorgio. "The State of Exception by an Unmotivated Emergency." Translated by *Positions Politics*, Positions Editorial Collective, 26 February 2020 at positionspolitics.org/giorgio-agamben-the-state-of-exception-provoked-by-an-unmotivated-emergency/. 2 October 2020.

Arnold, David. "Death and the Modern Empire: The 1918–19 Influenza Epidemic in India." *Transactions of the Royal Historical Society*, 29, December 2019, pp. 181–200; Cambridge Core, at www.cambridge.org/core/journals/transactions-of-the-royal-historical-society/article/death-and-the-modern-empire-the-191819-influenza-epidemic-in-india/7108A9A3EC7F29ED7566C9387ED24B73. 28 October 2020.

"Ashwagandha Can Be Effective COVID-19 Preventive Drug, Finds Research by IIT Delhi and Japan's AIST." *ETHealthworld.com*, 19 May 2020 at https://health.economictimes.indiatimes.com/news/diagnostics/ashwagandha-can-be-effective-covid-19-preventive-drug-finds-research-by-iit-delhi-and-japans-aist/75820118. 3 November 2020.

Harris, John. "There's Another Pandemic Stalking Britain: Hunger." *The Guardian*, 28 June 2020 at www.theguardian.com/commentisfree/2020/jun/28/pandemic-britain-hunger-boris-johnson. 15 November 2020.

India, Central Acts. "The Epidemic Diseases Act, 1897." *India Code* at www.indiacode.nic.in/bitstream/123456789/2326/1/A1897_03.pdf#search=epidemics%20act%201897. 28 October 2020.

"India Could Get COVID-19 Vaccine by Year-end, Says Harsh Vardhan." *The Hindu*, 23 August 2020 at www.thehindu.com/news/national/coronavirus-india-could-get-covid-19-vaccine-by-year-end-says-harsh-vardhan/article32421685.ece. 15 November 2020.

Kewalramani, Manoj. "Survey Findings: Perceptions of PRC amid Covid-19 Pandemic." *The Takshashila Institution*, 15 April 2020 at old.takshashila.org.in/survey-findings-perceptions-of-prc-amid-covid-19-pandemic/. 28 November 2020.

King, Nicholas B. "Security, Disease, Commerce: Ideologies of Postcolonial Global Health." *Social Studies of Science*, 32 (5), October–December 2002, pp. 763–789, JSTOR, at www.jstor.org/stable/3183054. 30 November 2020.

Klein, Ira. "Death in India, 1871–1921." *The Journal of Asian Studies*, 32 (4), August 1973, pp. 639–659, JSTOR at www.jstor.org/stable/2052814. 3 December 2020.

MacLeod, Roy, and Milton Lewis (Eds.). *Disease, Medicine and Empire: Perspectives on Western Medicine and the Experience of European Expansion*. Routledge, London and New York, 1988.

"Most People Proud How India Managed Coronavirus Crisis, Place Country at 3rd Spot Among 23 Nations." *The Economic Times*, 22 May 2020 at economictimes .indiatimes.com/magazines/panache/most-people-proud-how-india-managed-co ronavirus-crisis-place-country-at-3rd-spot-among-23-nations/articleshow/758 90567.cms. 12 December 2020.

Nova, Annie. "The Pandemic Is Driving Millions of America's 'Working Poor' to the Edge." *CNBC*, 19 September 2020 at www.cnbc.com/2020/09/19/coronavirus -how-the-pandemic-impacts-americas-working-poor.html. 15 October 2020.

Parsai, Harishankar. "The Days of Gardish." *Inspector Matadeen on the Moon: Satires* (Translated by C. M. Naim). Katha, New Delhi, 2003, pp. 157–161.

Patterson, K. David, and Gerald F. Pyle. "The Geography and Mortality of the 1918 Influenza Pandemic." *Bulletin of the History of Medicine*, 65 (1), Spring 1991, pp. 4–21, JSTOR, at www.jstor.org/stable/44447656. 25 October 2020.

Prasad, Prashan. *India: Dilemma of Development*. Mittal Publications, New Delhi, 1999.

Rai, Saurav Kumar. "Pandemic Through Indian Literary Lens." *Live History India*, Quintype, 6 July 2020 at www.livehistoryindia.com/cover-story/2020/07/06/ pandemics-through-indian-literary-lens. 22 October 2020.

Sengupta, Sohini, and Manish K. Jha. "Social Policy, COVID-19 and Impoverished Migrants: Challenges and Prospects in Locked Down India." *The International Journal of Community and Social Development*, 2 (2), June 2020, pp. 1–21. *Sage Journals*, at doi 10.1177/2516602620933715.

Smith, David. "'Don't Ask Me. Ask China': Trump Clashes with Reporters Then Abruptly Leaves Press Briefing." *The Guardian, Guardian News and Media*, 12 May 2020 at www.theguardian.com/world/2020/may/11/trump-us-latest -coronavirus-reporters. 27 October 2020.

Spinney, Laura. "Vital Statistics: How the Spanish Flu of 1918 Changed India." *The Caravan*, 19 October 2018 at caravanmagazine.in/history/spanish-flu-1918-ch anged-india. 15 November 2020.

Tavernise, Sabrina, and Richard A. Oppel Jr. "Spit On, Yelled At, Attacked: Chinese-Americans Fear for Their Safety." *The New York Times*, 23 March 2020 at www.nytimes.com/2020/03/23/us/chinese-coronavirus-racist-attacks .html. 15 November 2020.

Tomkins, Sandra M. "Colonial Administration in British Africa during the Influenza Epidemic of 1918–19." *Canadian Journal of African Studies*, 28 (1), 1994, pp. 60–83, JSTOR, at www.jstor.org/stable/485825. 20 November 2020.

"Trump Requests PM Modi to Release Hydroxychloroquine Ordered by U.S." *The Hindu*, 5 April 2020 at www.thehindu.com/news/international/trump-requests

-pm-modi-to-release-hydroxychloroquine-ordered-by-us/article31261271.ece. 5 November 2020.

"US Joins India in Trials for Ayurveda Formulations against COVID-19." *Biospectrum*, 15 July 2020 at www.biospectrumasia.com/news/49/16292 /us-joins-india-in-trials-for-ayurveda-formulations-against-covid-19.html. 5 December 2020.

Yi, Joseph, and Wondong Lee. "Pandemic Nationalism in South Korea." *Society* (57), July 2020, pp. 1–7, Springer, at link.springer.com/article/10.1007/s12115 -020-00509-z#citeas. 28 November 2020.

4

FROM 'COMMONWEALTH' TO 'GLOBAL SOUTH'

Engaging with African Literature in Indian Literary Studies

Mala Pandurang

I begin this chapter in an autobiographical mode to correlate circumstances which have shaped my personal engagement with writing from the African continent to a wider academic movement to dismantle Eurocentric narratives from their privileged position in literature programmes in Indian universities. I will begin by examining circumstances largely instrumental in introducing African writers into the curriculum of literary studies. I will also explore if, and how, this interest has been sustained over a period of four decades. The chapter will attempt to offer insights into cross-cutting issues that can be gained by studying and researching the remarkable body of narratives that the African continent has produced. My focus will be on writing in English produced by anglophone African writers.

In 1986, I registered for an MA programme in English literature at the SNDT Women's University, Mumbai. The syllabus comprised six papers on British poetry, prose, drama and fiction and followed the conventional pattern of being structured according to chronological periods of British history from the Chaucerian era up to the First World War. Also included in the curriculum were two papers on American literature and English language teaching. Later that year, in December 1986, Nigerian playwright, poet and critic Wole Soyinka became the first African to be awarded the Nobel Prize for Literature. He was also the first writer to receive the Nobel Prize from among the 'new literatures' in English that had emerged in the former colonies of the British Empire (Reed Way 1). This Eurocentric international recognition accorded Soyinka's work a stamp of credibility and overnight visibility in Indian academics, and the postgraduate department of English at SNDTWU felt it appropriate to organize a seminar on the

DOI: 10.4324/9781003399926-6

work of this exceptional Nigerian dramatist. While the scope of the seminar was expanded from a discussion of Soyinka's work to African literature in general, the presentations therein were limited to the three African texts that were available for circulation at that point in time, namely Alan Paton's *Cry, the Beloved Country* (1948), Achebe's *Things Fall Apart* (1957) and Ngugi wa Thiong'o's *A Grain of Wheat* (1964). Nevertheless, these narratives generated a great deal of interest as they offered a window to a new world of writing which was vastly divergent from the conventional prescribed texts of British Literature. My curiosity was ignited, and I made particular efforts to access more works by African writers such as Eskia Mphahlele's autobiography of life in South Africa under apartheid in *Down Second Avenue* (1959); Ayi Kwei's scathing satirical attack on corruption in post-independence Ghana in *The Beautyful Ones Are Not Yet Born* (1968) and Kenyan radical activist-novelist Ngugi wa Thiong'o's stringent critic of capitalist neo-colonialism in *Petals of Blood* (1977). My hitherto received image of the continent with its multiple heritage and complex history changed, and I decided to register for a PhD programme on postcolonial African fiction despite the paucity of critical material on this relatively uncharted area in Indian academics.

My resolve to research anglophone writing from the continent was further strengthened after I attended the annual conference of the Indian Association for Commonwealth Literature and Language Studies (IACLALS) organized at 'Dhvanyaloka' – the Literary Criterion Centre for English Studies and Indigenous Arts in Mysuru in 1990. The Centre had been set up by Prof. C.D. Narasimha in 1979 and has served as an important resource centre for scholars and critics keen on exploring newer arenas of literary studies that go beyond conventional texts offered under the traditional curriculum of English literature. To my delight, I discovered that the library at Dhvanyaloka had an extensive collection of current and past issues of the prestigious journal *Research in African Literature*, generously gifted by the late Prof Bernth Lindfors who was the long-time editor of the journal, as well as one of the pioneers of studies in African literature. Prof. Narasimha (or CDN as he was warmly, and respectfully, referred to) is also credited with starting a journal called *The Literary Criterion* in 1952 which provided space for publications of critical essays on writings from former British colonies of India, the Caribbean, Africa and Australia along with studies on American and Indian literatures. By the late 1970s, this area of study of anglophone literature generally referred to as Commonwealth literature increasingly caught the attention of Indian research scholars. The annual conference of the IACLALS became an important meeting point for young research scholars and college teachers faced with the challenge of teaching English literature in postgraduate and undergraduate departments across India and who strongly believed that a drastic change was needed in terms of the traditional frameworks in which literature was studied and taught. At these conferences, we would engage in debates on the use of English as a medium of instruction wherein English was perceived as part of an elitist identity on the one hand, but also acknowledged as a crucial tool of social mobility on the other hand. There was a shared sense of excitement at the possibility of a counter-discursive canon that would challenge the established alliance between English literature, history and ideology. We were like explorers venturing into hitherto unknown territories on a quest for narratives that could help our students to engage more meaningfully with issues of caste, class and gender. Indeed, conferences such as those organized by the IACLALS gave space to scholars in the late 1980s and early 1990s "to question their own place in the world, and hence to question the hegemonic closure of the texts upon which their epistemologies were based" (Ahmed 58).

Several crucial publications in the 1990s posed pertinent questions on the role and validity of English literary studies in the Indian context and stressed upon the need to rethink conventional pedagogic practices. Important among these are Gauri Viswanathan's *Mask of Conquest* (1989); Svati Joshi's Lie *of the Land* (1991); Rajeshwari Sunder Rajan's edited work *The Lie of the Land: English Literary Studies in India* (1992); Sudhakar Marathe et al. *Provocations. The Teaching of English Literature in India* (1993) and Susie Tharu's *Subject to Change: Teaching Literature in the Nineties* (1998). Edward Said's seminal work *Orientalism* (1978) and Bill Ashcroft, Gareth Griffiths and Helen Tiffin's *The Empire Writers Back: Theory and Practice in Post-Colonial Literature* (1989) are generally credited with playing an important role in ushering in what is today known as postcolonial studies as an academic discipline. However, as Diana Brydon reminds us, we tend to forget that as early as 1972 Ngugi wa Thiong'o, along with a group of colleagues at the University of Nairobi, had published a controversial document titled *Towards the Abolition of the English Department* which called for a rejection of an

> additive model of literary study centred on perpetuating the myths of empire and one that re-conceptualised curriculum from the group up, starting from the place where readers are located and working outward toward the world and backward through history from there.
>
> *(Brydon 3)*

Bernth Lindfors explores the opening up of African universities to non-Eurocentric texts in *Long Drums and Cannons: Teaching and Researching African Literatures* (1995). In a chapter exclusively on the Indian context titled "Achebe and the Indians", Lindfors draws from research which he had conducted in the later part of 1989 and suggests that the opening of the English curriculum to non-British subject matter in Indian universities was "a slow but more orderly process" (77). Lindfors describes this transition as proceeding in three distinct phases: first with American literature, which was "aided by a post-war innovation of Fulbright funds in teaching and research, infiltrating syllabus in a significant way in the 1950s" (77). The next phase was when Indian literature in English gained "a secure academic foothold" by the 1970s (77). And thirdly, Lindfors refers to how Commonwealth literature (by which he refers to literature of the rest of the English-speaking world) earned a small niche by the late 1970s and 1980s (77). He, however, stresses that the curriculum revision viz. the introduction of writing from other world literatures such as African writing was not a uniform move.

By the early 1990s, several postgraduate departments of English in Indian universities had begun to put into place major curriculum revisions wherein newer 'national' canons of American, Canadian, Indian writing and even Australian writing gradually emerged. The idea of a canon can be constructed as "an imaginary realm of its authorship" (Luhar 2), and therefore as and when a syllabus revamping occurs and a new set of texts are prescribed by the Boards of Studies, these are transformed into "a list of representative authors or social identities" (Luhar 2). By the mid-2000, specific theme-based papers such as aspects of diaspora and gender studies were also introduced wherein emphasis moved from location-based texts to allow for a wider selection of texts from different parts of the world. Such shifts in focus enabled Indian research scholars to explore comparative approaches between the work of Indian authors and their counterparts in these varied locations. Electives or optional papers were also introduced and titled 'New Literatures in English', 'Commonwealth writing' and Third World literature, which primarily included texts from the former colonies. In time, such nomenclatures gave way to the label of 'postcolonial writing' which has become an umbrella term to cover the literatures of regions such as the African continent, Australia, Canada and the Caribbean islands, as well as specific countries like Sri Lanka and Pakistan. Postcolonialism as a theoretical framework has gained in popularity as it offers scope for critical analysis to be extended to more contemporary issues such as globalization, social media and the environment. By the end of the first decade of the 21st century, syllabi revamping had been extended to most undergraduate programmes in English literature across India.

A selection of fictional and non-fictional writings out of the African continent thus entered into the curriculum of Indian departments of English as part of the wider counter-hegemonic strategy to decentre the cannon of Eurocentric literary classics as mainstream texts. African writers who have been accommodated across genres in syllabi from universities across India include Chinua Achebe, Ayi Kwei Armah, Nuruddin Farah, Ben Okri and Ngugi wa Thiong'o (novelists); Christopher Okigbo, Okotp'Bitak, Gabriel Okara, Kofi Awonoor, Chinua Achebe and Wole Soyinka (poets);

Wole Soyinka, Ama Atta Aido, Efua Sutherland, Athol Fugard (dramatists) and Buchi Emecheta, Ama Ata Aidoo, Flora Nwapa, Grace Ogot and Mariamma Ba (women writers). Not surprisingly, writers who have gained visibility in the West in terms of book awards and promotion campaigns such as Ben Okri (Nigeria), Chimamanda Adichie (Nigeria) and Nadine Gordimer (South Africa) have found their way into the curriculum probably due to easy availability of primary texts. However, the hitch is that it is merely one or two texts prescribed for study which are taken to represent the entire literary output of writing of the continent. Similarly, it is writers from Nigeria who are predominantly prescribed, once again restricting focus to a specific geopolitical region. Veteran novelist Chinua Achebe's *Things Fall Apart* has remained, to date, the most prescribed text by an African writer in Indian universities. The book is taught variously at undergraduate and postgraduate levels, mainly as part of postcolonial writing, wherein students are tutored to examine the text from multiple perspectives including "the colonial encounter and the fragmentation of the Igbo society; the loss of its self-regulatory power and moral base; the politics of identity and the problematics of gendered representation; and questions of leadership and tragic heroism" (Pandurang 19). Achebe's powerful reconstruction of Igbo society in the late 19th-century text lends itself well as a model narrative to illustrate the working of the postcolonial theory given the manner wherein it "imaginatively captures the key moments of African history from the beginning of colonialism to what has come to be known as postcoloniality" (Gikandi xiii). As Lindfors put it, "Most Indian students are introduced to African literature through Achebe and for the some of them African literature begins and ends with *Things Fall Apart*" (79).

The Board of Studies of English of SNDT Women's University took the interesting decision to replace Ernest Hemmingway's *Farewell to Arms* with *Things Fall Apart* as a compulsory text for the "General English' paper for its BA (Arts) second-year programme in 2002. In effect, this meant that the novel would have been taught to a large number of undergraduate women students who were not studying literature themselves. In a personal (unpublished) interview on the rationale for prescribing Achebe's pathbreaking novel in a curriculum intended for improving the language proficiency skills of students, former Head of the Postgraduate Department of English Dr Sunanda Pal explained that the novel had been chosen on three premises (Personal unpublished interview 2014). Firstly, it deals with the colonial experience, which is a shared context with India's historical past. Secondly, it was felt that the text would introduce an element of 'newness' in that it would interest and educate students about a continent they knew very little about. Thirdly, the Board of Studies opined that the narrative would be easy to handle because of Achebe's use of the English language which was perceived as 'simple to understand'. It is an exciting thought to assume that every student who studies *Things Fall Apart* would have set out on her journey of personal and collective postcolonial self-discovery. However, teachers who were given the task of dealing with the narrative in classes meant for English language teaching would undoubtedly have faced challenges wherein they would have had to engage the attention of students who have heard very little about Africa, and being part of a post-postcolonial generation may not have readily related to the narration of a colonial past. Most importantly, the lack of awareness on the part of the teachers of Igbo cultural practices as well as training in postcolonial theoretical frameworks is bound to have reflected in classroom teaching practices. Gaurav Desai's comment in the context of American academics is equally applicable to the Indian context. He points out that "the rise of a field of study designated postcolonial in literature departments has also meant that African novels are read and taught by those who may not identify themselves as Africanists" and therefore are not oriented themselves to the "conceptual, institutional and practical matters of the teaching of the African novel or any other genre for that matter" (Desai 8). The syllabi at SNDT have since been revised, and *Things Fall Apart* has given way to its replacement, an anthology of essays by Sudha Murthy.

There have been select universities across India that have offered exclusive papers on writing from Africa. In a presentation on "Perceptions of African Literature in Non-Western Environments: A Survey of the Status of African Literature in West Bengal" (2017), Kalapi Sen cites the example of Jadavpur University's Centre for Studies in African Literatures and Cultures (CSALC) which had offered a full course in literatures of Africa from 1999 which also included oral narratives, novels and poetry in African languages which were taught in translation since many of the faculty members had expertise in English, French and Portuguese, as well as in Swahili. Currently, Rishi Bankim Chandra College, Naihati (affiliated with West Bengal State University) offers two optional courses titled 'Literatures from Africa' which not only looks at literary texts per se but also takes into account practices of orature, literary and language systems. *E-Pathshala*, which is an online gateway to postgraduate courses, has uploaded detailed coursework online on African and Caribbean Writing with 35 modules on writers from both regions combined. Mumbai University's Department of English has introduced an elective paper in African literature under its MA Honours programme (2018–2019) while SNDT Women's University examines four writers under the category of literature from the Global South, namely Aime Cesaire and Ama Ata Aidoo (drama) and Nadine Gordimer and Nuruddin Farah (novel). By and large, however, the survey of syllabi across Indian universities shows that African writers still remain "fenced in" (to cite Chinua Achebe who appeals: "What I am saying really boils down to a simple plea for the African novel. Don't fence me in" (1974: 636). Despite the initial thrust of postcolonial discourse towards an inclusive approach, Africa as a geo-cultural location in 21st-century literary studies in India is still relegated to the margins of academic discussion. The model syllabus recommended by Curriculum Development Committee of the University Grants Commission makes no attempt to integrate African writers into mainstream courses such as 20th-century literature, the novel as a genre, critical theory, fine arts, theatre film and popular culture, all of which either still retain a Eurocentric core or have shifted to an Indian-centric perspective. Most African authors and their literary output remain restricted to elective courses that are not a mandatory requirement of the programme of work required of students. What emerges is an academic hierarchy resulting in an indirect ghettoization of narratives from particular locations. This is unfortunate given the variety of writing and the exemplary high literary standard of contemporary writing coming from the continent.

In 1995, *The Literary Criterion* published a special issue titled *African Literature Comes of Age*. This was followed by another issue, *New Directions in African Writing* a decade later, co-edited by Victor Dugga and Anjali Gera Roy. Dugga points out in the introduction to the collection that while African literature as a discipline was going strong in Europe and American centres, there were "fewer scholars from Asia and other former colonial territories who were taking an equal interest as the Euro-Americans to study African writings" (Dugga 11). He laments that "not even the spirit of south-south cooperation nor the similarity of postcolonial experiences has adequately stirred up the needed tonic of cross-cultural study" (Dugga 11). Another decade later, in 2015, Gaurav Desai describes how the African novel has steadily gained standing in North American classrooms over the past four decades with the culture wars of the 1980s and the emphasis on the values of multicultural curricula "resulting in an exponential growth in the classroom demand for it" (Desai 8). Sadly, in the Indian context, interest in the literary and cultural production from the African continent continues to be marginalized even in comparative frameworks engaged from within Indian academics. This is despite the close proximity of the African continent to India and centuries-old Indian oceanic connections wherein the Indian subcontinent has shared a historical connection with Africa that predates the colonial era. There are also multiple shared denominators in terms of the Indian and anglophone Africa's British colonial past. M.G. Vassanji's *The Gunny Sack* (1989), which is recognized as the first Tanzanian-Asian novel, offers a fascinating insight into the complex layered history of the Indian community in East Africa at the interstices of colonial and postcolonial histories of East Africa.

The downward curve in the interest in African writing as a choice of research is evidenced by the data available on Shodganga, the national digital repository of theses and dissertations submitted to Indian universities. A search on the number of theses submitted in the last academic year gives an indication of the number and nature of submissions on different aspects of African literature, from across Central and State-run universities in India. The focus of these projects largely remains on veteran writers like Chinua Achebe, Ngugi wa Thiong'o, Wole Soyinka, Ayi Kwei Armah and Buchi Emecheta. Scholars who had once actively taught texts from Africa (Harish Narang, Bale Kothandaram, T. Vijay, Anjali Roy Gera, Manju Dutta Gupta for instance) have either retired or moved on to other areas of research, as a result of which select universities that had early offered electives on African writing no longer do so. Scholars are working actively in the area, but unfortunately, this is a small group. The decline in serious research undertaken by faculty of English Departments will inevitably impact curriculum innovation, as these two areas are closely related. While there are Centres of African Studies in select Indian universities, as well as academic bodies such as the African Studies Association of India, the focus of these bodies is primarily on foreign policies and developmental issues. Funding is undoubtedly a vital element for any new initiative in area studies to go forward. Unlike the support extended to America, Canadian, Commonwealth and Australian literature over the past few decades, it remains difficult to get research and travel grants for exclusive Afro-centric humanities projects.

We are witness to a spurt in economic and political cooperation between the Indian government and the African States in the first two decades of the 21st century. There are growing concerns about the long-term impact of India's role as a player in the field of global capitalism as an increasing number of African countries become a marketplace for Indian manufacturers. Gyan Prakash traces the political idea of Afro-Asian solidarity back to the meeting of representatives of non-aligned Third-World nations in Bandung, Indonesia, in 1955. He makes an interesting reference to Prime Minister Jawaharlal Nehru's scheme to invite African professors and to include African subjects into curriculum so students could have "a more balanced approach to world understanding" (Prakash 194). Also referring to the idea of Asian-African solidarity, Antoinette Burton contends, "one of the tasks of the Nehruvian state was to establish a place for India not simply between two superpowers, but in relationship to the whole of the African continent itself" (Burton 132). The mindset of India-over-Africa at this time, according to Burton, was a legacy of the "superstructures of intracolonial interdependence that the British Empire had created, and from which India was poised to create a new postcolonial empire … a vision of power over the also colonized Other, an India-centered world order" (133). The Indian government is promoting marketing, trade and economic integration between the Indian corporate sector and African markets, but what remains to be addressed is the soft power of the humanities as a vital tool to develop a greater level of understanding among Indian and African communities. Speaking at the Parliament in Kampala in July 2018, Prime Minister

Narendra Modi defined his 'African Vision' in terms of the momentum of cooperation to be sustained through regular exchanges; preferential access to Indian markets for African products; assistance in harnessing digital revolution; improving Africa's agriculture potential and fighting climate change together.[1] Despite his declaration that the youth on both continents should aspire to work for a more democratic global order, there sadly remains a lacuna in structured platforms to promote the exchange of cross-cultural dialogue, which is crucial if we are to address the ostrich-like attitude of the average Indian when it comes to dealing with all things African.

Postcolonial African critics have repeatedly reiterated the importance of teaching the student to read non-Western text with particular sensitivity. The foundation of much of postcolonial writing from Africa was in response to the projection of the Africans as savage, uneducated and without a history. Sadly, students in India today are most likely to continue to associate the continent with images of poverty, illiteracy, famine and disease based on images that stem from the international media and age-old biases. Antoinette Burton offers a close reading of India's age-old relationship with Africa through an analysis of select Indian works of fiction and non-fiction in *Africa in the Indian Imagination: Race and the Politics of Postcolonial Citation* (2016). She argues that Indian discourse on Africa tends to engage in the "politics of post-colonial citation" which she defines as the "locative manoeuvre that serves as a racializing device, positioning Africans as black and Indians as brown, or at the very least as not-African and not-black" (Burton 4). According to Burton, Indian writers have cited or referenced Africa as a buttress of Indian identity "while at the same time, producing a hierarchal positioning of 'brown over black' that has served to refashion Africans as their racialized others" (Burton 4).

We need to therefore ask ourselves as to how far we have gone beyond how Africa, and the African, have been traditionally projected in the Indian imagination. How can we use literary narratives from the continent in a structured manner to challenge the general perception of Africa thus far as a static entity? An interesting alternative approach to the conceptual constructs of European historiography has been put forth by a group of African intellectuals known as 'Egyptians' who suggest how Africa's past be viewed beyond the framework of the colonial experience, which has been the lens largely used to approach African writing. Egypt, which figures prominently on the map of the African continent, was a British Protectorate until 1922. Yet writing from Egypt has not found inclusion in the larger theoretical and cultural discourse of even black postcolonial African intellectuals such as Wole Soyinka, Ngugi wa Thiong'o and Chinua Achebe. One could attribute the reason to cartography as black anglophone African critics have tended, as Schipper points out, "to see the whole area south of the Sahara as a relevant cultural delineation while others take the line between forest and savannah in a given region as a relevant boundary" (Schipper 130). Ghanaian writer Ayi Kwei Armah suggests that Africa's multi-millennial history can be traced back thousands of years to the rise of the ancient Egyptian civilization. Armah asserts that the existence of ancient Egyptian documents was sidestepped by Western historiographers. Ancient Egypt was a highly original civilization, and it was necessary to indicate a source for this civilization. Since the West had decided that Africans were a priori incapable of developing civilization, that source was located outside Africa (Armah 217). Egypt was thus isolated as a unique phenomenon connected to people in its African environment, and the study of Ancient Egypt was not a part of the study of Africa. Armah's sixth novel, *Osiris Rising: A Novel of Africa, Past, Present and Future* (1995), is an anthropological-historical novel, set in a mythical country called Hapag, which has geographical features and monuments that invoke Egypt, Ghana, Senegal and Tanzania. Armah intends for Hapa to be read as a microscopic representation of Africa. The novel centres on his African American protagonist's search for her African roots. In the context of curriculum innovation, Armah's protagonist Assar accepts a teaching appointment at Manda Teacher Training College in Hapa and participates in the designing of a revised curriculum for African studies. Chapter nine of the novel offers a joint position paper from the departments of African Studies, History and Literature wherein Armah argues that colonialism was "a post-conquest European strategy for keeping Africans useably underdeveloped and dependent" (Armah 214). He stresses the "need to liberate our productive intelligence" by creating "new, intelligently adapted curricula" (Armah 214). He advocates a dynamic consciousness of history as a process, inclusive of all sources, written and oral, and proposes a rational definition of the African people's history, of all the continent's inhabitants before Arab and European invasions. This, he proposes, can be done by ensuring that the curricula go "beyond European poles of reference to incorporate studies of Asian, Pacific and Amerindian societies" (Armah 215).

The label of 'African' was employed by the European colonizers to construct a monolithic entity out of a continent of diverse peoples, languages, religions and socio-cultural practices. The same term was adopted by early postcolonial critics from the continent as a point of reference for shared cultural and socio-political experience under colonialism. However, according to Taiye Selasi in her opening speech at the 13th International Literature Festival in Berlin in 2013: "This singular African to which we allude with African literature doesn't exist" (1). She therefore asserts that the very category of African literature itself is "an empty designation" and that "the practice of categorizing literature from the continent from which its creators come is past its prime" (1). She argues that in doing so, we demonstrate "disregard for both the complexities of African cultures and the creativity of African authors" (1). Africa is almost three times bigger in size than

Europe and consists of 54 nation-states recognized by the United Nations. The continent was colonized by the British, French, Portuguese, Germans and Belgians. Selasi reminds us that Africa may well be the "most culturally, religiously, ethnically and linguistically diverse over two thousand languages spoken on the continent, over 400 in Nigeria alone, South Africa has eleven official languages" (6). Selasi points out that while we may take the difference between European writers such as Russian, French and Spanish writers seriously or just as we may differentiate between Japanese and Chinese cultures, we remain indifferent to the nuances of the multi-lingual diversity and cultures within the continent. She therefore champions a "non-national, human-centric approach" to this rich body of writing. On the other hand, veteran novelist Chinua Achebe has pointed out, as early as 1965, that "any attempt to define African literature which overlooks the complexities of the African scene and the material of time is doomed to failure" (Achebe 1965: 27). It may therefore, be prudent to adopt a balanced approach given that the larger number of college-going students in India will require inputs on the cultural and historical particularities of individual African countries, starting with a basic orientation to the cartographic demarcation of the continent and then going on to the "specific thematic, political and aesthetic concerns of the authors who wrote the texts and the audiences and societies to which they were addressed" (Desai 4). The trick would be, as Gaurav Desai puts it, "to engage in a pedagogy that is at once intercultural without being trapped into a simplistic exoticism" (Desai 13).

I conclude with a few suggestions of possibilities of exploring the exciting body of writing from the continent, past and present, that deserves to be respected on par with literary and cultural production from any other part of the globe. Yvonne Vera's *Under the Tongue* (1996) and Mariamma Ba's *So Long a Letter* (1979) could well be taught to demonstrate innovative experimentation with form, whereas Ben Okri's The *Famished Road* (1991) lends itself well to discussions on magic realism. In terms of comparative approaches, there are certain narratives that would fit in well with discussions of South-South developmental issues, which could include Africa, Latin America, developing Asia and the Middle East. 'Global South' is a term that has been used to refer to economically disadvantaged nation-states. In recent years, however, the term is used in a post-national sense to address spaces and people negatively impacted by contemporary capitalist globalization. Mahler explains that critical scholarship that falls under the rubric of Global South Studies can focus on the formation of a Global South subjectivity and include the analysis of

the study of power and racialization within global capitalism in ways that transcend the nation-state as the unit of comparative analysis, and in tracing both contemporary South-South relations – or relations among subaltern groups across national, linguistic, racial and ethnic lines – as well as the histories of those relations in prior forms of South-South exchange. *(1)*

The application of such an approach will allow, for example, for the works of Somali writer Nuruddin Farah, such as *Maps* (1986) and *Gifts* (1992) to be read in the context of South-South development issues. Similarly, Nigeria is one of the world's largest exporters of petroleum and Nnedi Okorafor's science fiction novel *Lagoon* (2014), which is an Afro-futurist tale of an alien invasion of Lagos, lends itself well to the emerging body of petro-criticism or the study of the oil encounter in literature. The long-term degradation of the Niger Delta is central to Helon Habila's *Oil on Waters* (2010) and was the focus of the protest writing of the late Ken Saro Wiwo. Ngugi's *Wizard and the Crow* (2006) takes cognizance of growing urban discontents in terms of social malaise, degradation and political instabilities. Aminata Forna's *The Memory of Love* (2010) juxtaposes personal stories of love and loss within the wider context of the devastation of the Sierre Leone civil war and women writers from Zimbabwe have produced war novels on the role of women in war zones such as Yvonne Vera's *The Stone Virgins* (2002) and Tsitsi Dangarembga's *The Book of Not* (2006). Jack Mpange's *Gathering Seaweed: African Prison Writing* (2002) is a powerful collection of voices of dissidents imprisoned for views against those in power, while Chimamanda Adichie's *Americanah* (2013) and Helon Habila's The *Traveller* (2019) are insightful portrayals of life in diasporic spaces. Tayie Selasi's *Ghana Must Go* (2013) explores the idea of what she terms as an Afropolitan identity, which is rooted in the idea of cosmopolitism with African roots. In addition to this, there is contemporary production of graphic novels and chick lit waiting to be explored. Let us give heed to Ama Ata Aidoo's ardent request to readers to consciously look out for African women novelists, which is equally applicable to all writing from the continent: "Fish our books out", she pleads, "for either they exclude them, or even worse, where they also are present, they hide them behind shelves that carry the books of authors who are considered more displayable, racially or gender wise" (Aidoo 171).

Note

1 See https://www.narendramodi.in/pm-modi-addresses-the-parliament-of-uganda -540888 (accessed on 1 October 2019).

References

Achebe, Chinua, "English and the African Writer", *Transition*, 18, 1965, pp. 27–30.
———, "Thoughts on the African Novel", *Dalhousie Review*, 54 (4), 1974, pp. 631–637 at hdl.handle.net/10222/59628 (Accessed on 17th September 2019).

Ahmed, Aijaz, *In Theory: Classes, Nations, Literatures*, Verso, New York, 1992.

Aidoo, Ama Ata, "To Be an African Woman Writer – An Overview and a Detail", in K.H. Peterson (Ed.), *Criticism and Ideology*, Scandinavian Institute of African Studies, Uppsala, 1988.

Armah, Ayi Kwei, *Osiris Rising: A Novel of Africa, Past, Present and Future*, Per Ankh Publishers, Senegal, 1995.

Brydon, Diana, "Ngugi wa Thiong'o 'On the Abolition of the English Department' (1972)", *ESC: English Studies in Canada*, 41 (4), 2015, pp 3–3.

Burton, Antoinette, *Africa in the Indian Imagination: Race and the Politics of Postcolonial Citation*, Duke University Press, 2016.

Desai, Gaurav (Ed.), *Teaching the African Novel*, Modern Language Association of America, New York, 2009.

Dugga, Victor, "'Introduction', Special Issue on New Directions in African Writing", *Literary Criterion*, 39 (3–4), 2004. Pp. 5–14.

Dugga, Victor and Anjali Gera Roy. 'Introduction', Special Issue on New Directions in African Writing", *Literary Criterion*, 39, 2004.

Gikandi, Simon, "'Foreword', in 'Chinua Achebe and the Institution of African Literature'", in M. Keith Brooker (Ed.), *The Chinua Achebe Encyclopaedia*, Green Wood Press, Westport, CT, London, 2003, pp. vii–xv.

Hofmeyr, Isabel, "'Foreword'., in Burton, Antoinette (Ed.), *Africa in the Indian Imagination: Race and the Politics of Postcolonial Citation*, Duke University Press, 2016, pp. ix–xii.

Lindfors, Bernth, *Long Drums and Cannons: Teaching and Researching African Literatures*, World African Press, Inc., Trenton, NJ, 1995.

Luhar, Sahdev, "Literary Studies in Indian Universities: Notes on the Present Scenario", *Journal of Teaching and Research in English Literature*, 6, July 2015 at https://sites.google.com/site/journalofenglishliterature/archives/vol-6-no -4-3/6-literary-studies-in-indian-universities-notes-on-the-present (Accessed on 20th September 2019).

Mahler, Anne Garland, "What/Where Is the Global South?" *Global South Studies*, 2017 at globalsouthstudies.as.virginia.edu/what-is-global-south (Accessed on 20th September 2019).

Pandurang, Mala, *Chinua Achebe: An Anthology of Recent Criticism*, Pencraft, New Delhi, 2006.

Prakash, Gyan, Michael Laffan and Nikhil Menon. (Eds.), *The Postcolonial Moment in South and Southeast Asia*, Bloomsbury Publishing, London, 2018.

Reed Way, Dasenbrock, "Wole Soyinka's Nobel Prize", *World Literature Today*, 61, January 1987, pp. 4–9.

Schipper, Mineke, "Knowledge Is Like an Ocean: Insiders, Outsiders, and the Academy", *Research in African Literatures*, 28 (4), 1997, pp. 121–141.

Selasi, Taiye, "African Literature Doesn't Exist", Speech at The International Literature Festival, Berlin, 2013 at https://www.literaturfestival.com/medien /texte/eroeffnungsreden/Openingspeach2013_English.pdf (Accessed on 19th September 2019).

Sen, Kalapi, "Perceptions of African Literature in Non-Western Environments: A Survey of the Status of African Literature in West Bengal", Paper presented at the 9th University of Uyo Conference on Language and Literature on "Repositioning Research in Literature and Language in the 21st Century", University of Uyo, Nigeria, 21–24 February 2017.

Drama

5

THE STATE OF THE STAGE

An Interview with Mahesh Dattani

Angelie Multani

1. The 1990s were a key decade for Indian English theatre in general, and your work in particular. What do you ascribe the boom to?

   I am not sure I can ascribe anything to this boom. Perhaps the time was right; after over 40 years of Independence, we came to terms with the English language and made it our own. Although Indian English theatre existed since a couple of centuries, it was still covered with a mantle of colonial legacy. It is hard to say. Worth studying.

2. What is the state of theatre today, compared to the 1990s?

   Theatre is far more creative with form today than it was in the 1990s. There is a strong focus on the exploration of form. Many performances break rules, explore different aspects of performance and merge genres or mediums. All very exciting and different to the approach in the 1990s which was driven more by speech and text. New forms have taken the emphasis from the text and put it more on the body/space relationship. Anne Bogart, the founder of SITI Company, says something very interesting. She says (and I am paraphrasing but you can always get the right quote from the Net) that the traditional hierarchy of theatre has crumbled in the age after post-modernism. (I think she calls it constructivism.) The old hierarchy placed text at the top, then the director, the actor, the designers, etc. Now a performance and its narrative can emerge from anyone. A prop can be the starting point in a story or the architecture of the space. Mary Overly, a modern dancer of the twentieth century, recalls her first dance experience. She was to replace a performer. She wasn't sure what to do. (I assume there was no choreographer.) The

DOI: 10.4324/9781003399926-8

dancer who was leaving told her to simply absorb the architecture of the space and respond to it.

I remember seeing a production at Harkat Studios (a space that is so fringe and a hub for new talent). The audience were seated on stools in the hall (Harkat has no defined stage or performance space by design). The performances of three short stories were on the periphery of the space. The audience had to swivel in their seats to follow the action. Sometimes it was hard to tell between performer and audience. It created an intimacy that would be impossible to have in a proscenium stage.

3. There are many issues in your work that went largely uncommented on earlier, but which have now gained currency, such as the representation of sexualities. What do you think this is due to?

I guess when I wrote about them, they were not very fashionable. Now with the bombardment of information, political subjects such as gender and sexuality have taken the spotlight. This is a positive step. It is bound to be reflected in theatre. You are absolutely right in your observation. For instance, a play like *On a Muggy Night in Mumbai* had a tepid response in the 1990s and almost died a societal death with no performances save the first one by Lillete Dubey. But today, there are dozens of colleges, theatre groups all over the country who are keen to do the play.

The other play that just had a reading as part of Pride month is *Seven Steps around the Fire*. This is a detective story about a murder happening in the world of the Hijra community. In cracking the case, we learn more about their world. This has suddenly found favour with groups. There have been productions in Delhi, San Francisco, Canada. It was also done at the NSD [National School of Drama] as a student project production. While mainstream faculty from a previous generation don't think much of these works, they are very popular among students.

Tara is a bit of an oddity. I think it is popular because of its accessibility. It is generally interpreted as a play about saving the girl child. I wrote it as a metaphor for the male self and the female self, their disintegration through societal rules.

4. On the whole is academic attention to a playwright's work desirable? Do you think it changes the attitude/reception of the work?

It is desirable because it provides a context and critique to the work of the playwright that may get overlooked in performance. Sometimes a more in-depth study may help understand the playwright's work for posterity. I don't think it changes the attitude towards the reception of the work, at least not in India. But it will in future generations to come, who may access academic readings of the work before experiencing them in performance.

5. Theatre has changed a great deal in the last decade, thanks to technology and social media – what do you think about these changes?

Theatre has always reflected changing times and attitudes. Theatrical conventions change too, accommodating new norms. Sometimes, technology brings in a novelty factor, but people get blasé about it soon. For instance, not so long ago LED screens came into fashion as a novelty, but now they are more of a nuisance as they dwarf the actors and make them appear in silhouettes against the bright light. I personally hate the coldness of LED lighting although it is so much more convenient as you can change the colour at the click of a button.

Social media is a great tool for publicity. I think it has its limitations though. From experience, it is great to reach out and get people to like and respond to your event. But it doesn't translate to ticket sales. Social media has created a situation where nobody looks forward and sets aside a date for an activity. You decide immediately what you wish to consume.

However, some people use it creatively. For instance, there is a production, an adaptation of Chekhov's *The Seagull*, specifically designed for Zoom. All the characters meet online. The play within the play is also done online.

Maybe something will emerge from all this. It is too early to tell.

6. Almost all our art forms have been implicated politically in some way or the other, especially in the past few years. What is the role of art in a divided society? Does it have to be openly political and take a point of view, or should it 'simply serve itself'?

I don't think the two are opposed to each other. By serving itself, art makes very bold statements as a social piece, a political one and a personal one. Art is at its best when it raises empathy. It is the recognition of life experiences in others that raise our own awareness. This can cover governmental politics or social politics or personal politics. If we understand politics to be about power play.

Theatre puts you in touch with other human beings far more effectively because of the presence of the human being and not a representation of the human experience. Yes, theatre is also representational, but it lives in front of you, breathing at the same time as you in the audience. The human condition is represented by words in a novel, by metaphors in a poem or images in film. But in the theatre, it is the human body that represents the human being. Very much as in life, but with more beauty and form.

7. What are your views regarding the way in which dramatic texts are taught in schools and colleges of India? Do you feel it is an effective method? If not, can you suggest what changes should be made?

I remember once I was addressing a class who were studying my play as part of their MA literature programme. I asked how many have actually seen a play. Only about two or three hands went up. The play in performance is never a part of the study. Access to productions is a challenge I know, but isn't it possible for a class to read out the play and study characters through their actions? Or how a word sounds when spoken? It is usually the content of the play that is studied, never its dramaturgy or its emotional impact.

I am also surprised that many universities have an active drama department, but the students of literature who study the plays rarely interact with the department. The reverse is also true. Drama students can also benefit from academic discussions, but this just isn't an option considered.

This would not happen in a music class, would it? Even if you are studying music as an academician, there will be an attempt to hear the music. Dance historians spend hours looking at available footage. The problem is that there isn't enough documentation of performance, and this impedes the study of drama.

8. Have there been interpretations of your work that have made you look at the work differently? For instance, I remember a conversation you and I had many years ago about the performance of Tara in Delhi, where the slap that Bharati gets shifted from a real slap one night to a threatened slap the following night. I had an interpretation of how the change in gesture altered the meaning of the performance, and you explained that it was an expedient move as the actor playing Bharati had recently undergone surgery and the slap on the first night had caused some trauma!

Yes, I remember directing *Final Solutions* for Lady Shriram College almost a decade ago. As part of the rehearsals, I had sensitization exercises to help the actors (all supremely intelligent, confident and wise beyond their years) expand their perspectives and actually change viewpoints. Over coffee, one of the students told me that for her grandmother, no matter what she believes intellectually, she could never accept the presence of a Muslim in her home. It struck me that we are talking about human experience. I was surprised by my own shallow perception of prejudice. I always thought it was a result of ignorance and fear. But life batters out a wisdom that is unique to your own experience. A story that only you can tell from your point of view. From then on, I have viewed Hardika and Aruna with far more compassion. It is no longer about moving from ignorance to knowledge but moving from experience to experience.

Another interesting story is that with *Thirty Days in September*. In the play, I do have a well-meaning boyfriend who cannot understand the trauma of sexual abuse that Mala has gone through. There is a line where he says 'give me your hand', offering support and companionship. The actor would say it with great emphasis as if taking charge of the situation. Anuja Gupta and Ashwini of RAHI, a counselling centre for survivors of abuse, felt it sent the wrong signal to survivors. That they must put themselves in the hands of others, possibly leading to more abuse. Subtle as it may seem, it can be misread. Such sensitive subjects bring on an equally sensitive response to the consequences of portrayal.

9. Do you think that drama has been undervalued as a mode of education/ communication?

Absolutely. Maybe in some cultures it is not. But we do carry forward the traditional stigma against theatre. That it is an activity or occupation of the outcastes. No matter how urbane we get, somewhere we do see it as an inferior form of writing. Even in performance, it is seen as inferior to music. In reality, drama is an important tool in education because it employs all the skills necessary to live in an evolved society. Communication, physical and emotional culture, administration, language skills, empathy, instinct, philosophy are all aspects of life and drama.

10. What has been the effect of all the new multiple alternate theatre spaces that have emerged in the last few years? Theatre is now performed in cafes, bars, open air restaurants – is this only a temporary move to accommodate new audiences, or is it likely to have a real impact on the forms of theatre?

I think it has made an impact on forms of theatre already. Informal spaces offer a fluidity that a formal space may not. The architecture of a space has been a significant aspect of any form of theatre. The classical approach is to build a space that suits the conventions of theatre. The modern or post-modern approach is to draw inspiration from the existing architecture. Now, in the post-Covidien era, fluidity is key to creativity. We don't know if the spaces we know so well will be fit for performance anymore, not in the same way at least. It will be interesting to see how space is used in the months to come.

11. How do you think theatres will function in case the pandemic-like situation remains and social distancing becomes the norm? It will affect theatre of course. Do you see new possibilities emerging?

I think new forms relying heavily on technology will emerge. The question is will it still be theatre? Or something else? As far as theatre, which relies on sharing a space with your audience, I believe we will look at outdoor spaces. We might even look at silent theatre since the aggressive use of the voice may be considered unsafe. I pity the British actors who are so used to spraying the front rows with their spittle as they project. They will be banned. The Indian system of playback voices, especially with songs, has always been considered low art. It may just become the thing to do!

(Interview conducted over email)

6

PERFORMING THE DALIT

A Reading of Dalit Plays

B. Mangalam

Dalit literature has emerged as a discipline and received both critical and popular attention. Written in all the major languages of India, in multiple genres, translated into English and other languages, Dalit literary discourse is a significant, subversive, interrogative undermining of structures of power that hold sway over our social and political rubric. However, unlike poetry, fiction or autobiographies written by Dalits, plays have received far less attention in critical discourse. In the performative space, Dalit plays have ushered in radical re-formulations of the theatre idiom, stage-craft, choice of form and content. The plays initiate a dialogue with the oppressed, seeking to engender a critical awareness concerning modes of oppression, to inspire spectators (both Dalit and savarna) to shed their passivity and engage in a participative, agitationist response against casteist structures of power. Dalit literary discourse is further extended by these plays, to a performative, interactive, democratic space that enables a direct engagement with the community. The trajectory of Dalit drama is similar to that of autobiography and fiction, in terms of its substantial output in Marathi, followed by other Indian languages with a time lag of a decade or so. While many playwrights have made a significant impact on Marathi stage, I shall examine the plays of Premanand Gajvee as they offer a wide variety of experimentation in form and have been staged across Maharashtra and elsewhere to packed auditoriums. A Malayalam play and a selection of plays written by the Tamil playwright K.A. Gunasekaran would be studied to understand the dynamics of power, performance and resistance in Marathi, Malayalam and Tamil Dalit theatres.

DOI: 10.4324/9781003399926-9

Premanand Gajvee is a prolific writer, with a novel, short-story collections, a volume of poetry and more than 20 plays to his credit. Three of his plays, each one of them reflecting a different dramatic form to represent issues and concerns that lie embedded in Dalit community's struggles, aspirations and modes of resistance, would be examined to indicate key features of Marathi Dalit theatre. Gajvee's play *Ghotbhar Pani*, performed in 1977, has been staged for a remarkable 3000 and more shows across Maharashtra (translated as *A Sip of Water* by Shanta Gokhale). The play revolves around the issue of denial of water to Dalit communities, political apathy and a stark struggle for a dignified survival in the rural hinterland. The play shows how the conditions that precipitated the historic Mahad Satyagraha have remained unchanged even after three decades of independence and constitutional guarantees for the community. This short, One-Act play, hardly ten pages long, explores the hierarchies of power, enmeshed in caste and bureaucratic hegemony that dictate who can have access to water or, for that matter, to life.

The play has a stark structure, reminiscent of Absurd theatre in its use of a bare stage, with two male characters who play a series of roles to highlight a polarised society that uses caste privilege to uphold social marginalisation of Dalits. The two youths, simply named One and Two, visit a village as research students and enact the acute scarcity of water that they encounter as an engineered one by the upper castes, aided by the police officers, exploited by the politicians and a pliant media that ignores the site of agitation for water but is eager to interview the minister or offer him pictorial mileage in the newspapers. Gajvee's use of an absurdist structure is interesting as he posits it against a stark, realistic concern for a subject that is located in a social context, with a historical overview of its cultural divide. His use of folk idiom to reflect a see-saw movement amongst the castes, one oppressing, the other resisting, one assertive, the other resilient subverts the apolitical standpoint of Absurd theatre. The apparent similarity of a bare structure and deployment of role-play does not place this play with an Absurdist standpoint or reflect its ahistorical, universalist discourse. Gajvee employs an apparent absurdist feature to foreground recurring instances of oppression of Dalits and how craving for a sip of water has been imposed upon a huge populace as a form of structural violence. The play shows how such a mode of violence is aided by state institutions and media houses by concocting projects and reports on paper, far from the truths as they prevail on the actual site of contestation of the two communities.

The minister insists upon the presence of press photographers to cover his inauguration of a well that ultimately remains dry and half-dug:

ONE: Okay. Let's get a communal water drawing programme organized today.

ONE: Alright. But there must be full coverage with photographs.

(A Sip of Water: 2013: 13)

Dalit satyagrahis are assaulted by upper castes; the police beat them up, intimidate Dalit women with threats of rape or file false cases against them for drawing water from the village well. "Should humans drink the water that cattle drink?" (2013: 12). Ambedkar's satyagraha at Mahad in 1927 had raised similar questions. Gajvee's play posits such continuing modes of oppression of Dalits as unacceptable.

Throw away those yokes
Laid upon you through centuries
Live like sky-soaring birds...
A strong wrist is the way to freedom.

(2013: 17)

The play underlines the need to emulate the Ambedkarite edict to resist oppression in an organised, united mode. Gajvee uses theatre to educate the Dalit community of its rights, the nature of oppression/collusion of oppressors as well as the need for resistance. The performative dynamics embodied in the deployment of One and Two foregrounds the friction and social chasm between two communities, the hegemonic and the marginalised, modes of denial of resources and ways of reclaiming the same. *Ghotbhar Pani* is a critique of untouchability that lays bare the stasis pertaining to caste oppression in a democratic space, thereby undermining the basic principle of equality guaranteed to all citizens. The mass appeal of this play till date underscores the relevance of how access to water has remained enmeshed in power and a caste-demarcated matrix. This play also exposes Gandhian valourisation of villages as unfounded in everyday reality. "This rustic life is sheer death" brings out the symbolic as well as the reality of denial of water to a large section of citizens on grounds of their caste identity (2013: 9). If water is life-sustaining, its denial is an erasure of human dignity and right to life.

Gajvee's play *Kirwant* (1981) was performed in the 1980s but gained attention in the following decade when Shriram Lagoo performed the protagonist's role in the 1992 production. The 1990s witnessed a steady spread of Dalit literature in other languages and a concern for caste hierarchies being replicated amongst Dalit communities as a reflection of the internalisation of Brahminical ideology. Writers like Imayam in Tamil found favour amongst upper caste readers and publishers on account of his novels, in particular *Koveru Kazhudaigal* (1994; translated as *Beasts of Burden*, 2001), for their representation of intra-caste strife and discrimination amongst Paraiyars, Pallars and Arundatiyars in Tamil Nadu. The critical discourse in Tamil saw a shift from exploring the trajectory of caste discrimination to a rationalising of the same as Dalit castes too practise hierarchical social divisions. In this context, Gajvee's *Kirwant* acquires a significant voice in the performative domain as it exposed a discriminatory, dehumanising hierarchy practised within the Brahmin community. The Brahmin priests who conducted rituals related to death, cremation for the community, were not allowed to perform or even participate in pujas performed at Brahmin community gatherings. Horizontal social mobility as well as restrictions regarding marriage outside the Kirwant Brahmin-fold is imposed upon them. Gajvee examines this discriminatory practice as mirroring casteist oppression, hierarchical power structure that reduces human potential to a social identity yoked to one's birth in a specific step in the caste ladder. He thus shows caste hierarchies as dehumanising and inimical to all castes. The very reasons that pushed Imayam to critical acclaim and validation by savarna readers acted as pockets of censure in the case of Gajvee's play. It was viewed as diluting Dalit critique of Brahmin hegemony and shifting attention away from rigid hierarchies which oppressed the Dalit community. Gajvee's play, in fact, on closer scrutiny, emerges as a play that extends the ambit of Ambedkarite critique on varna and caste strictures. In *Annihilation of Caste*, Ambedkar pointed out, "caste system is not merely division of labour. *It is also a division of labourers*" (2002: 263).

Kirwant explores radical content through a traditional form, reminiscent of a Naturalist play of the early 20th century in its presentation of how a rigid, restrictive society stifles an honest, poor, hard-working individual in the name of safeguarding its tradition. The tragic disintegration of the protagonist who is unable to defy or endorse the inhumane *farman* of the powerful group presiding over his community captures the harsh bind of caste strictures as unrelentingly oppressive and cruel. The protagonist Siddeshwar's school-going son is forced to take up his father's profession and quit school upon his father's death. Siddeshwar's younger brother, Vasudeo who is drawn towards a Hindu *shakha* that works towards bringing all Hindus under one umbrella, is disillusioned by the group's rhetoric that erases the complex layers of the caste matrix. The confrontation between the two brothers despite their strong emotional bonding is yet another nuanced depiction of how caste controls family relations and personal loyalties. Vasudeo fails to persuade his brother to protest against the humiliation heaped upon him by Brahmins occupying a higher rung within the community. Siddeshwar's earnings are linked to his assigned duties as a Kirwant Brahmin. The reality of poverty does not allow him to join his brother in interrogating the gang of Brahmins who ill-treat him in public, taunt his son to read up *Garud Puran* instead of the school curriculum. The young boy is served tea in a broken cup, kept separately for him at his classmate's home. His wife is not allowed to socialise with other (Brahmin) women or attend social functions. The family is the only Kirwant Brahmin household in the taluk, but when Siddeshwar musters courage to refuse performing

Vedantashastri's mother's last rites, unless an apology is tendered to him for his public humiliation at a puja, the powerful Brahmins get another Kirwant from Sawantwadi and boycott Siddeshwar. Driven by poverty, caste pressures and his brother's exposure of the abysmal status of Kirwants as no better than the crows that are called upon to partake of the *pinda*, Siddeshwar's mind disintegrates. His hallucinations push him to caw like a crow, rave like a demented man, but he refuses to kill his son-like brother to earn a reprieve from the Brahmin lobby.

The dynamics of structures of caste, power and Hindu identity intersect, collude, conspire to target an individual more talented, scholarly than his social superiors. Siddeshwar's grasp over astrology or his predictions go unchallenged yet he is not allowed to make a living through his knowledge as only Dhabushastri, a crafty pretender but a Brahmin of superior standing, is entitled to interpret horoscopes in this community. Gajvee unmasks the caste structure as oppressive towards all sections of Hindu society. Vasudeo's comment expresses the play's central thesis: "Those who are untouchables themselves declare others untouchable. Talk about superiority! Talk about protecting cows and drive away human beings ... Those who drink urine and eat dung—they talk of purity, don't they?" (*Kirwant*; translated by M.D. Hatkanangalekar, 2013: 81).

The Brahminical rituals like the *sandhyavandan*, ritual changing of sacred thread, reciting mantras to the count of beads, the postures of *suryanamaskar* or the making of *pinda* rice balls in the shape of a woman's breasts at the crematorium show the gap between the authentic and performative gesture. This gap in turn indicates the construct of touchability and untouchability amongst different categories of human beings. The fact that the two categories belong to the same caste is ironic but does not negate the discriminatory, hierarchical, structure of caste that dehumanises the victim and the oppressor alike. Gajvee's play articulates the need to go beyond caste, the need to non-perform one's assigned casteist duty as an act of resistance. Vasudeo's intent to marry a non-Kirwant girl (whom he loves) does not enable him to prevent his nephew Madhu or his unborn children from being forced to perform the assigned duties as caste follows a patrilineal association of identity for every individual. He therefore announces that he shall remain a bachelor until his death. Thus, caste pressurises individuals to embrace the unnatural state of celibacy to escape its ordained strictures codifying an individual's role in society. If this is applied to the lives of millions of Dalits facing subjugation, a horrendeous cleansing would ensue, posing a challenge to the very core of social solidarities. Although the play *Kirwant* highlights the tragedy of individuals, it indicates resistance as a mode of deliverance for the entire Hindu society, as it has remained enmeshed in a casteist structure, granting power to some and denying it to others, depriving all sections from living in amity with each other.

Gajvee's Ambedkarite vision does not hesitate to subject Ambedkar to a scrutiny of his role during the freedom struggle and his relationship with Gandhi. His play *Gandhi-Ambedkar* (1997 per./98pb; translated by Shanta Gokhale) adopts an experimental form by depicting a conversation between Gandhi and Ambedkar, intermediated by a circus clown. Far from being a verbose, dialogue-centric play, Gajvee succeeds in making this an engaging and a riveting one. The play is written in the format of a discussion drama wherein the two historical characters are shown to be arguing, debating, rationalising and introspecting throughout the performance. But the play manages to hold the audience's attention on account of Gajvee's innovative positioning of a clown as an interlocutor who does not hesitate to make dents into the inflated notions of self-perception of both the deified personalities. Another important thread that sustains the play as an oblique dialogue with the spectator is the play's strong enunciation of a historical overview of the turbulent politics, struggle for power-sharing during the crucial decades of the 1930s and the 1940s that witnessed decisive, often bitter confrontations and debates between Gandhi and Ambedkar on a range of issues concerning social and political empowerment of the masses. In the course of the play, the Poona Pact, Gandhi's last fast, circumstances leading to the Partition, the role of the Muslim League and the assassination of Gandhi and Ambedkar's response to it form points of debate and dissent. The play also addresses the treatment and role of Kasturba and Ramabai in the domestic and public spaces and what they signified in the lives of their respective, illustrious spouses. Gajvee captures the different shades of the relationship that the two leaders shared. But what stands out in the contemporary audience/reader's mind is the fact that the possibility of a dialogue between the two is never ruptured, despite the significant differences of standpoint in almost every issue depicted in the play.

Gajvee's conceptualisation of the clown is innovative and radical. Both the leaders stand tall, valourised in public imagination and are role models to contemporary society, within and outside India. There have been critical readings of their life and works in the past, but they were laced with admiration, grudging or otherwise. Gajvee's play subjects both of them to a puckish, deriding, earnest interrogation, subtle subversion and a critical questioning of their standpoints on issues through the agency of a circus clown. The clown's affinity lies closer to the folk performative arts, although the *vidushak* of Sanskrit theatre comes readily to mind. However, unlike the *vidushak*, the clown in this play does not enjoy any privilege on account of his caste nor does he receive any patronage from the protagonists. The clown functions more as a spokesperson of the ordinary citizens who are turning to their icons but with an irreverence and a persistent questioning of their interventions. The role of a circus clown had been designed in the past to entertain the audience. But the clown in this play protests against his demarcated role: "But how long must this go on? How long must I slip and fall and why should I entertain you?" (2013: 93). Instead, he decides to draw the audience's attention to one's "relationship with history" (147). The clown subjects both the leaders to inconvenient questions, hints at their insecurities. He questions Gandhi for allowing/using Kasturba to plead with Ambedkar during his fast at Yerawada Jail, which paved the way for the Poona Pact or why Ambedkar who fought for women's rights did not attend to Ramabai's privations. The clown chides Ambedkar, "What? You quarrelled with Ramabai? ... I don't understand how these men who fight to win justice for the world quarrel like common men with their near and dear ones" (111). The clown calls out Gandhi, "Your mind was full of suspicion about every person who did not agree with your opinion" (114).

It is pertinent here to note that the clown's role was performed by a woman actor, Bhakti Barve, when the play was staged. The presence of a woman clown renders the interrogation of Gandhi and Ambedkar, regarding their domestic, conjugal spaces or their inattention to those spaces, more scathing. The play is set in a conversational mode, with a clash of ideas, beliefs and differing modes of decision-making as the salient features to sustain the dramatic interest. While *Ghotbar Pani* shows the confrontation between two sections of society, *Kirwant* depicts confrontation within a particular community. In both the plays, the mechanism of caste remains the core issue that aggravates divisiveness and discrimination. In *Gandhi-Ambedkar*, the dramatic confrontation is ideological and a clash of standpoints concerning the relevance and place of caste in our society. The confrontation impacts major decisions and processes pertaining to different stages of our anti-colonial nationalist struggle. The debate extends to the mantle of leadership over the Dalit community as well. Interestingly, Gandhi points out to Ambedkar, "As a matter of fact, there was no need for a second representative of untouchables when I had been their true representative even before you" (97). Ambedkar states categorically, "your pity is not going to help us" (96).

The play humanises both the leaders, letting us a glimpse of their frailties, their confession of admiration for each other or their anger and helplessness against the opposition posed by the other. The clown hears each one of them out, in private, even as he needles them or unmasks their idiosyncrasies and rigidity of stand towards the other's proposals. Gandhi is shown to have immense respect for Ambedkar's scholarship while Ambedkar is devastated by the news of his assassination. The play offers a rational estimate of the turbulent forties leading to the Partition. The clown's final address to the spectators underscores the need to engage with one's history, the individual's and of a nation's as the two remain intertwined. He points out that one cannot selectively access history. "History's voice has power. It rams through the impenetrable stone of time, uncaring about people's convenience or inconvenience. Remember, those who remember history make history" (147).

Premanand Gajvee's theatre foregrounds power relations based on caste or centred around the politics of caste. A reading of his plays draws our attention to one of the key features of Dalit theatre—engendering a dialogue with the oppressed and addressing the oppressor. This facilitation of dialogue, debate and a critical awareness of the course and processes of history emerge as the hallmark of Dalit theatre in Marathi. Gajvee's plays offer ample evidence of this aspect. The other significant voices in Marathi Dalit theatre in this period belong to B.S. Shinde, Datta Bhagat, Ramnath Chavan amongst many others. Gajvee examines Dalit as a category thrust upon the community by the Hindu caste structure and holds it to be an inadequate reflection of cultural and social marginalisation. In his later plays, Gajvee fused Ambedkarite thought with Buddhist edicts as a viable mode of representation of marginalised communities, their struggles and resistance. In the year 2000, he founded Bodhi Natya Parishad. The Parishad holds theatre workshops and script-writing sessions and provides a platform to stage new plays.

The Malayalam play *Kakkakkinavu* (2004; translated as *Crow-Dream*, 2013), written by A. Santhakumar, combines folk, mythic and resistance mode of dramatisation to foreground denial of aspirational and dignified lifestyle to Dalits. The play also indicates resistance movements, protest culture emerging amongst younger Dalits and how they have begun to spread and influence the elders in the community. The play projects its discourse through a flock of crows. The crows are endowed with human speech and are shown to be governed by dehumanising structures of power. Caste and patriarchy are shown to be working in collusion, although fledgling hope emerges towards the end of the performance. In fact, the play adopts a non-realistic, performative mode and a folk ballad structure. This play was staged at the *Yuvajanotsava* (Theatre for Youth convention), held in 2004 in Kerala. Watching the performance of this play is an experience worth a recall. The actors, dressed in black clothes, carrying branches of trees and dried twigs and multi-hued ropes hanging from the ceiling swirled around the stage in orchestrated movements. The ropes were used to incorporate the chasm between the ostracised community of crows pushed to live on the outskirts, and those of elite homes which imposed upon them a manual of conduct, codified eating habits and forbidden dreams. The dance of death to project Karumbi's stoning by human beings for polluting the water in their courtyard by her act of a birdbath was accompanied by beats of *parai* drum, associated with resistance in Dalit theatre in Tamil and Malayalam. The lighting was used to cast a surreal collage of death, dream, fable, protest by crow-chicks in a juxtaposition to a slow build-up of solidarity extended by the elders. Shades of blue evoked death of young ones and misery of mother-crows while hues of bright yellow and pink lighting conveyed the aspirational discourse, the dream songs recounted by the mother birds at the community panchayat where the male birds and the old chief accuse the she-crows of neglecting their maternal duty and of failing to protect their young ones.

The play draws our attention to gendered oppression of Dalit female subjectivity as the crow-panchayat orders the she-crow Karumbi to be pecked by the community till death as she had let her chick starve itself to death in the month of *Karkkidakam*, when *balichoru* was left in abundance near their nests by human beings as an offering to crows in memory of their dead ancestors. The practice of ritual offering of rice balls to crows is woven as a fable to indicate how one particular community is allowed to eat what has been designated to be their lot by a class of hegemonic arbiters of power. A hierarchical and arbitrary social structure places one group above the other and employs cruel, violent measures to maintain status quo. The image of *balichoru* (sacrificial rice balls) is juxtaposed with the image of *neyyappam* (a sweet snack made from rice flour and fried in ghee) to indicate the gap between the socially ordained mode of living and the aspirational one in the context of ground realities pertaining to Dalit community. Karumbi, a mother-crow, reports the death of her chick by starvation. Similar deaths are reported by other she-crows soon. Their old chief, Mooppan's scathing attack on Karumbi for not knowing "how to rear her chicks till they can fly" (2013: 147) seeks to transfer the burden of abiding by the social diktat of their oppressors on women, thereby indicating the dual curse of caste and patriarchy in the lives of Dalit women. Dalit discourse in Tamil raised concern and critique of Dalit patriarchy as early as the late 1980s/early 1990s. The Malayalam play extends that by showing it as penetrating every formulation of socialising in a society divided by caste.

Karumbi and other she-crows recall the tale of Chekon who had snatched a *neyyappam* from a human child and was stoned to death. Chekon is revered as a martyr, and his subversive act is narrated by mother birds to their chicks. The chicks begin to demand *neyyappam* and refuse to eat the *balichoru*, thrown around the tree trunks or at their nests by the ruling masters. The practice of ordaining a specific community to receive offerings related to death rituals and treating them as untouchables is a recurring motif in many Dalit writings across languages and genres. The crows resist eating the *balichoru* as they are leftovers, dirt that they are destined to eat to rid human beings of their debts to their ancestors but are, in turn, labelled as symbols of sin. The practice of untouchability and social labelling in a hierarchical binary is represented through a medley of fable, body language, interplay of cawing, lullaby, screams, beats of *parai* drum, orchestrated, gliding movements and images of scattered feathers.

The performative possibilities are matched at the level of narrative by the tale of overreachers who would settle for no less than a dignified living and striving for what is deemed to be forbidden in their lives. The snack *neyyappam* gains a symbolic resonance in the play as the chicks in the crow-clan prefer to drop down dead, one by one, rather than feed on the rotting balls of rice lying around their habitat. The role of Dalit women as subversive facilitators is highlighted in this play as the chicks are shown to be fed on dreams, tales of resistance and heroic martyrdom of Chekon by the mother-crows. Karumbi informs the other she-crows who wonder at the spate of deaths amongst their chicks, "Often chicks see what we grownups fail to see" (151). She points out that times are changing and that parents need to understand the aspirations and overcome their own fears of reprisal from upper castes (human beings) towards their resistance against their continued subjugation. They should no longer perceive their state as their 'fate':

> *Karumbi:* Their chickhood is not like our chickhood … there is a dream in their little eyes …
> *Chakki:* So, our chicks dream of what we were not able to dream of. Is that so?
> *Karumbi:* … We too can also dream such crow-dreams.
>
> *(2013: 151–152)*

Chekon's act of stealing a *neyyappam* from a human child underlines the need for sharing of resources amongst all equally. If denial of water to Dalits is resisted in *Ghotbar Pani* through a folk idiom of role-play, in *Kakkakkinavu*, the fable of crows snatching a sweetmeat underlines the sites of inequality in our society. Chekon confesses that he got

> tired of eating *balichoru*, the dirt and such nasty decayed things. This *neyyappam* … let me give sweet meat to my chicks … Not only by the human children … let the sweetness of this stuff be tasted by the chicks of crows too.
>
> *(152)*

Food and water are not only essential for sustenance, they also guarantee dignity to life. Caste structure imposes stringent code on access, consumption, storage, an aesthetic engagement with food and water and denies Dalits what upper castes enjoy materially and aesthetically. Dalit theatre offers visual representation of movements of resistance by the oppressed community that are put down by the oppressor community in the real world, day in and day out. Dalit theatre addresses the oppressed and the oppressor simultaneously to forge solidarities arising out of self-reflexivity and collective action amongst its spectators. It initiates a democratisation of performance within and by implication outside the theatre arena. In *Crow-Dream*, the assertion by those who have been put down for ages that "crows cannot remain sinners anymore without committing any sin" is an apt reflection of Dalit identity assertion (153). No wonder that Chekon was surrounded and stoned to death by the powerful savarnas. However, his death is not allowed to remain a static, past memory. It is retrieved by the women (despite death threats from male elders) to be narrated to their young ones who learn to resist, defy and act to give momentum to a collective movement against the privileged few who hoard the resources.

The play concludes with Karumbi's defiant birdbath at the courtyard of human beings, braving the stoning that ensues in response to her act. But now, the young chicks raise their cawing to a battle pitch, the adult crows rush to her rescue, Moopan orders the crow-clan to "snatch things which we too deserve" (157). The collective act of resistance resorts to violence and snatching as weapons are needed to fight a battle for survival and dignity. The stage directions indicate the necessity of mobilisation of community and organised retrieval of resources to resist discriminatory, unequal structures:

> (*Hearing this, spreading wings widely and screaming violently, the crow-clan gets ready to fly with all vigour ... to the courtyards of human-homes ... to the kitchens ... of human beings*)
>
> *(2013: 157)*

Dalit theatre works towards building a critical awareness of oppression—how they have operated historically, sociologically, at our homes in our day-to-day social interactions. Parattai, a theatre activist in Tamil Nadu, holds that Dalit performative arts are "weapons of liberation, tools of empower-ment" (*Kalaga Mozhi*, 2003). Dalit theatre as well as Dalit feminist theatre in Tamil offers an important critical discourse in the performative arena, through an interactive, revisionist theatre. Playwright, critic, academic and activist K.A. Gunasekaran underlines the need "to instill a critical awaken-ing among the spectators who are thereby motivated to participate in the liberation movement" (2006: 81). He advocates discouraging "passive recep-tion" to the act of performing the Dalit and suggests that Dalit writings, in particular, plays, should "adopt strategies of agitation" (81). He rejects the relevance of *Natyashastra* to the framework governing agitationist, inter-ventionist theatre. He holds the view that oppressed people "need a separate theatre for themselves" to evolve a line of communication with their com-munity, to view performance as indicating agenda for collective action, to deploy the agency of theatre in the cause of Dalits (78). *Natyashastra* has been traditionally viewed as *Pancham Ved*, the fifth Veda by theatre prac-titioners and critics. K.A.G., as Gunasekaran is popularly called by theatre lovers, rejects at the outset such a standpoint. He believes that "as the Vedas uphold *Varna Niti* which does not consider Dalits fit to be categorised as human beings within the four varnas, the Sanskrit theatre, and this fifth Veda also remain alien to Dalit sensibility" (2006: 78).

K.A.G.'s plays, performed between 1993 and 2004, offer an apt illustration of his theorisation on Dalit theatre. His knowledge and work at the grassroots as a folk theatre performer and folk singer add a layered texture to his scripts. The use of *parai*, a musical instrument used during death rituals or to make announcements at crossroads by Paraiyars, is both extensive and subversive in his plays. His plays offer a deft interplay of folk dance forms, performative aspects of *Cindu, Nayyandi, Opparai, Thalaatu* (ritual songs during a religious procession like *kavadi*, satiric/subversive songs, dirge, lullaby, respectively) and the dynamics of *Therukoothu, Karagaattam, Silambaattam, Thappattam, Urummiattam* (street theatre as a folk form, a folk performance involving a balancing of pots on one's head with intricate footwork, a form of martial dance with the use of sticks, a vigorous dance to the beats of *parai*, a dance to the beats of *urumi melam*, respectively). As the *parai* is made of cow-hide and *urumi melam* is made of goat-skin, the instruments are associated with Dalit culture. The playwright uses these instruments as images of Dalit assertion and to evoke notions of cultural liberation from casteist markers.

His plays range from a re-reading of puranic tales from a Dalit feminist perspective (*Sathiya Sodhanai*, 1993), a re-working of archival material or inscriptions pertaining to oppression of Dalits (*Bali Aadugal*, performed in 1993) on marginalised communities like the transfolk (*Martram*, 2004), on power politics concerning untouchability (*Thodu*, 2002, *Mazhi*, 2004), a feminist re-writing of popular, musical plays written by Sankaradas Swamigal (*Pavalkkodi alladu kudumba Vazhakku*, 2001, *Kandan/Valli*, 2004). He wrote and performed many more, and his published plays carried an interesting provision for theatre practitioners. K.A.G. has made it clear that "These plays have not been written to be read. They have been written to be performed in public (people's) stage. Anyone is free to use these plays for purposes of staging/performance" (Preface to *Sathiya Sodhanai*, 1993, translation mine). His theatre praxis was essentially interventionist, agitationist and community-centric.

In *Sathiya Sodhanai*, he highlighted the trials, privations and social ostracisation of Chandramati, the wife of Arichchandiran, the king who sold his wife and son and worked at the crematorium to uphold truth. A feminist re-reading of a well-known tale that had come down to generations of readers as a homily on adherence to truth and one's word of promise. Gandhiji had been tremendously influenced by this tale as noted by him in his autobiography. Gunasekaran presents Chandramati as an impoverished mother who has to care for her son through her labour as a slave on account of a pompous, self-righteous husband. The play juxtaposes her life with that of Chandrika, an activist from contemporary society who confronts the police on their inaction against women's complaints against domestic violence, dowry-deaths and works towards bringing together victims and activists to resist misuse of power by the police and fight for justice. She is shown to confront misogynist comments and patriarchal brushing aside of women in public spaces by those occupying positions of authority. The interplay of the puranic and the contemporary perspective alerts the spectator to continuing forms of subjugation and the collusion of the state and the ruling elite to uphold patriarchy and caste hegemony. The use of Brahminical register for the oppressor and the colloquial, slang, conversational for the intervention-ist characters in the play captures the caste and class divide. The presence of *Kattiyakkaran*, a narrator-figure borrowed from *Therukoothu* adds an element of subversive humour and acts as a structural link to the stories of Chandramati and Chandrika. The play uses folk music, intertextual refer-ences to Sankaradas Swamigal's musical play on *Arichchandiran*, extensive use of musical instruments like the *parai*, harmonium, 'military band music' at the police station scenes as a counter-discourse to its nineteenth-century model. The performance of music associated with *mulaipaari kummi* by the actors to synchronise with Chandrika's enumeration of the suffering of Sita, Panchali, Nalayini, Kannagi, Chandramati underlines the need for women to rise in rage as a *Pudumai Penn*, an image of modern woman visualised by the nationalist poet Subramanya Bharati. *Mulaipaari Kummi* is a folk, ritual music performed at temples of little goddesses with rows of sprouted greens dotting the stage. The sprouts associated with this *kummi* are suggestively used in the play to mirror the sprouting of a feminist consciousness enabling an interrogative discourse under Chandrika's leadership. The *agni chatti* dance, performed by dancers carrying pots with burning embers, highlights the rage against injustice towards Dalit woman activists. Chandrika gets punished by the court for disrupting public servants (the policemen) from discharging their duty, and she questions the spectators at their silence.

The staging of this play is a powerful representation of the dynamics of power, performance and resistance in theatre. At its first performance, the stage was visualised in a dual space to demarcate the puranic from the con-temporary, highlighted through the use of lighting. A live orchestra on one side of the stage was the highlight at the performance, watched by nearly 4000 spectators at Tiruvannamalai in Tamil Nadu. Gunasekaran (1955–2016) preferred to stage his plays in the open maidans, at the crossroads, in fisherfolks' *kuppam*, in *paraiyar cheri* and at university spaces.

Dalit theatre in Tamil offered an articulate critique of caste and gender-related oppression in the 1990s. Amongst Dalit writers in Tamil, Sivakami and Bama were the foremost to critique Dalit patriarchy as they highlighted the exploitation of women's labour at home and in the fields or factories as well as sexual violence faced by them at the hands of their upper caste employers and their husbands, brothers, fathers or partners. The plays of K.A. Gunasekaran endorsed this standpoint and correlated it with the sys-tematised subjugation of women, Dalits, Dalit women, Adivasis during pre-colonial, colonial and post-independence periods. In his play *Arikuri*, K.A.G. depicts casteist discrimination at university spaces against scheduled caste students at the hands of upper caste students. The play presents a collage of the bullying faced by Dalit students in university hostels, the heckling of their woman friends, the angry, spiteful outbursts against the scholarships which they receive from the government. The Dalit student Muniyan is humiliated for eating beef, and trumped-up charges are brought against him. The upper caste students are let off as the warden believes they are unlikely to misbehave with anyone as they hail from respectable castes!

The play begins with beats of *parai* drum and is used as a background score during the disciplinary meeting held by the warden. Actors can be seen to move their lips and gesticulate, but their voices are drowned by the *parai* drummers who take over the stage to register, through their performance, Dalit dissent, resistance and subversion of stage-managed inquiry committees set up by the authorities against Dalit students. A mask of a cow's head adorns the stage prominently throughout the staging of this play as a mark of Dalit assertion. The deployment of this mask and live *parai* drumming in different beats to indicate simmering anger, dissent and outburst of defiant rage form a parallel performative discourse that offers an unmasking of caste biases and injustice meted out to students who avail of affirmative reservation at institutes of higher education.

Muniyan hails from a rural background and his poor, widowed mother's hut is burnt down by upper caste landowners for protesting against their ruining of her vegetable garden, her only source of income to finance Muniyan's expenses in the city. The village panchayat's flogging of a Dalit schoolteacher for crossing the path of upper caste women on his way to his school deters Muniyan's mother from approaching the panchayat for redressal. Muniyan's mother is left homeless with no means of survival, and Muniyan's plea for justice goes unheard. The privations of the mother and son, of an old widow and a young man, of a rural labourer and a university student in the city are represented on two sections of a stage intersected by the group of *parai* drummers and the cow's head looking down on the action in both the spaces. The performance concludes with the cow's head charging forth, breaking into a *veriyattam* synchronised with the vigorous beating of the *parai* drum. *Veriyattam* is the dance of possession that involves a ritual of prediction of the future by the dancer under a state of trance. *Parai* is an *arikuri*, a mark of Parayar's identity and pride. Consumption of beef by Dalit communities is widespread in Tamil Nadu. K.A.G. presents the twin aspects as symptomatic of Dalit resistance to hegemonic culture that gloats over its vegetarianism and rhetoric of compassion to mask its bias against Dalit empowerment through education or self-sustaining labour. The *veriyattam* performance offers a variation to the notion of Hindutva which made its militant mark in the early 1990s. Hindutva's rhetoric of cow protection is perceived by as a sub-narrative that is antithetical to Dalit culture, in the context of eating habits, occupational affinity, economic survival and the community's creative labour in the making of percussion instruments through the processing of cow-hide. When the mask breaks forth into a live cow, with an actor's enactment of *veriyattam* to the beats of the *parai*, it seeks to represent the *arikuri*, the mark of Dalit assertion and the performative dynamics of resistance by the Dalit community. The play *Arikuri* is a powerful indictment of undermining of rights of Dalit students in university spaces and the collusion of privileged castes and authorities in stifling their aspirations and potential. Muniyan's testimony, "I have done no wrong and justice is on my side" is repeated as a refrain in the final sequence of the play (1999, my translation).

Gunasekaran's *Bali Aadugal* (Sacrificial Goats) fuses history, ritual practices and resistance to inhuman treatment by Dalit women in a fascinating way. It also embodies many of the striking features of Gunasekaran's plays including a gendering of the narrator and the chorus, use of mime, music, dance forms of Dalit communities, innovative use of *parai* and a feminist underpinning to Dalit discourse. The strategy of dividing the stage into dual spaces, use of two registers indicative of a casteist vocabulary and a deliberate interplay of the historical past and contemporary present are deployed in most of his plays including *Bali Aadugal*. These strategies draw our attention to the continuing polarisation of our society on caste lines, on the lines of the oppressor and the oppressed, the hegemonic and the subjugated. It is to Gunasekaran's credit that through theatre, he initiated a recovery of *parai* from its traditional association of drum beats announcing death and related rituals by making it integral to performative spaces as an instrument signifying Dalit assertion, affirmation of solidarity amongst those who emulate the edict of Ambedkar to "*educate, agitate and organize*".

Mulk Raj Anand's interview with Ambedkar is played as an audio text at the beginning of *Bali Aadugal* and intermittently throughout the performance. Ambedkar's exhortation to Dalits to be like lions, as the savarnas sacrifice only goats at the altar of their deities, casts a strong sub-text to the core of this play. When the chariot of the deity does not move forward despite efforts, the upper caste panchayat decides to offer a human sacrifice. Chinnandi, a Dalit, is chosen by the panchayat to be offered as a sacrifice to appease the goddess. Uduman, another Dalit, supports the panchayat's diktat and is put down by the community as a stooge of the upper castes. A transvestite person (called *Ali* in Tamil) helps Chinnandi and his wife in running away from the village. The panchayat now zeroes in on Uduman as the chosen *bali*, underlining the reality that joining forces with the oppressor class does not guarantee any safeguard from being oppressed oneself. Uduman persuades the panchayat, headed by Brahmins, to offer his wife as a human sacrifice as gods do not discriminate between men and women! A lament by the *Ali* brings out the position of Dalit women as the most subjugated one in our society:

> You men join hands to slaughter a woman like this? Women are a caste lower than the *parai* caste. Why do you trample women like withered grass?
>
> *(1999: 32–33, translation mine)*

In the printed text of the play, Uduman's wife is killed with a trident by one of the Brahmin priests, and the women's chorus surrounds the dead body and laments on women's fate:

> Our talis have turned into fences
> In each caste, women are enslaved
> Bound by family burdens
> Women are unpaid workers
> Female deities at the temple sanctum
> Female infants in the garbage bin
> Endless is the tale of women's misery.
>
> *(36, translation mine)*

The play seeks to foreground intersectionality of caste and gender in the context of Dalit lives. K.A.G. allows improvisation in the staging of his plays and the performance held during the theatre workshop organised by the NSD and the Rotary Club (30 August 2002 to 28 September 2002) in Puducherry, Uduman's wife addressed the spectators thus:

> You are the witness.
> You carry the burden.
>
> *(translation mine)*

The priest performed a *samiyattam* (dance of a devotee possessed by a deity) before killing her. The killer priest was surrounded by people, many of them from the audience, and was driven out. The *Ali* led the Dalit group in singing a song of protest. Actors carried posters and placards with messages written to condemn untouchability, highlighting how caste crimes are crimes against humanity. Posters displayed by Dalit activists at the World Conference against Racism in Durban in 2001 were held by the actors. Ambedkar's message to the community to act like lions and not goats was played out. The chorus of Dalit men and women lined up to take their final bow while *parai* was played in a fast tempo.

Bali Aadugal is a significant Dalit play not only on account of its radical content but also for its performative dynamics, its visualisation of power, its problematising of gender and use of slides, posters, songs without diluting the folk format that K.A.G. associates as Dalits' heritage. His representation of the oppressor as a group wearing masks, sacred thread, saffron/yellow/red *veshti*s, breaking out into aggressive gestures or loud laughter, reciting dialogues in a mantric tone or chant a set of dialogues one after another in a ritual mode, conveys brahminisation of religious festivals and village processions. The practice of targeting vocal, lower caste dissenters or those who demand their rights, be it legitimate wages for the work rendered, is depicted in the play in the context of a religious procession hijacked by upper castes. Chinnandi in the play points out that the priests resent his questioning of decisions by the panchayat as against the interests of Dalit community. The Panchayat's decision to offer him as a sacrifice to the village deity has to be located in the context of upper castes' strategy to control Dalit leadership.

The oppressed community is represented by a group of actors who are wearing only a *kovanam*, a bare essential piece of cloth tied around the waist on a string to cover one's private parts. They either sit on a corner of the stage with knees bent or lie sprawled on the front of the stage, tied up with thick ropes, moaning in pain or defiantly laughing at the poonal wearing group for kicking them. Four sets of ropes are placed strategically on the stage to indicate the four varnas. The head priest is carried by four actors to mime a palanquin, and he speaks in a sanskritised Tamil, in a Brahmin register, quotes from the Eklavya episode of the *Mahabharata* to rationalise the decision to offer a Dalit as a sacrifice to appease the goddess and let the temple chariot move ahead. As he speaks, the white *veshtis* of the savarna group turn a deep blood-red in colour through the use of stage lighting. The actor who enacts the role of Ali is not presented as a stereotypical transvestite as in the populist tradition. Instead, an actor with a moustache and a beard speaks the lines of this character.

Gunasekaran referred to Augusto Boal's Theatre of the Oppressed and Brecht's Epic Theatre in his critical writings but placed his theatrical praxis as a critical re-working of the Dalit/folk performative arts, subversive use of Dalit musical instruments, the *Gana* tradition of Tamil Muslims and a re-working of musical plays of Sankara Das Swamigal wherein the form is retained but the content is revisionist and subversive. His contribution to the Festival of Dalit Arts held every year on 6 December, since 1995, extended to organisational, staging of plays, dissemination of Ambedkarite thought and performances of Dalit music. In the 1980s, he had organised concerts of Dalit folk musical performances on the lines of Carnatic classical music concerts which galvanised Dalit movements and solidarities. He released audio cassettes of songs set to folk tunes, accompanied by instruments popular amongst Dalit communities, to disseminate Ambedkarite perspective on caste, rendered incidents of atrocities on Dalits like the Keezhvenmani massacre, burning down of Dalit hamlets into songs, urging Dalits to resist violence by land-owning upper castes. His plays *Thodu* (Touch) and *Mazhi* (Shave) depict the inhumane aspects of untouchability where lives of upper castes are saved by Dalits, but they are humiliated and physically shunned by upper caste survivors. In *Thodu*, the deployment of *Silambattam* is used to convey the subversive anger of Dalits against the practice of untouchability. *Mazhi* shows the courage of an insulted barber to say 'No' to the overtures of his oppressor in a moment of personal distress. The play uses songs and poetry from the Sangam period and interplays them with folk melodies.

Dalit theatre, in all major Indian languages, has represented the structures of caste as upholding the interests of the privileged and the powerful. Through the extensive use of performative dynamics of theatre in the plays of Gajvee, Gunasekaran explicates the rationale for the community to adopt the act of performing the Dalit as an act of resistance, as a strategy to subvert the casteist assertions in the domain of ideas, culture, electoral politics as well as against the unleashing of violence and marginalisation in academic and corporate workspaces. The impact of Dalit theatre during the period 1977– 2004 corresponds to the spread of Dalit movement, the emergence of Dalit literatures in various Indian languages and the discipline formation of Dalit Studies in the corresponding period. Dalit theatre has enriched mainstream theatre in different regions in its successful incorporation of native, folk elements, in its theatrical innovations and re-visionist formulations of traditional motifs. It has posited the subject of caste oppression as a violation of human dignity. Its efforts in empowering Dalits to deploy their cultural practices as a political subversion of dominant structures of power have inspired spectators and readers alike. The democratisation of theatre spaces facilitated by Dalit theatre has paved the way for a dialogue between the savarna and the Dalit audience, creating a congenial platform for re-configuring an interactive, intersectional negotiation of sociocultural concerns. Dalit theatre holds out forging of solidarities amongst the oppressed groups across caste, race, sexuality, class and other marginalised categories, a possibility. Performing the Dalit is an act of resistance against casteist structure of power, but this negotiation holds out political possibilities for many other oppressed groups as well. And, *that* indeed is the most significant contribution of Dalit theatre.

References

Gajvee, Premanand. *The Strength of Our Wrists 3 Plays*. Trans. Shanta Gokhale, M. D. Hatkanangalekar. Delhi: Navayana, 2013.
Gunasekaran, K. A. *Arikuri* in *Bali Aadugal*. Chennai: New Century Book House, 1999; rpt. 2003.
Gunasekaran, K. A. *Bali Aadugal*. Chennai: Kavya, 1999; rpt. 2003.
Gunasekaran, K. A. *Kandan/Valli* in *Thodu*. Chennai: Thamarai Pb., 2004.
Gunasekaran, K. A. *Matram* in *Thodu*. Chennai: Thamarai Pb., 2004.

Gunasekaran, K. A. *Mazhi* in *Thodu*. Chennai: Thamarai Pb., 2004.

Gunasekaran, K. A. *Odukkapattor Arangiyal*. Chennai: New Century Book House, 2005.

Gunasekaran, K. A. *Pavalakkodi Alladu Kudumba Vazhakku*. Chennai: Adaiyalam, 2001.

Gunasekaran, K. A. *Reflections on the Need for a Dalit Theatre*. Trans. B. Mangalam. JSL, Special Issue on Theatre/Performance. Ed. G. J. V. Prasad. Delhi: JNU, Autumn 2006, pp. 76–81.

Gunasekaran, K. A. *Sathiya Sodhanai*. Chennai: New Century Book House, 1993; rpt. 1995, 2002.

Gunasekaran, K. A. *Thodu*. Chennai: Thamarai Pb., 2004.

Imayam. *Koveru Kazhudaigal*. Chennai: C-rea, 1994.

Larpir, Mohan. P. Ed. *Kalaga Mozhi*. Madurai: Dalit Aadaraa Maiyyam, 2003.

Rodrigues, Valerian. *The Essential Writings of B.R. Ambedkar*. Delhi: OUP, 2002.

Santhakumar, A. *Crow-Dream*. Trans. Vellikkeel Raghavan, A. Anagha. Delhi: Sahitya Akademi, 2013, Vol. 57, No. 4(276), pp. 146–157.

7

INTERPRETING EURIPIDES'S *MEDEA* IN THE CONTEMPORARY INDIAN CONTEXT

Anuradha Marwah

In this chapter, I attempt to interpret Euripides's *Medea* (431 BCE) in the context of its 15 performances in Delhi and Rajasthan. From April to November 2019, eight of us from the pandies' theatre – cast-cum-creative team and I, the director of the play – toured Delhi and Rajasthan with our *Medea* (Hindustani; 55 min).[1] We performed in disparate spaces ranging from a literacy camp in a village to a cultural hub in the centre of the metropolis. Our audiences included school-going adolescents, undergraduate and research students, first-generation literates, migrant labour, rural and urban village communities, academics, MNC executives and theatre aficionados. Invariably, the audiences brought contemporary concerns into the discussion of the play that followed the performances. We found that conversations took off on complex subjects like marriage, sexuality, motherhood and migration and after sailing in uncharted personal experiences anchored in universal human rights. This happened not only in Bastis (urban villages) and rural spaces but also in middle-class venues like schools, colleges and city theatres. As we went on with the performances, *Medea* was selected by The United Nations High Commissioner for Refugees (UNHCR), for a show at Delhi University to raise awareness about refugees. It was performed for a postgraduate Psychology class for their course on motherhood and for rural girls as part of an awareness and empowerment initiative. It was also selected to be the concluding play at India's first community-curated festival organised by the Left theatre group JANAM at Studio Safdar and May Day Bookshop. Thus, our performances of the ancient Greek play were received as contemporary and issue-based in twenty-first-century India – something that gratified us as an activist theatre group but also something that needs

DOI: 10.4324/9781003399926-10

to be referenced and contextualised in terms of both the history of the play's reception and present-day conditions.

The Debate on the Feminist Appropriation of *Medea*

Euripides's *Medea* is about heartbreak and revenge. The Colchian princess, Medea, falls madly in love with Jason, the Argonaut. They marry and settle down in Corinth where Jason betrays her trust by secretly marrying the daughter of the King. The King sentences Medea to exile. Medea extracts a promise of refuge from Aegeus of Athens. She then goes on to wreak terrible vengeance on Jason by killing not only the King and his daughter but also her own two sons by Jason.

The play *Medea* became quite a favourite with the first-wave feminists. Sybil Thorndike, an actress who played Medea to great acclaim, recalls Gilbert Murray, an Oxford Fellow and the notable translator of Euripides saying that Medea "might have been written for the women's movement." Quoting Thorndike, Edith Hall observes that Murray had supported the aim of the women's suffrage movement since 1889: "He believed that the ancient Greeks were the first nation that realised and protested against the subjection of women" (35).

Indeed, *Medea* was staged countless times during the suffrage movement in England when there was an upsurge of interest in women's rights. In Robert Brough's highly popular burlesque "Medea, or the Best of Mothers with a Brute of a Husband" (1856), Medea explains the reasons for committing infanticide in the following way:

> What can a poor, lone, helpless woman do —Battled on all sides — but appeal to you? (To audience) My plot destroyed — my damages made good. They'd change my very nature if they could. Don't let them — rather aid me to pursue my murd'rous career the season through; Repentance is a thought that I abhor, What I have done don't make me sorry for.
>
> *("Medea, A Performance History")*

By the twentieth century, the fact of Medea being a Colchian princess and an outsider to Corinth (she is called a "barbarian" by Jason in the play) began to be foregrounded in several powerful performances that represented Medea as the racial other in society. The Greek tragedy was thus performed as the 'Other-ed' wife and mother's devastating protest against institutionalised discrimination.

Some contemporary scholars and classicists are, however, uncomfortable with the iconising of Medea as protofeminist for a variety of reasons. It is well known that Greek tragedy was a 'popular' form that was patronised by those in power. Its famed multi-vocality was definitely a way of providing expression to contesting points of view, and scholars like Edith Hall have marked Attic theatre as "the natural complement to the Assembly" (the body of decision-makers in Greek democracy) ('Democracy and the Ancient Greek Theatre'). However, it can be argued that privileging one point of view over the other in a contemporary performance would amount to a 'misinterpretation' of the play. Justina Gregory summarises Jasper Griffin's strong objections against over-emphasising the liberative elements in Greek tragedy:

> Griffin maintains that it is anachronistic to define tragedy as didactic in the sense of encouraging a critical examination of prevailing social standards. Although he allows that tragedy is rooted in its contemporary reality, Griffin concludes that 'the political element can be greatly exaggerated and misconceived … interpretation in excessively political terms can lead to damaging mistakes'.
>
> *(144)*

Besides the danger of "misinterpreting" the play, there are added concerns for a practitioner with *Medea*. It is by no means easy to stage "sympathetically" the story of a mother who plans out the murder of her children and dissembles in order to enlist support. In her article on twentieth-century performances of *Medea*, Helen P. Foley describes the reception Medea's first speech receives about the unfairness of being a woman in Corinth in a critically acclaimed performance of Euripides's play in 1994:

> the New York audience at least (I cannot vouch for London) disconcertingly laughed out loud at the play's explicit references to gender conflict and sexual stereotypes. This may have been in part a response to the actress' very cerebral performance, which to some extent distanced the audience from the heroine's anger and passion; but it also seems inevitable.
>
> *(10)*

She quotes a classicist to trace the reason of this disconnect to the plot and storyline of the classical play:

> Nancy Rabinowitz' *Anxiety Veiled*, for example, argues that the play's problematic agenda deliberately includes convincing its male audience that women who step out of line are threatening to male children, and that female subjectivity or encroachment on masculine territory is dangerous. She finds all attempts to appropriate Medea from a modern feminist perspective to be problematic.
>
> *(10)*

Indeed, many contemporary scholars – and actors and audiences too – are wary of the theme of infanticide. In the twentieth and twenty-first centuries when children's rights are foremost in the discourse of human rights, to present a mother who kills (especially in a premeditated and chillingly sane fashion) as protofeminist or human rights hero, is to strike a false note. Foley goes on to articulate why Medea's drastic revenge might seem extreme:

> Women may not yet easily maintain the independence or even the desire that would enable them to turn their back on male betrayal or to own their children, but the rebellion of any serious modern counterpart to Euripides' *Medea* would be likely to entail something far more subtle than resorting to physical violence.
>
> *(12)*

The Objective of Our Endeavour with *Medea*

I must state right in the beginning that propagation of feminist values was not the primary objective for me when in 2018, I started to work on a Hindustani version of *Medea* even though the theatre I work with – the pandies' theatre – and I, in a personal capacity, identify as feminist. With this project I was aiming to take 'great' theatre classics where they have never been before – the *bastis* of Delhi and rural spaces in Rajasthan, where we have done community/workshop theatre. Our primary objective with project 'Samtal' (On Level Ground) is thereby articulated in the following way: to make profound themes and aesthetic values that are associated with elite theatres in India accessible to everyone, especially to those in underserved spaces.[2]

However, it was not an easy task to select a play for our first set of performances. At the pandies', we discussed and debated the feasibility of staging *Medea*. With its rich history of performances not only in England and the US but also in Africa and Asia, *Medea* may be defined as a living world classic. Moreover, as indicated above, it has been remarkably amenable to anticolonial interpretations. I could see that there would be an added advantage in performing the Greek tragedy as it would resist religious or communal stereotyping. The vote in the theatre group was overwhelmingly in favour of *Medea*.

Thus, the work cut out for me while adapting Euripides's *Medea* into Hindustani for a performance in the round was to cull the full-length original script for what would speak to 'everyone.' We had decided to limit the play to an hour because in our long experience of working in the *bastis* we have found that in these community settings the timespan can stretch only about this much before the exigencies of everyday life begin to intrude. It was a challenge I was eager to meet. While working on the script, I had before my mind's eye the performance spaces in Shaktishalini Kushalta Vikas Kendra (also a shelter home for women) in Nehru Basti and the Barat Ghar in Nithari Basti where we were going to have our premiere shows. In my mind, I was already addressing the residents of the Shaktishalini Shelter Home and people from Nehru and Nithari Basti.

Aiming for the Heart

We had 60 precious minutes to build up to the act of Medea killing the children. I felt that the play would have to convince and horrify in equal measure; the familiar and the monstrous would have to be blended in the right proportion in order for it to speak to my proposed audiences who were uninitiated in classical theatre but highly proficient in the drama of lives led in the margins. I intuitively aimed for a fast-paced and emotive script.

I give below a rough translation of a section from my Hindustani script as an instance of my edits. Abandoned by her husband, Jason, Medea now faces the prospect of being banished from Corinth by the King whose daughter is Jason's bride:

Creon
Be gone with you. I will have you evicted from my land by force.
Medea
No-no Creon, please listen to me. I beg of you with folded hands.
Creon
Woman, you are hell-bent on creating a scene.
Medea
I am not petitioning you to reverse the sentence of exile.
Creon
Then what is the mayhem in aid of?
Medea
I am only asking for a few hours. Let me stay on in Corinth just for
   today, so that I have time to work out my future. I have to plan
   for the children as well; their father has made no provisions for
   them. My children are my biggest anxiety, Creon. Please try and
   understand, I am a mother.
Creon (assessing the effect of Medea's plea on the Chorus)
I do not have the nature of a tyrant. But being merciful has led me
   into trouble more than once. Even now, I feel I am making a big
   mistake. I grant you your wish. However, I am warning you,
   Medea. Tomorrow as soon as the day dawns, if you or your chil-
   dren are sighted within my territory, you will die. This is my final
   command.

Exits
Chorus (3)
All men are false. Their promises and vows are writ in water. Medea, you set forth from your father's home with fire in your heart and navigated the ocean. But today, you have lost everything in a foreign land. Like a refugee you're being thrown out, and being divested of your own home. The other woman has usurped your bed and queens it in your home.

(Performance Script, Translation: Anuradha Marwah and Nirbhay Bhogal)

Along with making the dialogue crisp (Greek tragedy comprises long speeches) and cutting out scenes extraneous to the main plot, I also worked to heighten aspects of the play that our audiences would identify with. In this section for instance, I added the line "I am a mother" and also used the term 'refugee' to indicate Medea's status, retaining the English word in the Hindustani script as it is widely used in the country. Residents of Shaktishalini Shelter Home that houses abandoned women along with victims of domestic violence and abuse were going to be part of our first audience. In informal conversations that I had had with them, many had narrated how being the parent who is considered primarily responsible for bringing up children, made their plight even worse. My own experience of being a divorcee with two children had been similar. So, I assumed that Medea's pain and subsequent rage at being abandoned by Jason and then exiled by his father-in-law would resonate if the fact of her being a mother is highlighted. Besides, there were refugee women from Afghanistan in the Shaktishalini Shelter Home. To add to this, the *basti* audiences in both our first shows, especially in Nithari, were likely to have a large proportion of migrant labour families. Migrants in Delhi (as well as in other cities) experience prejudice and stereotyping much in the fashion of minority communities and refugees. Like Medea, they too are accused of 'uncivilised' practices foreign to the host city.

I must emphasise, however, that we made sincere efforts to remain faithful to the balance of the original play in which Medea's revenge on Jason, his new wife and Creon is pitiless and heart-rending. This was sought by giving requisite space to the horrifying description of the murder of Jason's bride and his lamentations after the killing of their children by Medea.

As an instance, I am giving below a section from the penultimate section of our play. Hearing the shocking news of the murder of the two children, Jason accuses Medea of being "unnatural" and "not a woman but a monster" but even more strongly, he challenges her murderous actions by asking whether betrayal on his part can be a justification for her act:

Medea
What did you think? That you could humiliate me and continue to live
your happy life? Yes, you can call me a witch – the ocean-haunting
Scylla! I too have wrested control over your heart.

Jason
You feel no grief at murdering the children?

Medea
Yes, my grief is everything! You can't jeer at it.

Jason
O children! To be slain by your own mother! A witch, a demoness,
for sure!

Medea
They died of a disease they contracted from their father.

Jason
No, that's not true. Lying, traitorous woman! Murderess!

Medea
What happened to your swagger about your young, virginal bride?

Jason
And for that you slew the kids?

Medea
Do you think love is an insignificant thing for a woman?

Jason
For a sensible woman, nothing is more important than her children.
But you are Evil personified.

Medea
Your children are dead, Jason. I will keep repeating this to inflict the
greatest pain on you. You are left with no heirs.

> *(Performance Script, Translation: Anuradha*
> *Marwah and Nirbhay Bhogal)*

Having presented Medea as both the victim and the cruel perpetrator, I
was unsure whether the performances of *Medea* should be followed by a
discussion with the audiences in the fashion of all the pandies' plays. I felt
that the emotional impact of the play would be too overwhelming for any
theorising on social or gender disparity to follow immediately. So, for the
first two shows we did not announce audience interaction as part of the
programme.

After the Tears: In Nehru and Nithari Bastis

I was proved wrong on the day of the premiere. It became very clear to us
with the first two shows that the performance could not end with the actors

taking a bow. The performance in the round had coopted the audiences in a deeply immersive experience, and it seemed grossly unfair to not let them respond to the play.

After the Shaktishalini show, a woman from Nehru Basti, who I had noticed particularly because she had come to the show with *henna* still applied to her hair, came up to me. It was a Sunday morning, and I at once empathised with her loyalty to her weekly beauty routine. She had come to watch *Medea* with a scarf covering the henna paste on her head and had not bothered to hide her tears during the show. I was taken aback when she hugged me as though to condole with me the bloodshed that she had just witnessed. I asked whether she had liked the play, and she answered with tears welling up in her eyes once again, "I liked it very much." She pressed my hand to her heart and then seemed to look over her shoulder almost guiltily. "What did you like about it most?" I asked her. By that time two other women had also walked up to us. "She shouldn't have killed her sons," she replied evading the question and stepping away for me. One of the women who had just joined us nodded and said, "Your play was very good but Medea was wrong to have killed her sons."

I couldn't help wondering what the lady with the *henna* would have said to me if others hadn't joined up at that moment. Would she have expressed an unconditional affirmation of Medea if she had some support from the residents of the Shelter Home or the NGO workers? I was asking myself. It was obvious to me that the women of Nehru Basti were vigilant about any messages that the avowedly feminist space of the NGO 'Shaktishalini' disseminates in their community reach programmes. They were attracted to the socially sanctioned work of providing support to victims of domestic violence and abandoned women, but such participation also involved policing each other (and themselves) against any empathy that might prove disruptive to the male-centric domestic life they probably led – like in most homes in the country. Some of them were domestic workers and privy to the hypocrisies of 'progressive' middle-class homes where, in the name of equal distribution of domestic work, it is actually passed on to low-paid female workers. I was put in mind of the Chorus of Corinthian women (citizens in my adaptation) and their uneven support to Medea. The Chorus expanded to include the audience and I, as a visibly middle-class woman who had brought them *Medea*, felt that I was being reminded of the 'real' station and standing of women by the matrons of the community.

In Nithari Basti too, groups of women and girls chatted among themselves with the latter literally mobbing the actors, especially the lead actor. The woman 'sarpanch' of the area spoke to me at length about training young people of the community to do theatre like this one. She avoided talking about the play but was reluctant to let me go. "It is a real story," she said in response to my question about what she thought of the play. To my question whether such things happen in real life, she replied, "Of course, they happen. But it is not right. The children had done no wrong." On the whole, the men left earlier, although only after complimenting all of us on bringing them a 'unique' performance.

For most of our initial viewers, our shows being their first regular theatre experience made more ethereal by the presence of costumed and made-up actors in such close proximity. They had wept with Medea and a bond had been created; connections established. They had things to say to us. Shedding my initial hesitation about starting a conversation with an audience after the performance of a tragedy, we formalised the post-performance discussions as part of the programme in all the 13 shows that followed.

Collation of Some Responses in Shaktishalini

A meeting was organised by the coordinator at Shaktishalini KVK to discuss the play a few days after the performance. The following report was shared with me:

The morning of April 21st raised the curtains for 'Medea' in one of Delhi's significant communities, among a curious crowd and a canopy of sarees. When Euripides wrote the play, one wouldn't have imagined its everlasting relevance in today's contemporary times, those that reflect and inform the fault lines of gender. Medea is a Hindustani play directed and performed by the pandies' theatre group and premiered at Shakti Shalini's skills development centre in New Delhi under the former's project 'Classical Theatre in Communities'. The fifty minutes drama was accompanied by bursts of live music and cathartic dance movements. It saw an ensemble cast delivering a profound narrative of women empowerment, with ways we look at vengeance, agency and kinships. The crowd for whom this was staged come from deeply marginalised communities of varying degrees of violence, both within their homes and at the mohalla, the bazaar and the streets. The purpose therefore as pandies writes, was to ask the "questions relevant even today in our still gender-unequal world."

The play began with much fanfare from the communities, as they poured in with children, eyeing for the seats under the shade. As it progressed, a handful of men joined at the rear side and were seen quite eager, if not very forthcoming with their responses. Post the show, some women came forward and expressed what they saw and how they felt. Quoting some of them (translated), 'the murder was unethical but the man's negligence and untoward behaviour towards the spouse was also unethical'; 'we always look at the angry man, but we must also look at the angry woman, one who is often denied justice'; 'we see such incidents in our communities too, where the man leaves his spouse and furthermore isolates her from her support systems, it is disturbing'; 'its heartbreaking to see the murder of one own children, but equally the heartbroken woman who had to take such a step.' While most disfavoured the ways in which vengeance was acted upon by the proletariat, there was a delicate persistence on unlearning one's ways. In such ways, the play stood out as a stunning complement to Shakti Shalini's Artivism program. As change makers on both sides of the aisle, art was not just a way to share history and make the present more informed, and more empowered, but also initiate ways to engage interpersonally, of unpacking gender in their lived experiences, even if only as extraordinary afterthoughts.

Audience Responses in Delhi and Rajasthan

Opening up the play for post-performance discussion in the 13 performances that followed the Shaktishalini and Nithari shows proved to be extraordinarily successful in terms of realising the scope of *Medea* in contemporary India. In a research article 'Raging in Delhi and Rajasthan: Post-show Audience Discussions of *Medea*,' I do a detailed analysis of audience responses in four spaces. Here I am making a chart to indicate the kind of audiences we addressed and enumerate the topics that came up during discussions.

Venue: Audience Profile; Number of People Present; Duration of Post-performance Discussions

21 April 2019
Shaktishalini Kushalta Vikas Kendra, Nehru Basti – Women's shelter home residents, NGO workers and community members (mainly migrant labour) (100 approx) (30 minutes, informal discussion)
Nithari Basti – Migrant labour community (200 approx) (20 minutes, informal discussion)

28 April 2019
Studio 81, VK (2 shows) – University students, academics, upper middle-class residents, professionals, regular theatregoers (55 + 46) (60 minutes + 40 minutes)

20 Sept 2019
Gargi College for Women, Delhi University – Students of BA (Hon) English and the English Department Faculty (150 approx) (65 minutes)

25 Sept 2019
AUD – Postgraduate and research students, professors and academics (100
approx) (55 minutes)

29 Sept 2019
Arain – community leaders, NGO workers, housewives, and students from
local colleges (50 approx) (30 minutes)

30 Sept 2019
St Mary's Convent, School for Girls – Grade XI students and faculty (167)
(32.16 minutes)
Savitri Girls' Government College – College students (BA and MA) and
faculty (150 approx) (25 minutes)

1 Oct 2019
Khwaja Model School (co-educational) – Grade X, XI and XII, faculty and
members of the Trust (140) (25.03 minutes)
Mangliawas – Open school dropout girls between 15 and 20 years of age
from nearby villages in a residential SRHR and gender equity programme
and girls from other programmes run by Doosra Dashak, Peesangan,
NGO workers and community members from Mangliawas (130) (36.12
minutes)

7 Nov 2019
Indraprastha College for Women, Delhi University: Students from Delhi
University, Faculty, UNHCR officers, Afghani community members
(130 approx) (46.51 minutes)
23 Nov 2019
India Habitat Centre: Regular theatregoers (90 approx) (34.52 minutes)

24 Nov 2019
Studio Safdar (2 shows): Community members, regular theatregoers,
JANAM associates (50 + 50 approx) (15 minutes + 30 minutes)

The topics of discussion can be put under the following headings:

(i)   *The newness of the experience*
(ii) *The skill of the actors with reference to performance in the round*
(iii) *The use of 'Hindustani'*

(i)   *The surprising resonance of the ancient play in contemporary times*
(ii) *Contemporary examples (news reports) of cases of abandonment*
      and murder
(iii) *Abandonment and sexual jealousy*
(iv) *Female infanticide, in vitro female infanticide, abortion laws, traf-*
      ficking of women

(v)   *Ancient Greek Theatre*

(vi) *Our music-scape and Indian folk theatre*

(vii) *Greek myths and Indian myths especially 'Kali' the avenger, and 'Ganga' who also kills her sons (and debates about their comparative richness)*

(viii) *Jason's typically masculine behaviour. Contemporary instances of misogyny gender roles in India and double standards*

(ix) *Medea's courage and fearlessness: Her refusal to be victim*

(x)   *Prejudice: Stereotyping and 'othering' of minorities, outsiders and women*

(xi) *The extent of Medea's culpability (debate whether the monstrous ending came about due to her 'faults' or that of Jason and Creon/ patriarchal society)*

The last point was the one that was extensively discussed in all interactions and audiences' observations touched upon both ethics and the psychological and social dimensions of Medea's act. At times this was the very first question to be asked from the troupe as though to ascertain our 'motives' in staging the play. Our Medea had moved hearts but Jason's grief felt real too. The young man who played Jason was our most experienced actor, and I had accorded full play to him. Medea answers his charges forcefully and divines an inglorious end to his life. At times it seemed that the highly charged debate between Medea and Jason was continuing seamlessly in the post- performance discussions. Would this have happened in the polis of Ancient Greece? I found myself asking, especially, if theatre was a natural corollary of the Assembly as claimed by scholars?

In his article, Caraher marks out a distinguishing characteristic of Euripidean tragedy – "the disappearance of the hero" – and the installation of "an agon or contest between two paired characters, notably Jason and Medea and Pentheus and Dionysus, but also Admetus and Alcestis and Hippolytus and Phaedra" (157).

It would be difficult to ascertain who came out stronger in such contests in 431 BCE, but the very existence of the 'agon' tells a liberative tale with *Medea*. Its continuation in our post-performance debates was especially significant as in four of our videos – recorded in Ambedkar University Delhi, Mangliawas village in Rajasthan, the India Habitat Centre and Studio Safdar in New Delhi – Medea's team for defence is all women while the prosecutors are men. As I discuss in the article 'Raging in Delhi and Rajasthan', our *Medea* was pitting women against men in a debate about the contemporary Indian gender-scape and it is anybody's guess as to which side was coming out more persuasive. Women called out Jason's 'hypocrisy' while accepting that his grief was real. They didn't defend Medea but asked some difficult questions. Why did Jason abandon his family if the children were so precious to him? It was due to his excessive ambition and lust for a younger woman, wasn't it? Why did Creon, his father-in-law, sentence Medea to exile? Perhaps some questions are as eternal as 'great' theatre classics.

Indian Melodrama

My attempt to mark out the Indian context, especially of a Hindustani (combination of Urdu and Hindi) performance like ours, would be incomplete if I do not refer to the ubiquitous Bombay cinema that has preserved and developed this register in modern India.

Even while scripting the play, in my subconscious mind, I had as a reference point, moving scenes from the film *Mother India* (1957). The film details immense hardships endured by an abandoned woman with children and her heroic act of killing her beloved son to save a woman he is abducting. In addition to this classic of Indian cinema, there are recent 'revenge films', ranging from the extreme and gory *Khoon Bhari Maang* (1988) to the polished and riveting *Kahani* (2012) about women who are 'wronged' and who go on to kill. Women protagonists are built up as larger-than-life avengers in them. Bombay cinema on the whole has often been discussed in terms of being 'melodramatic'. Revenge films specially, or at least some overly 'high-pitched' scenes from them, have been criticised as "melodramatic tear-jerkers" by film critics and elite audiences alike. The twentieth century's most-performed Greek tragedy, *Medea*, was born in an altogether different context and time, but some sections of the play may be seen to anticipate the Bombay films.

On entry, Medea makes a resounding public pronouncement that – as reported by Foley and mentioned earlier in the article – made New Yorkers laugh. That speech is a protest speech against the unfairness of being a woman and could have fitted seamlessly into one of the above-mentioned films. Long emotive speeches describing inequality and injustice and foreshadowing or justifying the retributive act of violence are a characteristic of this kind of Bombay cinema. Medea also accuses Jason of breaking his oath; pleads cravenly with Creon, the King; sets up an elaborate ruse to avenge her humiliation and fortifies her murderous intent by explaining her reasons persuasively to the Chorus. In the last scene, covered in blood, she metamorphoses into demigoddess or witch. Although known to be unusually intelligent, venturesome and politically savvy, Medea is also a Colchian woman 'wronged' by the institutions of the State and the Family, wreaking vengeance. She declaims throughout the play. Awang Bin Othman observes that Medea speaks "from the outside in the outside" (in the outside space known as the public space — the *polis* — as a feminine who in turn is a marginalised subject who is "outside" a privileged position) (178). It is the location of Medea on the extreme periphery, as a lone individual in conflict

with age-old institutions, that has an eerie similarity with the woman protagonists of the films I mention. Like them, Medea has been pushed there by
circumstances beyond her control, and the actions she impels are reactive. I
am perhaps talking about the seeds of 'melodrama' in Euripides's play that
resonates with the use of melodrama in Bombay cinema.

Euripides's plays have been discussed as precursors of melodrama which
is intended to appeal to emotions and which became the prevalent mode in
European theatre in the eighteenth and nineteenth centuries. Marking the
difference of Euripides's *Medea* from other Greek tragedy (Aeschylean and
Sophoclean), Caraher categorises it as "melodrama of horror":

> Euripides gives voice to victims of adventurism, aggression and betrayal
> in the name of 'reason' and the 'state' or 'polity.' Medea constitutes one
> of the most powerful mythic forces to which he gave such voice by melo-
> dramatizing the disturbing liminality of Greek tragedy's perceived social
> and cultural order. The social polity is confronted by an apocalyptic shock
> to its order and its available modes of emotional, rational and social inter-
> pretation. Euripidean melodramas of horror dramatize the violation of
> rational categories and precipitate an abject liminality of the tragic vision
> of rational order.
>
> *(143)*

Caraher submits that *Medea* resists the delineation of the tragic hero by
Aristotle. He describes her as a wronged woman and an avenger:

> Medea oscillates between the figure of avenger, "that essentially melodra-
> matic character who haunts the stage for two millennia", and the charac-
> ter of a tragically conflicted and grievously wronged woman.
>
> *(Heilman 1968: 266–267) (160)*

Caraher's article is suggesting that the play has a deeply destabilising impact
due to the seeds of melodrama. Rather than affecting the Aristotlean cathar-
sis with its connotations of restoration and renewal, it served to split up
the space of the polis in a way that our post-performance discussions were
unconsciously mimicking.

The term 'melodrama' in a pejorative way about Bombay cinema too has
in recent years given way to a serious engagement with its mode of negotiating the public space. Identifying "scenarios of extremity" and discussing the
"melodramatic embodiment of gender and identity" in Bombay cinema of
the 1940s and 1950s, Ira Bhaskar says:

> As one of the most popular and enduring cultural forms through which
> contemporary social and political crises are cinematically represented

and negotiated, melodrama's "capacity to respond to the questions of modernity" accounts for its pervasive influence in different cinemas of the world. Theorized as an aesthetic form that emerges in transitional periods, melodrama has been seen to negotiate the dislocating traumas of class and gender struggle, and to answer the doubts and aporias consequent to the breakdown of the "traditional sacred."

(Seminar)

Indeed, scenarios of extremity and Bombay cinema were never very far from us. In the end Jason is on his knees, begging for the corpses of his children and Medea marked by their blood and bearing the corpses in a white sack slung across her shoulder ascends beyond human reach. The Chorus beat their breasts in choreographed symphony and invoke the absent Gods. In Mangliawas, a viewer observed, "We watch *scenarios* [*sic*] on our mobiles and television but this is better. It was right here – so close to us" (translated. from Hindi). Operating in real time, the live performances collapsed centuries and a tale from another time and place became ours.

Notes

1 'Pandies' is a Delhi-based activist theatre group of which I have been member for 21 years. The cast and creative team of *Medea*, my first directorial venture, comprised Janees as Medea; Zeeshan as Jason; Priya as the dancer and Chorus; Arham as the Nurse and Chorus; Sameer as Creon; Nirbhay as the Tutor and the Messenger; and Akash and Robin as Chorus.
2 Greek tragedy is performed only in hallowed spaces in India. Coincidentally, in the year we performed *Medea* in Delhi and the villages of Rajasthan, an elaborate English version of it by Nautankisa Production, directed by Ira Khan, was mounted in Mumbai. The cheapest tickets were for Rs 500. All our shows were free entry except for the two Studio Safdar shows. Studio Safdar charged Rs. 20 (or less if necessary) from community audiences and Rs. 200 from others. Thus, through Samtal we tried to democratise the performance of Greek tragedy.

References

Awang Bin Othman, Johan, 'Can Medea Speak? Tracing Euripides' Medea's Complex Performative Gendering in Her Speech from the Outside in the Outside', *Procedia – Social and Behavioral Sciences*, 208 (2015), pp. 175–181.
Bhaskar, Ira, 'The Limits of Desire' in Circuits of Cinema: A Symposium on Indian Cinema in the 1940s and 50s', Seminar No. 598, June 2009 at https://www.india-seminar.com/2009/598.htm (accessed on 8 June 2020).
Caraher, Brian G., 'Tragedy, Euripides, Melodrama: Hamartia, Medea, Liminality', *Amaltea*, 5 (2013), pp. 143–171.
Foley, Helene P., *Reimagining Greek Tragedy on the American Stage*, University of California Press, California and London, 2012, p. 190.
Gregory, J., 'Euripides as Social Critic', *Greece and Rome*, 4.2 (October 2002), pp. 145–162.

Hall, Edith, 'Medea and British Legislation before the First World War', *Greece & Rome*, 46.1 (April 1999), pp. 42–77.

Hall, Edith, 'Interview with Alessandro Brambilla, Democracy and the Ancient Greek Theatre', 2015 at http://www.leussein.eurom.it/author/alessandro -brambilla/ (accessed on 8 June 2020).

Marwah, Anuradha, 'Raging in Delhi and Rajasthan: Post-show Audience Discussions of *Medea*', *New Theatre Quarterly*, 38.1 (February 2022), pp. 75–90; and Nirbhay Bhogal, *Medea*. Translated from the Hindustani (Performance Script). Unpublished.

'Medea, A Performance History' at http://www.apgrd.ox.ac.uk/ebooks-medea (accessed on 8 June 2020).

SUB-THEME III
Poetry

8

POETRY, PLAGUE AND LOCUSTS

About Writing Sonnets on the Black Death

Keki N. Daruwalla

The title, deliberately dismal in keeping with the overhang of the corona-virus raging on the planet, could be reminiscent of a Wagnerian movement or Thomas Hardy at his most pessimistic. Hence apologies in advance. The chapter may not really raise the spirits of the readers. But raising the spirits of an assortment of readers can never be the objective of poetry. To digress a bit, does poetry have objectives, I mean cut and dried and ready to be served at the reader's or the publisher's desk? I am no scholar of history, but Paul Celan has written about the gas chambers. He was at Auschwitz as a kid where he lost his mother. So poetry has been written in catastrophic times about those times. After all, over six million people were gassed by the Nazis. I remember fondly a poem by Thomas Hardy on the sinking of the Titanic. For the flighty bourgeoisie that ship and the iceberg must have been the talk of the western world for years. Keats wrote his ode on melancholy. What I wish to stress is that each time you touch the melancholic vein, you are compelled to be reflective. You have to burrow into your psyche to write or compose music.

History can at times throw up vaguely, and erroneously, what we dub as parallels. One is not hard to find one for the current coronavirus. You have the Black Death in the 13th century, the plague that came and rav-aged Europe. The disease dribbled down into succeeding centuries. It took between 150 million and 200 million lives in all. It was rodent-borne and left a terrible impact on civilization. I am surprised that Christianity sur-vived. However strong one's faith is, and however grounded one's piety is, how does it survive a tempest of death that goes on and on, killing people of the church and laity, saint and sinner, alike. Didn't the Divine intervene?

DOI: 10.4324/9781003399926-12

Was he asleep? That saint who never hurt a fly, fed the poor, nursed the sick, caught the chills and was dead in a few hours.

Excuse me saying this, but while I am writing, a solar eclipse has taken place. So in Delhi where I live, we have had earthquake tremors, an eclipse, locusts nearby from Pakistan, a pandemic from China—a truly Biblical scene. Most cultures have memories of floods (parlay) and visitations that have devastated civilizations. When I was studying for my novel *Swerving to Solitude: Letters to Mama*, I found that in Punjab the plague took away 20,000 every week in the first decade of the 20th century. People blamed the plague on the canals that the English had dug! The Bible, rather the Section Exodus, is full of plagues. I read *Exodus* by Leon Uris before I came to Exodus in the Bible. The Pharaoh will not let the Hebrews leave Egypt. His heart is hardened. The Israelites are enslaved by the Pharaoh and the Egyptians, and the Lord says to Moses and Aaron that when the Pharaoh asks you to perform a miracle, "take your staff and throw it down before Pharaoh and it will become a snake." When this was done, the Pharaoh "summoned the wise men and sorcerers, and the Egyptian magicians did the same by their secret arts" (Exodus 6:12). Then follow a list of plagues, the plagues of blood when the Nile turns to blood and the fish die, the plague of frogs, which cover the land, the plagues of gnats, flies and the plague of boils. The only time the magicians are stumped is when the plague of boils attacks the Egyptians. "The magicians could not stand before Moses because of the boils that were on them and on all the Egyptians" (Exodus 8:14:12). Incidentally, such stories abound in all faiths. A false sun is created by the magicians, and Zoroaster shows it for what it is, in Zoroastrian lore. The pious had to be against sorcery. Sorcerers were cheats.

Why did the Lord harden Pharaoh's heart? So that each time the Lord God of the Israelites could show his miraculous powers. The plague of boils almost resembles the buboes of the plagues. There is also a plague of locusts, these days they were coming across Pakistan. So plagues, locusts and migrations (as shown in Exodus) have been a part of human and civilizational history. And after all Moses crosses the Red Sea with his flock and all is hunky-dory. Regrettably our migrants don't have a similar tale to tell.

Migrations are always difficult
ask any drought,
any plague;
ask the year 1947.
Ask the chronicles themselves:
if there had been no migrations
would there have been enough
history to munch on?

(From the poem "Migrations")

I am not a historian, certainly not a medieval historian. The Welsh poet DafyddapGwilym (1315–1350) or (1340–1370) wrote a poem called "Rattle Bag," referring to the sound made by the buboes. A civilization became conversant with the universality of death, as shown by *La Danse Macabre*, which became a signpost for the age. People thought the world was ending. The Muslims believed the world was ending in the 1970s when a self-styled Mehdi took over the Kaaba. Germans had to be called in and the fellow shot—so were his followers I believe. The world's end was very much of an intellectual and religious baggage which people carried. In a poem by Thomas Nashe, the playwright gives an idea about the drooping pessimism the plague brought about in the continent:

> "A Litany in the Time of Plague"
> Adieu, farewell earth's blisse
> This world uncertaine is
> Fond are life's blissful joyes,
> Death proves them all but toyes
> None from his darts can flye
> I am sick, I must dye
> Lord above have mercy on us.

A belief system of an age comes through in a short seven-line poem—foolish (fond) are 'life's blissful joys,' death is supreme, the poet is sick and must die. But there is no deviation from belief in the divine. Even doubt is not expressed. There were collective hallucinations. People heard a horse clattering away at night ridden by a skeleton. It reflects on the collective terror. As far as the plague narrative goes, the great Bard, appearing over 200 years after the first shock of the dread disease, is a bit disappointing.

> Not from the stars do I my judgement pluck;
> And yet methinks I have astronomy,
> But not to tell of good or evil luck
> Of plagues, of dearths, or seasons' quality;

The sonnet ends with the lines to his beloved:

> Or else of thee this I prognosticate:
> Thy end is truth's and beauty's doom and date.
>
> *(Shakespeare's Sonnet no. 14)*

Francesco Petrarca, better known as Petrarch (1304–1374), was fortunate or unfortunate to live through the Black Death. He is remembered more for his sonnets and the love poems to Laura, a figment of the imagination. In the final year of his life, he said that his society had lived with "This plague without equal in all the centuries." The arrival of the Black Death is 1348, but its havoc lasted till 1353. The Florentines fled on their periodic return. The Black Death sharpened his sense of the "sweetness and fragility of life." What was the meaning of life after so much death? Had it transformed him or anyone for the better. His patron Giovanni Colona died along with members of his family, all of whom he had served in Avignon. He wrote numerous letters to friends and printed some of the correspondence. He was a scholar of the writings of Cicero, and to him we owe the quote from Cicero that "letters make the absent present." He mourned the loss of his friends. The father of humanism as he is called, he derided astrologers and dubbed predictions that "turned out right as accidental truths."

"Why do you feign futile prophecies after the fact or call chance truth." He asked. His life was spent wandering from place to place. When plague returned to the Venetian Republic, friends pleaded with him to leave. His answer was "It has often happened that a flight from death is a flight to death." He was not a cantankerous man, but said of astrology, "we do not know what is happening in the heavens." And he ridiculed the common people who waited on every word from astrologers, characterizing the scene as that of "Parched minds and thirsty years." He did not think much of the science of medicine then and said that ignorance itself was pestiferous.

The Knockdown

We all have a private side, the one through which we dream and talk to ourselves. Let's call it imagination. Writers, artists hug this side very carefully, sometimes secretively. Any poet or artist makes the most of this intensely personal hour or two. I am no different. A creative writer relies on imagination, whatever be his bedrock of experience. If at the end of a poem or story the imagination has not taken some sort of a flight, there is no point in writing.

I had found the earlier years under the current establishment a bit of a lockdown. I am basically a good democrat, can't see politics being channelized towards majoritarian rule. I can't stomach someone getting on to TV at 8 PM and announcing that my hard-earned money is no longer legal tender or that I clap and burn candles at 7 (which I did) or that I can't stir out—all at 4 hours' notice. This is not the freedom I am born into. Just to remind you of the one full year I spent in Oxford writing on democracy in South Asia.

Like others, I come to my writing with complexes, inhibitions, proclivities, habits. My writing often tends towards bleakness. I avoid it, especially after an accident and a mishap in the family which left its imprint on all of us. I made a purposeful break. I also need to abjure violence in my writing, for in my first two books, there was a bit of it, and not very intelligent critics latched on to it.

So during the semi-intellectual lockdown I wrote short striking poems. These were pointed and aimed at targets. One was on the murder of Gauri Lankesh which was rather harsh. But if a society or *sanstha* murders a right-thinking bold editor, surely it needs the harshest slap in print. I have written too harshly. I tried writing on Shaheen Bagh, and I couldn't. You can't write poetry on anything you want. Poetry is not a servant; it is the master. You, the writer, are the horse. It gives you rein. I find that if halfway through writing a poem you get up to have a cup of tea or water, the poem often disappears. If you get up for whisky, the poem stays. It was right there, and it is gone. My notepads are full of half poems, and you can't turn them into poems.

So let us start with the intellectual lockdown. We were told that only belief systems that count are the ones that are home-grown like *arharki dal*. Anything that came high jumping over the Hindu Kush was not Indian, and such believers were to be treated as foreigners. When you write on matters socio-political, write stridently. But there is always room for satire. I wrote one on Sadhvi Bindiya. And another on Manu Rishi.

Then comes the coronavirus and the logical lockdown. Am not sure which of the two was worse. For me the lockdown has been no problem at all. This tragedy of the coronavirus is unprecedented—it is worldwide, flung by China on the planet. How does poetry deal with a tragedy of such proportions? It does. In fact, it is surprising there are very few poems say on plagues—the Justinian or the Black Death which did away with 150 million people.

If one may put it grotesquely enough, there are two ways of "exploiting" the circumstances. You can write about the horrendous details, those being enacted in front of you, the misery of the migrants, for instance, the detailed horror of 40 million souls being uprooted by unemployment and hence lack of money and food, people being overrun while sleeping absurdly on rail-way tracks. That is one dimension. I have a poem called "Migrant Notes." There is an element of reportage here, but it is a poem taking you to the desert and the deer dying, since it has got lost trying to find an oasis, pana-cea. Allegory is a European category, Europe has grown up in it, Bunyan's *Pilgrim Progress* and so on.

What happens when you grapple with something equally horrendous, you wrestle with it and pillage it from history. To be a poet of any standing you have to be a good thief. Empty the granary of the guy you rob. So after thieving from history or myth, you start mulling over the event, the saga, reimagining the landscape of grief and havoc a similar event caused, mean-ing the Black Death. It took away 150 million people if not 200 million. No one knew what it was. People blamed witches and Jews—they were always the bête noir, the whipping boys. The ones who had borrowed from them

were the ones who accused them, so that they could get away without paying. You have to first study the history, but facts have to be touched upon
lightly. After all you are not writing history. You are imagining a historical
era and the landscape of grief and havoc the plague left behind with a bewil-
dered people—prayers, terror leading to hallucinations. People start hearing
a horse cantering away at night, and there are people who will swear that
a skeleton was riding on it. By now I hope the readers have got the flow of
what I intend to say in this chapter.

I didn't want to start dismally. So got the Devil to speak of what he was
at, in the first poem of the prologue.

Prologue to the Sonnets

The Devil never left Black Death in the foyer
to be discussed at length in devastating detail.
Cleverer than Satan and Iblis, those soul-sawyers
he couldn't ever fail!

He checked out of Hilton, memory had him dismayed:
Didn't the hotel echo some rhymester of yore?
Yes of course the guy who needed Hearing Aids,
his verse sonorous as a river gorge!

Having planted Brexit, the Devil thought of exits
make a run for it, buddy, though sad to leave Hilton,
in poor English he said, "this place is truly gala".

His task severe, bury memories of Black Death
in some catafalque, beyond the reach
Of sonneteering bums like Daruwalla.

Another sonnet had to follow, a rhymeless one where the scribbler is penal-
ized. Then we come to the actual Black Death Sonnets. When writing
poetry, not even fiction, the writer is negotiating through shoals, by which I
mean craft, beliefs, history (which was very unfair to Jews). If you read the
Inferno, Dante was pretty unfair to Islam and saw it burning in hell. I give
a quote from the Canto VIII, Lines 70–72 (translation by Dorothy Sayers):

Dante says to his guide Virgil

And I "Already I see its mosques arise
Clear from the valley yonder—a red shell
As though drawn out of glowing furnaces."

In their notes both Dorothy Sayers and Michael Palma clarify these lines— am quoting Palma, who has translated the *Inferno* brilliantly, "The mosques suggest the medieval Christian view of Islam as heresy, a rebellion against God." Almost as an aside in my sonnets I say discussing in just three lines the blame for the plague:

> "They did it," the court says, "beggar, witch, Jew
> and migrants; were there minaret and dome
> dusk-lit, they'd have blamed it on mosques aglow."

So a poet carries what he has read with him, and when he gets his chance rebuts something unfair. Jews had a very hard time of it during the Black Death, and there are three other lines which spring to the defence of the Jew. Incidentally, the very people who were in debt to the Jew spread the canard that they had brought in the plague. To quote from the sonnets would be unfair to the publishers (the anthology has yet to come out). But I must emphasize that none of this comes out as an overt effort. The subconscious, and all that one has seen and imbibed over a lifetime, comes out.

Questions like whether you should try to heal the world or rage against the dying of the light never occur. A novel is better equipped to bring in a social change rather than poetry. If I had started documenting the plague, it wouldn't have remained a poem. And yet if you are just floating in the air, you are being less than a writer. I agreed to a mix. For the kind of Covid we are facing, personally, forms like the ballad and haiku are irrelevant, too slight. The sonnet is weighty. And since I have experience in this form (my book *Fire Altar* contains more than 20 sonnets), I find it the more malleable. What can't be used in one sonnet turns out to be the basis of the next!

Poets are neither philosophers nor activists. But they can be decent thieves and do some pinching from both these guys. As I mentioned in passing, a poet can come to a formidable subject with complexes. If you are writing on Black Death, it will be all gloom and doom. In the prologue I brought the Devil in and the fellow is living it up at the Hilton. In the next one the Cardinal sentences the writer to a year's hard labour. He has written a sonnet without rhyme. The Black Death Sonnets are a unit by themselves. The poems are more or less written in the first person by the king of Byzantium, John VI Kantakou Zenos, who has lost his 13-year-old son to the plague. I do not wish to elaborate on each sonnet. For instance, I have negated the popular belief about Jews and witches being behind the epidemic.

This is a rather scholarly or stodgy manner of writing poetry during a lockdown. I was asked if I would write for an anthology around the theme: Singing in Bad Times. This clutch of poems was the result – the sonnets that are yet to be published. Time and the corona hung like a pestilential canopy.

One just hunkered down. But my urge towards medieval Europe and the Black Death helped me tackle the subject.

A Select List of References

Shakespeare's Sonnet no. 14 can be accessed at https://shakespeare.folger.edu/shakespeares-works/shakespeares-sonnets/sonnet-14/, 25.11.2022, 20:10 hrs.

Keki Daruwalla's poem 'Migrations' can be accessed at https://www.poetryinternational.com/en/poets-poems/poems/poem/103-2893_MIGRATIONS, 25.11.2022, 20:14 hrs.

The poem 'Rattle Bag' by Dafydd ap Gwilym can be accessed in translation at https://soundcloud.com/konchpoetry/the-rattlebag-by-dafydd-ap-gwilym-translated-by-joseph-p-clancy-read-by-anne-marie-copestake, 25.11.2022, 20:35 hrs.

Swerving to Solitude: Letters to Mama Hardcover by Keki N. Daruwalla, Simon & Schuster, 21 August 2018, ISBN-10-9789386797223.

Exodus by Leon Uris, Bantam Doubleday Dell Publishing Group Inc, ISBN: 9780553258479, 9780553258479, Edition, 1999.

Paul Celan is known for his writings on the Holocaust. An interesting essay on him entitled 'Language and the Holocaust: Reflections on the Poetry of Paul Celan' by Emery George in the *Michigan Quarterly Review*, Volume XXXVI, Issue 3, Summer 1997, can be accessed at https://quod.lib.umich.edu/cgi/t/text/text-idx?cc=mqr;c=mqr;c=mqrarchive;idno=act2080.0036.318;g=mqrg;rgn=main;view=text;xc=1, 25.11.2022.

Poem entitled 'The Convergence of the Twain' (Lines on the loss of the 'Titanic') by Thomas Hardy, accessed at https://www.hardysociety.org/media/bin/commentaries/1532429316.pdf, 25.11.2022.

Ode on Melancholy' by John Keats can be accessed at https://www.poetryfoundation.org/poems/44478/ode-on-melancholy, 25.11.2022.

Fire Altar: Poems on the Persians and the Greeks by Keki N. Daruwalla, HarperCollins, 13 December 2013 ISBN-10-9789351160793.

9

TRANSLATION AND VARIATION

Literary Studies, Reading Practices, and the Vernacular

Udaya Kumar

While working on the thought of Sree Narayana Guru (1856–1928), the renowned spiritual and social thinker from Kerala, I faced some difficulties in translating passages from some of his writings into English. I was translating these for citation and analysis, and not for stand-alone publication. English renderings of these passages became especially challenging when analysis tried to follow the movement of thought by focusing on particular words or concepts and on the connections that the text seemed to forge among them. The problem was not really about equivalences between words in English and those in Malayalam, although equivalence and approximation are particularly unstable when we deal with conceptual vocabulary. Translation seems to work precisely in that uncertain territory of promise and of the risk of similitudes without guarantee. This experience is all the more pronounced where the languages involved have no clear linkages through evolution or adjacency in contemporary life. The histories, the neighbourhoods and the resonances of individual words differ, and the loss and the unjustified gain involved in the decisions of the translator resist being computed in advance. But here I am concerned less with this lexical dimension of translation than with the connectedness, the flow and the force of textual sequences.

This issue confronted me forcefully when I worked with Sree Narayanan's rare prose writings where he adopts a diction that is different in its rhythms from familiar idioms of prose and verse writing in Malayalam. For instance, in the opening of *Atmavilasam*, which may loosely be translated as *the play of the self*, we find a register that oscillates between the mystical and philosophical. After much effort, the opening paragraph entered English like this:

DOI: 10.4324/9781003399926-13

Om! All this seems to be like a shadow that appears in a mirror placed before us. How amazing! The eye that sees everything – it is not seen by the eye. When we hold a mirror before the eye, the eye appears as a shadow in the mirror. Then the eye sees the mirror as well as the shadow. The shadow is lifeless (*jadam*). It does not have the power to see the eye. The eye does not have the power to look directly at itself. Thus, when the eye and its shadow are not visible in our eye, it is we who see the eye there. Similarly, we do not see the we who sees the eye.[1]

I aimed to show that the articulation of a sense of the self in these lines worked through a demonstration that focused on exteriority and involved the mirror, the shadow, the gaze, and the elusive figure of the viewing subject. The English rendering, with quite some difficulty, managed to indicate the scenography of the self in this passage to the reader, but it failed to convey the energetic charge of the original, its tempo and its rhythm. Even more elusive was the gestural quality of the locutions, which approximated bodily expressions of surprise and delight in what is seen and revealed. The passage at times has an intensive sense of certainty and surprise, indicated by the suffix 'thanne' in the first sentence (nizhalpolethanne – exactly like a shadow). The single-word exclamation (adbhutam!) that follows works as an echo of this expression of certainty. Alliteration (*kannine, kannu, kanunnilla, kannadi*), arising from the repetition of 'kannu' (eye), 'kannadi' (mirror), and several forms of the verb 'kanuka,' seem to produce an effect of acoustic confusion which arguably parallels the perceptual bewilderment at the core of the experience invoked in the passage.

I have presented this as a problem of the difference between languages, but this may be somewhat limiting as an approach. Can we really speak of the differences between languages as if they possess stable, self-contained identities? Naoki Sakai has persuasively argued that

> it is not because two different language unities are given that we have to translate (or interpret) one text into another; it is because translation articulates languages so that we may postulate the two unities of the translating and the translated languages as if they were autonomous and closed entities through a certain representation of translation.[2]

The thrust of Sakai's argument is to challenge the model of homolingual address which seems to underpin stable notions of language identity, associated prominently with cultural nationalism. Sakai argues that the translational process, predicated on heterolingual address, creates a certain protocol which produces as its effect the idea of separate languages with distinctive identities. Viewed in this way, arguments about proximity and distance, neighbourhoods and territories, may appear less dependable in their presupposition of clearly demarcated spaces. We seem to be in a domain of expanding neighbourhoods rather than in that of territories with sharply policed regulations of entry and exit. In other words, even within what we consider as the unity of a language, we are in a state of heterolingual address, and processes of translation are underway in acts of reading and interpretation. Our linguistic inhabitation is not in a self-enclosed territorial space but in a plane of continuous variation.[3]

This approach enables us to examine the nature of the difficulties that I indicated in the opening paragraph more closely. The sonic and gestural feel of the passage from Sree Narayana Guru's *Atmavilasam* actively mobilizes many such variations. It is not even clear if this text has a purported addressee. The tone is that of registering and documenting an experience of discovery by articulating it, saying it, or writing it. However, the utterance and the act of articulation are part of the experience of discovery and realization, and not external to it. Metaphysical propositions appear here not as presented in a neutral space but simultaneously as the experience and recording of a vision, where it is difficult to determine who the viewer and the objects of vision are.

The problem I faced while translating this passage is not unique to English. If one writes on this text in the register of modern academic writing in Malayalam, problems of a similar nature are likely to arise. Part of the problem comes from the difficulty in grasping and engaging the force of alliteration and the gestural and sonic inflections as part of philosophical writing. One is not sure as to how to determine its value and its effects on an academic reading. The distinction between English and Malayalam as stable linguistic entities with their distinctive features and expressive possibilities will not be sufficient to grasp this. The internal dynamics of Malayalam, both in Sree Narayanan's times and as it operates in our present, appear to play a role in configuring the terms of our reading. This is not a matter of Malayalam alone; we will find similar issues in most, if not all, Indian languages. It may not even be a matter of Indian languages versus English. Some of the discourses in the English language in India too deviate from the protocols of the academic register and may show energies similar to the one we mentioned above. This may have much to do with the complex effects of the colonial encounter on the concept, practices, and normative structures of language.

The concept of the 'vernacular' has been used sometimes to thematize the deployment of force that characterizes the uses of language I mentioned above. Rather than employing this concept to designate individual languages that do not have cosmopolitan scope, one may use it to refer to domains of exchange and inhabitation within languages that are at variance with the protocols of 'official' and 'formal' discourses. Partha Chatterjee advanced a case for such a use of the term 'vernacular' after the publication of *History in the*

Vernacular, pointing to a domain of production of knowledge that remains outside the ambit of disciplinary discourses in professional academic structures and spaces.[4] While elaborating on this distinction, Chatterjee pointed out how many key themes in Indian social sciences research – such as 'caste' in the case of sociology – first emerged as issues with political charge in the vernacular domain before they entered academic, disciplinary discourse.[5] He even proposed that issues identified as political in the vernacular domain of knowledge often turn into methodological problems after they enter the disciplinary domain. We often see academic and vernacular discourses trade charges against each other for being 'political.' For both parties the allegation of being 'political' signifies the operation of vested interests, although its sense may not be identical. For academic discourse, the political character of the vernacular usually signifies an absence of methodological rigour and a deviation from the protocols of academic objectivity and veridiction, while for the latter the entire edifice of the academy appears at times as a self-concealing repository of institutional vested interests that obstructs an egalitarian passage to justice.

The distinction between the vernacular and the professional academic was primarily elaborated in the context of knowledge production in a postcolonial context. But the distinction can be useful for understanding the arrangement of and transactions between discourses in a wider sense. We may be able to approach the problem I began this chapter with in the light of this discussion. How would we characterize a text like *Atmavilasam*? It does possess a close relationship to knowledge and to doctrines developed and debated in philosophical discourse. Signs of training in philosophical thinking are evident in the text. However, overriding the tone of the erudite philosophical thinker is a feel of animation and energy. The latter refers to immediate experience, articulated in a language close to ordinary life and not processed through the degree of linguistic refinement that usually characterize the discourse of abstract thought. More importantly, the relationship between the speaking voice and the text of the utterance seems to be different from what we usually find in conceptual philosophical discourse. The speaking voice in *Atmavilasam* conveys not only insights and truths arrived at but also the delight and the excitement of the experience of this arrival. Several locutions in the text have a gestural quality, which comes from an oscillation between immersion in various activities in the world and watching these from a distance as if on a screen. The image of the mirror in the passage I cited inaugurates this configuration of action and observation. One might say that this oscillation shapes the implication of the speaking voice in discourse.

It is difficult to characterize this voice as belonging to an individual subject in the usual sense. The word that refers to the first person is 'naam' which is in the plural, the equivalent of 'we,' but it can be used for referring to oneself in the singular too, as in the honorific use of plural pronouns. This usage suggests a tone of impersonality which moves away from the claim of unique interiority that first-person references invoke in modern contexts. Interestingly, the speaking voice in academic discourse, be it that of philosophy or other disciplines, also resists being understood as belonging to individual subjects. First-person singular references have a peculiar status in that, in relation to the arguments proposed, they refer not to a biographical subject but usually to an order of impersonal demonstration. Even when personal or biographical references or anecdotes from one's own life are invoked, they are often subject to ironic amelioration in that they serve as pretexts for entry into a domain of analytic or speculative thought where we leave behind the world of references to identifiable individuals in their specificity.

I wonder if some of the difficulties I had in translating texts such as *Atmavilasam* had to do with transiting between these two orders of impersonality, especially since my attempt involved embedding or incorporating the locutions of one into the other. The translations I did for citation led to arguments that framed the passage in terms of my commentary and analysis. Among other things, there was the problem of tone: while the impersonality of academic discourse presumed reasoned argumentation and reflection, the text in the vernacular appeared to work a different, more robust tenor. The prose has a gestural quality, something almost physical, and informal, while at the same time staying a little elevated from the level of the ordinary and the everyday by the sheer charge of an intensity that propels it. These features are precisely the ones that I found difficult to carry over into the English I made from the text for academic discussion.

In describing this, I am not making a case for the impossibility of translation or for the loss inherent in the passage into another language. My interest is rather in the narrower of question of the permeability and resistance of texts in the vernacular to academic contexts and reading practices. Such permeability may indeed be a feature of all texts, but my concern here is with some issues that arise when one transits between different registers of thought and expression, which cannot be fully understood through a framework of discrete language identities conceived on a model of well-policed territorial units. This is more of a division or a variation within language itself. The vernacular and the professional academic are only two instances or modes of existence of this spectrum of variation. We need to be careful not to replicate the model of territorial differentiation and see them as stable subdomains within a language. In other words, communication within a language involves translation between unstable variations of meaning and energy. These are not transactions between two independent and completed entities as much as connections established within the oscillations of a fluctuating medium, between low and high intensities or force. The distinction between object language and meta-language, which thinks in terms of vertical levels, is perhaps better seen as an effect of the translational process which tries to regulate and order variation by splitting and freezing it into planes arranged hierarchically.

I began with Sree Narayanan for other reasons as well. His compositions spanned three languages: Malayalam, Tamil, and Sanskrit. After learning Tamil in his childhood, he acquired deep proficiency in Sanskrit under the tutelage of Kummampilly Raman Pillai Asan, whose writings included not only commentaries on Sanskrit texts but also those in Tamil.[6] This trilingualism in the context of nineteenth-century Kerala, especially in Travancore where Tamil also had a specially privileged status in the royal court and in the bureaucracy in the capital, is closer to the situation of variation rather than to one of co-existence of discrete languages. This is evident in the history of literary production in Malayalam in what we refer to as the medieval period. Whether it be in the Manipravalam tradition, in which Sanskrit words share poetic space with elements from bhasha, or the pattu tradition where the presence of Tamil words and word endings predominates. It is difficult to demarcate the locus of Malayalam or what was referred to as 'bhasha' territorially. It is rather to be understood through subtractions and eliminations. *Leelatilakam*, a text on Manipravalam from the fourteenth century rediscovered in the early twentieth century, seems to have regarded the space of bhasha as what is left in Manipravalam after the subtraction of Sanskrit words.[7] However, this is also a variant, as it is characterized as the language of the three upper varna groups (*traivarnikas*) as distinct from that of people of low birth (*hinajati*). Rich Freeman pointed out that the variant associated with the *hinajati* as described in *Leelatilakam* displays features from the use of language in the east coast, thus indicating overlap between various idioms of differentiation, resulting in an intermeshing of regional self-awareness and linguistic practices anchored in cultures associated with *varna* and *jati*.[8]

This is not specific to medieval times when the linguistic identity of Malayalam was not established with clarity; its traces can be found, as I have tried to show, in Sree Narayanan's prose writings from the late nineteenth and the twentieth centuries. The spectrum of variation that gives the lie to pictures of stable language identities is visible in contemporary writing too, notably literature from speech communities that stand at a distance from what is generally regarded as the dominant standard in literary usage. Dalit writers from various parts of India have mobilized the energies of this variation powerfully. The emergence of Dalit literature as a pan-Indian category in publishing and in literary analysis, especially in English, has some relation to the circulation of English translations of these texts and to the currency acquired by this category in the media and the academy. Insofar as certain features of language use and specific strategies of writing are marked as characteristics of Dalit writing, the formation of this category in academic discourse may need to be seen as reliant upon a degree of disciplining of the energetic use of variation, which initially contributed to its significance and impact. Dalit writing is not the only site where these processes are evident. Concepts used in literary studies, whose definition is anchored in variations from the dominant standard and understood as based on the distinctiveness of language used by social groups or regions, tend to evidence intimate tensions between variation and disciplining.

In the remaining parts of this chapter, I hope to think with two questions that emerge from this: (a) how does a recognition of variation, rather than solidified linguistic identities, as our point of departure affect our conception of translation? (b) how can we describe the operations that academic criticism performs on vernacular literary production if we approach it through the dynamic of translation sketched above? In order to address these questions, a closer engagement with literary cultures and reading practices becomes necessary. I shall therefore begin with that.

In her very important essay 'Nationalism and the Imagination,' Gayatri Spivak proposed an important set of arguments about subaltern literary cultures in contemporary times. She stresses the 'oral-formulaic' as an important element of literary production among the tribal communities with whom she worked in rural West Bengal. In Spivak's use, this term refers to an iterative production of utterances that serve as the locus of inventive improvisation, thus permitting the incorporation of elements of various kinds and origins, without being constrained by the demands of epistemic coherence. "The oral-formulaic can appropriate material of all sorts into its machine, robbing the content of its epistemic charge if it does not fit the inventiveness of the occasion."[9] The rhythmic, iterative impulse that works with a principle of equivalence appears here as a mode of imaginative production that has survived over time and is perhaps on the verge of forgetting and disappearance. What were the modes of oral imaginative production at work in the compositions of a poet like Sree Narayanan worked in a milieu of linguistic variation, the amplitude of which spanned over at least three languages in the modern calculus of enumeration?

I am not suggesting that the energies of the vernacular ought to be understood in terms of the oral as opposed to the literal. The relationship between the oral and the written is often complex: Aniket Jaaware, for instance, has contested the claims made about the oral in the Brahminical Sanskrit tradition by arguing that the oral which is aimed at invariant repetition ought to be seen as a form of indelible inscription:

After mastering the text in a variety of combinations of letters, forward, backward, skipping, or exchanging every second or third letter, and so on, the text is as stable in memory as any text written down and preserved in that material form; it is as good as a written text, and the distinction and supposed difference between the written and the oral collapses. ... In fact, it is further possible to argue that the material on which the text is preserved in writing is more capable of corruption than this solemn, sacred, and dutiful memory – it is more written than texts written on material surfaces.[10]

The work of invention that we found in the oral-formulaic is absent here; it is even forbidden and guarded against. Interestingly, the distinction between these two modes also seems to possess a gender dimension. Jaaware associated the Brahmanical oral transmission of an identical text with "the principle of inheritance, which can, as with property, so with memory, easily be equated to that of male lineage." In the subaltern tribal context, Spivak linked the oral-formulaic with Sabar women while men "inhabit an enforced illiteracy rather than an orality at home with itself and with the great genealogical memories."[11]

I invoked these two nuanced accounts to foreground contrasting pictures of what is usually described as oral. They might serve as important background for considering the interplay of the textual and the oral in a figure like Sree Narayanan. It is said that many of Sree Narayanan's verse compositions initially existed orally and only later were set in writing. Some others were composed without the aid of writing and then dictated orally to disciples for transcription. These practices were quite common in Kerala, and elsewhere in India too, especially at that time; even now, they may not have disappeared altogether. One might say that these poems of Sree Narayanan were initially composed in his mind, but we must distinguish this idea from the modern conception of the mind as the locus of the poet's individual interiority, as a sort of otherness that can be contrasted with bodily and public existence. Furthermore, the space of composition here is not anterior to its emergence in sound. Metrical regularity, rhythm, and the sound structure of verses take shape in a mental space that is indistinguishable from the public domain of the voice. One has to move beyond any direct opposition between the oral and the written to grasp the dynamic of their interrelationship in such instances.

In the spectrum that extends from the reproduction of the identical in the Brahmanical tradition invoked by Aniket to the inventive deployment of equivalence in the subaltern, tribal tradition in Spivak's account, orality had a range of relations with textuality and remembrance. Sree Narayanan's mastery over the Sanskrit and Tamil textual traditions was marked by the audacious inflection of the robust vernacular. One might say that the vernacular element in Sree Narayanan's innovative iteration came less from the tradition of Malayalam writing as from the domain of life practices including those of local and regional traditions' spiritual practice. The famous statement attributed to him when challenged about his ritual qualification for the consecration of the Aruvippuram Shiva Temple – that it was an 'Ezhava Shiva' that he installed and Brahmins need not worry – illustrates this well.[12] The statement works not through argumentation but through a gestural move towards deflation of the claim that serves as the ground of the challenge. A similar gestural quality – arguably corporeal rather than textual in its expressive orientation – is evident in anecdotal accounts of Sree Narayanan's conversations. His verse writings span a wide range, from devotional compositions of ardent passion to abstruse metaphysical propositions and arguments. And prose writings, smaller in number, evince to varying degrees a state of heightened intensity, of energetic articulation, which transgresses the formal restraints of literary prose.

His metaphysical verses such as *Swanubhavagiti* or *Arivu* show an intricate play of pronouns and numbers which make the listener or writer work with intense concentration. Simple, ubiquitously used demonstrative pronouns like 'this' (*ithu*) and 'that' (*athu*) and numerals such as 'five' (*anchu*), 'six' (*aru*), and 'eight' (*ettu*) are repeated in tightly composed verses where their referents need to be identified through a careful unravelling of the verse and parsing of its syntax. This process is not a matter of the eye; it is only by enunciating the verse, sensing the syntactic connections between words which may not always follow the sequence in which they appear in the line that the reader comes to grasp the meaning. And the pleasure of this intricate arrangement arises from a smooth and continuous re-enunciation of the verse in its entirety after figuring out these connections. Does this work belong to the order of the oral or the literal? Parsing makes it necessary for us to hold the lines in our mind, going back and forth over them, and this makes it akin to what Jaaware describes as an orality that is akin to writing. However, the pleasure of the verses comes from a sensitivity to variations and the surprises it experiences. Here repetition works not at the reproduction of the identical but drawing on the resources of equivalence that we encountered earlier while discussing the oral-formulaic. The pleasure of these surprises is similar to that of verbal puzzles. In unravelling the verse, the listener works not in an ideational but in material and corporeal engagement with the words and sounds.

These compositions presuppose a culture of reading where embodied practices of listening, retention and performative improvisation are central. In the vernacular literary culture of nineteenth-century Kerala, proficiency in verse idioms was more preponderant than in prose. Verse was not reserved for literary and devotional compositions but also for obituaries, scientific information, and even news. C. Kunjurama Menon, the editor of *Keralapatrika*, an early twentieth-century newspaper from Travancore, remembers the difficulty of finding news reporters who could send their reports in prose, as many of them preferred to file them in verse![13] The verse form with its relationship to rhythm and memory perhaps points to a set of more proximate relations between bodily existence and the literary. The gestural quality of the prose of *Atmavilasam* which we discussed at the beginning of this chapter is a sign of this relationship.

The problem with which I began was that of translation – what is it to translate instances of literary production from a culture of reading and writing to another? In this question, as I pointed out earlier, two distinct problems overlap. Firstly, there is the question of languages, Malayalam and English. Secondly, there is the problem of variation, between the vernacular and the academic registers. I was translating in order to cite and analyze. One could say that the translated text was meant for purposes that were totally different from those of the original. More importantly, the practices that the reader/listener engages in these two cases are substantially different. In discussing *Atmavilasam* my aim was to understand this text within a history of idioms of writing about the self in modern Malayalam. Although I began my project as an exploration of the emergence and evolution of the genre of autobiographical writing in Malayalam, I quickly realized that autobiography may not be the only or even the most important place to look for the key moments of such a history. Idioms of self-articulation emerge not only in forms that are explicitly identified as self-narratives; they are forged with resources from a variety of forms of writing in nineteenth-century Kerala, which do not often tally with the distinct literary genres with which academic literary studies work now. *Atmavilasam* is an example of this. It is difficult to determine if it is prose or poetry, mystical or metaphysical writing.

This difficulty is not merely one of analytical and interpretative protocols appropriate for the text. It is also about the practices within which the text circulates and lives its lives. What are these practices? Are they those of a literary reading leading to an aesthetic effect, which may in turn be excavated through an academic investigation that seeks to lay bare the textual mechanisms and strategies behind it? Are they practices that seek to realize a 'spiritual' experience of dissolution of the self? If this is so, are we to see textual mechanisms as leading to this experience in the same way as in literary reading? I am not concerned so much about the distinction between what I have called 'spiritual' and 'literary' experiences as with the differences between the practices involved. Texts such as *Atmavilasam* appear to presuppose a certain disposition that is, strictly speaking, not that of erudition, although the text might be informed by a deep knowledge of Advaita thought. The address of the text to its reader or listener is belied by a sense of the absence of an addressee for the statements that appear within the text. The latter seem to be in the nature of documentation, or a narration addressed to none other than oneself, although the scope of the idea of oneself remains unspecified and potentially expansive. The reader/listener, uninvited to this internal world, partakes of it by attending to it and thus learning from an experience of witnessing. A practice of spiritual pedagogy which does not involve direct address from the Guru to the Shishya seems to be at work here. This pedagogy teaches neither doctrine nor skills or techniques, but a non-reciprocal receptivity or permeability which may open the way to a peculiar emulation of the Guru. Peculiar because of the impossibility on which it is predicated: the Guru appears at an unreachable height and remains intimate in his indifference and non-reciprocity.

We may perhaps be able to understand the problem of genres better if we take it away from the specific literary context in which it is usually considered in academic literary studies and consider them in terms of the practices in which they are embedded.[14] The specific force of the vernacular, in the sense in which I described it earlier, may be more clearly sensed if we see it as working the relationship of address, witnessing, and pedagogy we encountered above. Rather than engaging in an analytical deciphering of sentences in the text and their interpretative appropriation, the addressee assumes a posture of absorbed witnessing. The vernacular, gestural quality of the prose, confers on this relationship a dimension of energy and intimacy. These tonal or textural attributes are not external or supplementary to the content; they are at the core of the work that the text performs and the practice in which it is embedded.

Translation of texts like this for citation and analysis in academic discourse thus conceals a second order of translation, from the practice-embedded, non-interpretative protocols of a vernacular text to the analytical unpacking of textual machinery. It is important not to see these as two self-enclosed domains, and translation as a bridge of traffic effected between them. Rather these two modes of textual existence ought to be seen as instances in a field of variations, and the possibility of transit between one and the other is at the heart of our life in language. The vernacular and the academic are thus unstable economies, open to one another.

This enables us to understand better one of the challenges that English literary studies in India is faced with today, how an awareness of modalities of textual existence and reading cultures can be incorporated into its core conception. This problem came to the foreground with special force in the 1990s when literary texts from Indian languages were introduced into English literature syllabi in many universities in India and became objects of doctoral research in some universities abroad. The frequent acknowledgement of the limits and difficulties involved in this has usually focused on the differences between Indian languages and English. One insufficiently examined consequence of this approach is the stability it confers on both these languages and the reduction of the transactions between them into the plane of textual and narrative structures. This often has the effect of reproducing a nationalist idea of language leading to a negotiation of the terms of exchange between languages on the basis of this model. This pushes us to a strange paradox; the decolonizing and post-colonial thrust in English studies resulting in a nationalist consolidation of modern Indian literature. Arguments for pluralizing this model by the inclusion of diverse identities and communities and traditions do not perhaps go far enough, as they do not necessarily challenge the model of language identity and literary textuality that frames the institutional space.

I have tried to argue against this approach. The discussion above points to the centrality of variation and to the suggestion that translation is intrinsic to linguistic practices. The challenge posed by the Indian language literary text in the English classroom may then be seen as one of recognizing the dependence of literary studies on translation, not only in the sense of an inter-linguistic transaction but also between variations between practices within what is identified as one language. The challenge faced by English in its encounter with these texts is mirrored to an extent by modern academic criticism within Indian languages. This can be addressed only by attending to the diverse nature of literary cultures and to the practices from which texts emerge and in which they stay embedded. Questions that emerge from this turn are fundamental: what do we mean by the word 'literature' in the Indian literary studies classroom? What modes of translational activity is this usage dependent upon? Which histories have determined its regulation and the emergence of the discourse of academic literary studies? Finally, this move may enable a re-estimation of the value and power of 'criticism' by affecting a shift in priorities away from unveiling the hidden, through the interpretation of textual strategies to attending to the practices in which texts serve as props – objects that are indispensable to the performance of acts but that do not hold the key to secret meanings.

Notes

1 Narayana Guru, "Atmavilasam", *Sreenarayanaguruvinte Sampurna Kritikal* (T. Bhaskaran Ed., *Complete Works of Sree Narayana Guru*), Mathrubhumi, Calicut, 1995, p. 630. English translation is from Udaya Kumar, *Writing the First Person: Literature, History and Autobiography in Modern Kerala*, Permanent Black, Ranikhet, 2016, p. 64.
2 Naoki Sakai, *Translation and Subjectivity: On Japan and Cultural Nationalism*, University of Minnesota Press, Minneapolis, 1997, p. 2.
3 The idea of variation used in this chapter draws on the discussion of language in Gilles Deleuze and Felix Guattari, *A Thousand Plateaus: Capitalism and Schizophrenia* (trans. Brian Massumi), Athlone, London, 1987, especially Chapter 4, pp. 75–110.
4 Partha Chatterjee, "Introduction: History in the Vernacular", in Raziuddin Aquil and Partha Chatterjee (Eds.), *History in the Vernacular* Permanent Black, Ranikhet, 2008, pp. 1–24.
5 These points were made by Chatterjee in his presentation at a panel discussion on "The Possibility of a Contemporary History: Disciplinary Formations and

the Social Sciences in post-1947 India", at the Institute of Economic Growth, Delhi, on 29 February 2008. For a brief discussion of this panel, see Prathama Banerjee, "The Social Sciences in Post-1947 India", *Economic and Political Weekly*, 43 (16), 2008, pp. 22–25.

6 For a discussion of Sree Narayana Guru's education, see M. K. Sanu, *Narayanaguruswamy*, Sahitya Pravarthaka Co-operative Society, Kottayam, 1987, pp. 43–68.

7 See Rich Freeman, "Rubies and Coral: The Lapidary Crafting of Language in Kerala", *Journal of Asian Studies*, 57, 1998, pp. 38–65, and M. R. Raghava Variar, *Madhyakala Keralam: Sampattu, Samuham, Samskaram [Medieval Kerala: Resources, Society and Culture]*, Cinta Publishers, Trivandrum, 1997. For an edition of *Lilatilakam*, see Ilamkulam Kunjan Pillai, *Lilatilakam: Manipravalalakshanam*, Sahitya Pravarthaka Co-operative Society, Kottayam, 1955, Reprint 1985.

8 Rich Freeman, Ibid., p. 55.

9 Gayatri Chakravorty Spivak, "Nationalism and the Imagination", *Lectora*, 15, 2009, p. 83.

10 Aniket Jaaware, *Practicing Caste: On Touching and Not Touching*, Fordham University Press, New York, 2018, pp. 119–120.

11 Gayatri Chakravorty Spivak, no. 9, p. 81.

12 For a reading of the consecration of a Shiva temple by Sree Narayana Guru, see Roby Rajan and J. Reghu, "Backwater Universalism: An Intercommunal Tale of Being and Becoming", in Vinay Lal (Ed.), *Political Hinduism: The Religious Imagination in Public Spheres,* Oxford University Press, New Delhi, 2009, pp. 66–67. See also Udaya Kumar, no. 1, pp. 61–63.

13 Ashokan Nambiar, "Print, Communities and the Novel in Nineteenth-Century Kerala", Unpublished Doctoral Dissertation, University of Delhi, 2015, p. 71.

14 Michael Warner's discussion of the relations between reading practices and disciplines of subjectivity has suggestive observations that point in this direction. See "Uncritical Reading", in Jane Gallop (Ed.), *Polemic: Critical or Uncritical*, Routledge, New York, 2004, pp. 13–38.

10

OF DREAMTIME AND DREAM-TRACKS

Revisiting Australian Indigenous Identity Construction with Reference to Select Poems by Oodgeroo Noonuccal and Kevin Gilbert

Santosh K. Sareen

Which identity or plural does Australian Indigenous poetry of the twentieth century quest for and design, how does it curve an autonomous space of representation? The question mark initiates a challenge to the pre-dominant 'White' image of Australia, positing that the hegemonic culture that identifies itself – in the sense of the modern 'nation-state' – with the landscape and has thereby come to constitute 'quintessential Australianness', could also be mirror-imaged as an 'alien' to the soil, its history having been defined since the late eighteenth century by the invasion of the land and its Indigenous people by the British. Over two centuries of colonization, effectively led the other'ed, invisibilized, dispossessed, brutalized, assimilated/acculturated and appropriated Indigenous people to gather and re-assert their Indigenous identity. This involves reclaiming the land and its tracks as the original inhabitants' memorialization of an alternative, yet more authentic Australianness, shaped almost in inverseness to the hegemonic 'White' Australia.

Since time immemorial Indigenous people had lived on the island continent of Australia, the land roots/routes their notions of identity and belonging (Sareen 62–74). It defines for them a geosophy, the concept used by Max Charlesworth in his 1998 volume *Religious Business: Essays on Australian Indigenous Spirituality* as a portmanteau of geography and philosophy. Much like the subcontinental sacred geography or spiritual topography, "geosophy" implies a perspective on the land that exceeds chartered cartography and attaches to it an epistemic, mnemonic-intense valency (Charlesworth xix–xx). As in case of nature worshippers, the landscape represented for Indigenous Australians the sacred and inspiring, in a departure from what Bill Ashcroft terms the "terrifying sublime" of untamed space for early white Australian settlers (Ashcroft 22). They belonged to the land and

DOI: 10.4324/9781003399926-14

did not seek to abuse but rather to live in and on it and revere it as the sacred source. It is for this reason that the land and its spiritual connotations resonate in every nuance of Indigenous life. Another important aspect of their identity is the sense of being part and trans-tense continuation of an ancestral matrix, akin to the Hindu way of thought in which a certain part of the year, almost a whole month, is earmarked for remembering and paying obeisance to the ancestors. In the case of Indigenous people this has been expressed and understood by the West through the notion of "Dreaming". While it "refers to a complex of aspects of traditional Indigenous belief, including mythology, law and history" (Hodge and Mishra 27), it remains outside the historicist comprehension of the modern European mode of thought. The latter mode denies alternative ways of exploring life and its meanings and reduces the possibility of such Indigenous alterities to what was labelled by Hegel as the "fantastic symbolism" of Hindu thought (Hegel 47–65).

What has been termed as the Aborigine notion of "Dreaming", together with its weave of myths and legends provides texture to the identity of the Indigenous people since it relates to their sense of continuum with land and ancestors, entwined. As Anita Heiss puts it in *Token Koori*, "my genealogy, bloodlines and heritage are part of the history of this land since time began" (Heiss 6). Creation and Dreamtime ancestors are symbolized by the motherland, inalienable features of Dreaming being sanctification and personification of the land, identification of self with land and the land with forefathers. George Tinamin, for instance, expresses it thus, "Ngangatja apu wiya, ngayuku tjamu", indicating that "This is not a rock, it is my grandfather", a spring-spout for dreaming "right up from inside the ground" (*Spirit Song* 4). The issue of identity, when situated in a network of continuities, seems less fraught. Given this ecology, receptive to the land and intimate ur-voices from other tenses, contradictions could converse and converge in creating Indigenous identity as a fecund node, in excess of the tyranny of antipodean whiteness and its erasure-oriented Science-sanitized rationalism.

In case of Indigenous Australians, the issue thus pertains as much to the loss of identity as to assertion of identity. In Kim Scott's *Benang* (1999), the genetic absorption of the Indigenous people by the settlers is compared to the ingress of a small stream of dirty water into a large clear stream – a popular image from the 1930s. Re-definition in a grid of whiteness was obviously being attempted but that could not erase previous definitions. For instance, land was not seen in terms of ownership by the Indigenous people till the point they were dispossessed. Land was "mother" to them, akin to the concept of 'matrbhumi' in Indian thought. Eva Johnson implores the land-mother for the return of "our people / Their spirits", "our culture" in a poem titled *Land Our Mother*. For the "world of wonder and beauty" seems to have been exiled post the "rape of this our land", and Indigenous people, "the children of the earth", dispossessed from their rituals, language and place of birth – "our language, our dreaming, / our lore" – all effects of what she ironically codes as "civilized passing" across Australia (*Spirit Song* 43).

What mattered was emotional ties, a sense of togetherness, of extended family. "Dreamtime" represents generations of interaction with the land that had birthed plural Indigenous cultures with distinctive traditions of myths, rituals, song and dance, distinctive ways of life and religious beliefs handed down through generations via the oral medium, and yet symptomatic of a collective non-exclusive nation-wide Dreamtime Indigenous identity that binds and gathers together the many tribes, constellated under the demonym 'Koorie', from regions as varied as New South Wales and Victoria.

"Dreamtime" in fact posits a continuity between the different tribes, for even if traditions and cultural formations may vary across tribes, the essence of its creation converges in the interaction with an alive landscape. If Indigenous languages have been lost and along with them the distinctive Indigenous cultures, Indigenous poets give expression to Aboriginal identity that refuses to get erased and resurrect alternative possibilities of Australianness, residual and emergent, through their dream of 'Dreamtime' and the recounting of oral traditions, opening doors to myriad shades of memory, loss, politics, economics and history. Through the language of power, i.e. English, they dig into the residue that trickled down despite systematic 'White' acculturation of more than two centuries, hoping to trace continuities that may recover the susurrus, even some of the essence of their cultures, lost.

We attempt to illustrate this through the poetry of Oodgeroo Noonuccal (1920–1993), earlier known as Kath Walker, and Kevin Gilbert (1933–1993). Both as activist and in her work as a poet, Oodgeroo pioneers the representation of Indigenous voices, their identity, cultures, rights and grievances. Gilbert spent 14 of the best years of his life in jail for the crime of allegedly killing his white wife. During the prison term, he educated himself and upon release turned out to be one of the most prolific writers and activists of Indigenous Australia.

Oodgeroo, known as Kath Walker after her marriage, adopted a tribal name in 1988, followed by the name of the tribe she descended from, Noonuccal. In 1970, she was awarded MBE (Member of the Order of the British Empire) but returned it at the time of protest against the bicentennial celebrations of the first European landing and settlement around 1988. Her personal experiences, convictions and actions as a champion of Indigenous rights get reflected in her poems. Her poem *Colour Bar* represents the anguish and anger of the Indigenous people faced with discrimination right from the tender season of childhood, as the absurd derision of the 'White' man's racism on the basis of skin colour bewilders the uncomprehending mind of the child, naked before the infinite injustice of an adult world. The poem invokes the invasion by the colonizing British people which led to a loss of innocence for the Indigenous people. Their traditional world had been built on comparatively more intricate ties with the land than that of the virulent technologies of violence. So Oodgeroo faced with monumental injustice writes how "fierce anger sears" when a taunted child comes home humiliated, all teared up by "The colour bar!" as perpetuated by "the meaner mind / Of moron kind" (Cochrane 46).

Perhaps she suggests that centuries of racist degradation, she hoped, would have toughened the Indigenous people and they would at last have learnt to bear its sting and remain unaffected, having re-asserted their independent identity and reclaimed the value of their culture to the point that the venom of white 'superiority' could no longer poison the world of a child or that of the vulnerable. Her free expression of anger in this poem aims to possibly rally her Indigenous compatriots in a solidarist realization of the injustice of 'White' racism and unite them against 'White' supremacism and further "loss of innocence". Poetry here morphs into a political gesture, giving it the role of activism while channelling emotional release along with a salve for bitter experiences. She ends the poem with an exposure of the violent exclusionary foundations of the illusion of 'White' civilization, their rationality, their religion, all built on "brothers banned from brotherhood". The white Australian's professed Christianity then turns into a lie and pride in justice to "a cant of hypocrites, content / With precedent". The fact that the 'White' population dominated Australia for well over two centuries on the premise of self-proclaimed superiority will no longer suffice as justification for their continuing Aborigine-humiliating hegemony.

Oodgeroo's poems are haunted by a powerful sense of sorrow, the melancholy that besets the Indigenous mind when it reviews the dark history of exploitation, brutality, cultural strangulation, the monumental betrayal of humanity involved in the destruction of their world. Such an originary destruction preluded the setting up of another 'White' world in its own image by the colonial power of Britain which till today pervasively imprints Australia, despite the occasional apologies and reluctant dole of equality, and continues the process of acculturation in an attempt to mould the entire nation after its hegemonic identity. So effective has been the thrust of colonization through systematic eradication, followed by government-sanctioned assimilation and acculturation of the children of lost, i.e. annihilated, incarcerated, dispossessed generations, that the Indigenous people have been reduced to a wither of their former selves. They or rather their shadows still grope with traditional ways to find that that world is gone and the landscape appropriated into 'White' man's Australia, so much so that "We are as strangers here now, but the white tribe are the strangers" (Cochrane 132).

Oodgeroo reveals the true identity of the Indigenous through the intrinsic relationship with the land. In her poems, the Indigenous individual becomes one with it through 'Dreamtime' – "We are the wonder tales of 'Dream

Time'" (132) – his identity segues into the land, a homecoming renewed and remembered through the 'sacred ceremonies, 'laws of the elders', tribal legends', 'the hunts and the laughing games', etc. that inextricably link him to his native environment, the source spring of this culture. In *Bwalla the Hunter* Oodgeroo Noonucal demonstrates through diction and imagery the use of the traditional oral practice, the rhyme and rhythm made simple and easy to remember and passed down through tribal generations, though presented here in translation. During the hard times of drought and famine, Bwalla the hunter followed by his wife and children are all on walkabout driven by hunger, and they find no kangaroo, emu or seed, though "the children all time cry for feed" (*Kath Walker Collection* 30).

And yet, in her well-known poem *We Are Going* written to commemorate the eight-kilometre march for Indigenous rights organized in Sydney in order to demonstrate against the official bicentennial celebrations scheduled on 26 January 1988, Oodgeroo sounds a warning that in 'White' Australia's continual process of acculturation and assimilation/appropriation, this world, this relationship is dissolving, disappearing forever, and with that terminus the last vestige of an independent Indigenous identity will dissolve into its end. All are gone and ghosted, almost – the scrubs, hunting and laughter, the eagle, emu and kangaroo, the bora ring and corroborree – and with "all the old ways / Gone now scattered", even the "nature and the past", the poet ominously concludes, "And we are going".

However, in *Son of Mine* written for her elder son Dennis, who, perplexed by the normalized discrimination and repression he faced in white settler Australia, found expression for his angst through violent means, Oodgeroo expresses the belief that beyond the point of sorrow and anger at the traumatic past of colonial atrocities, there is need for reconciliation in the present, for passage towards a harmonious future. As a measure of hope and healing, she is keen to touch some core of human understanding, of compassion and coexistence. Perhaps in her son's dilemma, she realizes that instead of looking back at the dark Indigenous history of colonial devastation, comprising "crimes that shame mankind", heartbreak, hatred, "brutal wrong and deeds malign" (Cpchrane 57) – that can only arouse uncontrollable passions not only of sorrow but also anger at the historical injustice of these crimes against humanity, that callously destroyed one world to create another, based on assumed grounds of civilizational superiority and hypocritical postures of morality and religiosity, hurtling the Indigenous down the abyss of reactionary, retaliatory hatred and violence, it is perhaps richer to look ahead at possibilities for a more harmonious future, where an attempt could be made to change racial prejudice with the hope of touching the human chord of fraternity across shadowlines, the hope of mutual understanding and imagination that might reconcile the Indigenous to the sufferings of their past. This future Australia, home to alternative possibilities "brave and fine", could possibly house "lives of black and white entwine[d]" and combine men in brotherhood, as limned in the last lines of the poem *Harbour Another World*.

Kevin Gilbert, 13 years younger to Oodgeroo, again gives vent to anger, angst and sorrow, characteristic of Indigenous verse in his poems. In *Memorials* he reads, Indigenous skulls "weighed heavy with bullets" or in case of children, "crushed and caved in" and can hear the white man's cry: "Slaughter the breeders / wipe out the babies and wipe out the gins" (12). In the first part of the poem, *The New True Anthem*, he unequivocally condemns the 'White' settlers rationalizing that they corrupted the land accidentally, as innocent 'aliens' set to adopting a fresh continent. They had polluted the rivers, littered every road, scarred former treescapes with "barbaric graffiti" and the beaches, mountains "are covered with your shame", as the poet reminds the civilizers and as the country bears testimony (Gilbert 36).

Gilbert thus critiques the entire process of colonization, appropriation of the land and its white settler acculturation for creation of a national identity, which to an extent or even completely wiped out their former/ originary culture and made of them "bicultural Blackfellas", stripped of cultural heritage, pride and self-identity and removed from their land, to be abandoned to the charity of 'Missions'. The white settlers transformed the landscape and tried to eradicate or acculturate the Indigenous people they had dispossessed. In the second part of the poem Gilbert expresses sorrow at the degeneration of the ideal of Australia as a 'nation', which could perhaps be read as an appeal to create a non-racist plural 'Australia' where Indigenous people would no longer be racially persecuted. This would be a rainbow Australia without a dominant 'White' image where there would be no hate, no tyranny, no land theft and racial murder, and "black bodies writhing/humanity locked in chains" would be restored to their sanctity (Gilbert 36). He thus condemns the colonial atrocities for the wounds that fester within the nation and stand in the way of the possibility of a glorious Australia idealized in the concluding lines of the poem, an Australia that could finally "stand tall and free" without being fuelled by "bitter anguish" (Gilbert 36). It is possible that in the use of the term 'free', Gilbert, as a staunch Indigenous activist, demands full Indigenous rights which include the claim to ownership of the land and posits the notion of a postcolonial Australia emancipated of colonial rule, implying freedom from the 'White' settlers and a nation of Indigenous peoples with the stain of colonization wiped. It could also, on the other hand, create the hope for a nation free of racist prejudices of colonization, where 'White' Australia would emancipate itself from the illusion of superiority and treat Indigenous counterparts with respect, fraternity and understanding, making Australia in truth an egalitarian nation.

In *Shades of Grey*, Gilbert seems to propose a reconciliation, but of a markedly different kind. He proposes self-reconciliation, where the Indigenous has to engage with the dichotomy within the 'self', created by two centuries of 'White' acculturation splitting him along the colour line. In this short poem, he addresses a monumental issue. As a consequence of the annihilation, systematic eradication of the direct representatives of the Indigenous in Australia during the early stages of the colonial process – through policies of segregation, the stolen generation, practice of separating children from their families, discrimination on the basis of colour, a 'caste' politics as Ruby Langford puts it – those remaining belong to mixed parentage, or lead a traumatized hybrid existence at the abject margins of society, having been forcefully acculturated for years, and dislocated and distanced from their traditional lands, way of life, customs, culture and traditions. This hybridity, often only the compelled capital for mere survival in a changed world, is easily appropriated as fief of a 'White' identity. This remains quite apparent in the politics of representation of protest in Australian Indigenous poetry, the protest has to be performed in the language of power, i.e. English.

It is only in recent decades that Indigenous people have begun to acknowledge the Aboriginal dimension of their heritage and celebrate their proud descent from the traditional tribes, against those who found it simpler to assimilate within the dominant identity of 'White' Australia, despite never having been fully accepted and partitioned by skin colour, *The Chant of Jimmie Blacksmith* being a classic example of such failure. Even for those who acknowledged themselves to be Indigenous and stood up for their rights and voices to be heard, the fact remains that like Kevin Gilbert they had to translate themselves into English to visibilize themselves within the Australian literary circle and abroad as Indigenous writers and activists. Their names in translation, e.g. that of Gilbert, are not even remotely Indigenous. The politics of representation thus grows increasingly complex. Gilbert dares an Indigenous boy to "look under / your own black skin one day" and recognize the "white men lurking" beneath as the intimate enemy to be traced, known and defeated (Gilbert 30). He seems to suggest here a confrontation of this 'whitization' of the Indigenous 'self' and reconciliation to the Indigenous independent identity by defeating, erasing two centuries of acculturation. This is perhaps in keeping with his possible suggestion in the previous poem of an independent Indigenous nation or "nation within a nation" finally exorcized of an exclusive, supremacist 'White' identity. He thus seeds in his poems the emancipation of the Indigenous mind, through de-colonization and a possible return to the rhythm of a traditional life or re-assertion of an autonomous Indigenous identity in case of coexistence. After all, as Oodgeroo put it in her poem *The Past*, "Let no one say the past is dead, / The past is all about us and within" (*My People* 93).

Finally, in his poem *Last Word* Gilbert, like Oodgeroo, Gilbert seems to suggest that anger per se can accomplish nothing but destruction

caught in the web of
Nothingness you wrought

(Gilbert 56)

The anger may be justifiable, but Gilbert seems to suggest that in retrospect, the emotion albeit attractive as a passion seems futile, a "sad estate" cold and grey, razed to deserts "where once bloomed / such lovely flower" (Gilbert 56). We find here a more reflective poet, suggesting like Oodgeroo, that anger, as the Indigenous people look backwards on an unjust past of inhuman persecution, may only consume the person and not result in anything fecund or fruitful. Identity construction must then undergo change and healing, not through mere reconciliation but rather on terms that guarantee the craft of the making of a distinctive Indigenous identity, a coexistence and epistemic acceptance of Dreamtime and Dream-tracks in excess of the kitsch of an absurdly asymmetric equality.

References

Ashcroft, Bill, "The Sacred in Australian Culture," in Makarand R. Paranjape (Ed.), *Sacred Australia: Post-Secular Considerations*, Clouds of Magellan, Melbourne, 2009, pp. 21–43 (Print).

Charlesworth, Max (Ed.), *Religious Business: Essays on Australian Indigenous Spirituality*, Cambridge University Press, Cambridge, 1998 (Print).

Cochrane, Kathie, *Oodgeroo*, University of Queensland Press, Queensland, 1994 (Print).

Gilbert, Kevin, *The Blackside: People are Legends and Other Poems*, South Yarra, Hyland House, Victoria, 1990 (Print).

Hegel, G. W. F., *The Philosophy of Fine Art 1835–38* (Trans. F. P. B. Osmaston), G. Bell and Sons, London, 1920 (Print).

Heimann, Betty, *Indian and Western Philosophy: A Study in Contrasts*, George Allen & Unwin Ltd., London, 1937 (Print).

Heiss, Anita, "Identity," in *Token Koori*, Curringa Communications, Sydney, 1998 (Print).

Hodge, Bob and Vijay Mishra, *Dark Side of the Dream: Australian Literature and the Postcolonial Mind*, George Allen & Unwin Ltd., Sydney, 1991 (Print).

Mafi-Williams, Lorraine (Ed.), *Spirit Song: A Collection of Aboriginal Poetry*, Omnibus Books, Norwood, South Australia, 1993 (Print).

Noonuccal, Oodgeroo, "Oodgeroo Noonuccal, 1920–1993: The Legacy of a True National Treasure of Australia," Interview by Bruce Dickson, May 1981, at <http://www.dropbearito.com>, 22nd June, 2020.

———, *My People: A Kath Walker Collection*, The Jacaranda Press, Brisbane, 1970 (Print).

————, *The Dawn Is at Hand*, Jacaranda Press, Brisbane, 1966 (Print).

————, *We Are Going*, Jacaranda Press, Brisbane, 1964 (Print).

Sareen, S. K., "Self, Identity and Belonging: The Aboriginal Case," in *Australia and India Interconnections: Identity, Representation, Belonging*, Mantra, New Delhi, 2006, pp. 62–74 (Print).

Scott, Kim, *Benang: From the Heart*, Fremantle Press, Fremantle Western Australia, 1999.

Shoemaker, Adam (Ed.), "Oodgeroo: A Tribute," *Australian Literary Studies*, 16 (4), University of Queensland Press, 1994 (Print).

Translation and Transcreation

11

AN EQUAL MUSIC

C.S. Lakshmi

I met G.J.V. Prasad in the early 1990s in a conference organised by Katha, to discuss translation and related matters. I was a bit surprised when he said in the conference that he could help translate from Tamil to English. At that time, I did not think highly of Delhiwalas who were Tamilians, for I had met some who were Tamilians settled in Delhi but not familiar with Tamil literature or with contemporary fiction in Tamil. Apart from the well-known writer and critic Ka.Na.Su (K.N. Subramaniam) and the critic Venkat Swaminathan, there were not many translators from Tamil to English. The first collection of my translated stories (*A Purple Sea*) translated by Lakshmi Holmstrom had just been published. Professor K.R. Indra from Chennai was also doing translations from Tamil to English. So I did not take Prasad's claim that he could translate from Tamil to English, seriously. But we became friends as writers. His novel *A Clean Breast* had been published, and I enjoyed reading it, and when I visited Delhi, I often went to his place and had long chats with him and Kamala on many things including modern Tamil fiction and became aware that he did keep in touch with Tamil literary magazines. I also liked his non-aggressive ways of asserting his views. I am not sure but I may have been the first Tamil writer that he had invited as a scholar-in-residence at JNU despite my telling him that I did not know much about English literature. He said he was inviting me as a Tamil writer. Staying at the campus brought us closer, and when my latest collection of stories came out in 2018, I asked him with great hesitation if he would like to translate it. I had enjoyed working with my earlier translators (Lakshmi Holmstrom who is no more and Anirudhdhan Vasudevan and Gita Subramaniam with whom I still work), going through several drafts of

DOI: 10.4324/9781003399926-16

translation in the process and with a lot of discussion and some fights too! I wondered if a professor of English would be so open to discussions and arguments.

To say that I hold some definite views on translation will be an understatement. I hold extremely strong views on translation from Indian languages, especially Tamil, since that is the language I write in, into English and have fought constantly for the author to be in an equal relationship with the translator and not to be placed in a hierarchical relationship with the translator calling the shots. I had said in one of my articles on translation:

> The translator who translates into English an Indian language always feels that it is an act of favour where the Indian language writer is being raised to a different level. The Indian language writer also feels this act of translation to be some kind of a 'promotion'. It is almost like a magical transformation where an ugly frog becomes a handsome prince or a divine blessing where a cursed stone turns into a woman when a divine man steps on it. In the process of this transformation the writing is turned into a consumable product that can be easily consumed by a market of different kind of readership. Many things are involved in creating this product to be consumed by a choosy readership. In the first place the product has to be turned exotic and ethnic, an exhibition piece that can please a certain readership. Hence stories that 'belong to the soil', stories of 'protest', 'suffering' and stories that have explicit cultural elements like arranged marriages, dowry deaths, witch-hunting and poverty become more saleable than other kind of stories. Some other elements are also seen as part of our culture. These have to do with India being a land of desires, of sensuous women, the land of Kama Sutra. The second method of turning the writing into a market-friendly product is to give as many footnotes as possible. The writing must be made as transparent as possible. No space must be left for opacity. So idli will become steamed rice cake, and dosa, a salty pancake and murukku, rice dough twisted into round shapes to make a design and deep fried in oil. Jilebis and other food items will similarly be explained as if the writer were serving a menu instead of a story. Clothes are also given such elaborate footnotes. I remember reading once a footnote for dhoti: it said it is something similar to a sarong. Will the sarong be further footnoted, I wondered, or was it an image accepted by this market as an exoticism understood? Turning a culture into footnotes is a power politics a writer has to constantly resist. When we were young and read French and Russian novels, even American ones at times, I don't think footnotes were provided. One did not understand certain references to Greek and other mythologies nor some references to certain kinds of food. One did not quite know how

champagne tasted and for a long time pronounced it as champ-page-ne. But it did not in anyway take away what the book contained. Literature of that category when it came to us was seen as something that was flowing down to us. We had to receive it the way it came and raise ourselves to its level. But our literature is seen as something that is flowing upward and something that takes that kind of a direction has to suit itself to the needs of that upward path.

It is not that in translations from one Indian language to another, such questions do not become crucial. Once a Telugu translator who was translating one of my stories changed a word I had written: She felt a caterpillar squirming in her mind. The Telugu translator wrote: A snake was squirming in her mind. I asked her why she had done that. She told me that the Telugu reader will relate to snake better. 'Why, aren't there caterpillars in Andhra?' I asked her. Another Telugu translator changed the name of the main character in my story who was a woman because she thought the Telugu readers will not relate to that particular Tamil name. Also, some Indian language writers are not particularly interested in being translated into another Indian language; they would rather reach the world through English and other European languages. There is no other way one can get the Nobel Prize. Whether it is an effort to reach another language culture within India or another language culture in the world, what is translated and how it gets translated gets decided by the translator, and the author is expected to acquiesce without any resistance; and mostly that has been the politics of translation.

Every time one works with a translator, all these questions come up. However, the discussions about how to take a story from one culture to another without it getting mauled and distorted or beautified and enhanced in unrecognisable ways or growing fangs it never had to begin with are endless and very much a part of the process of translation when it comes to translation into English. The English translator is in the role of a benefactor, and the author who resists and struggles to hold on to whatever is in the original is seen as someone who is biting the hand that feeds. I have been lucky that my battles with my translators have been fierce but also interesting and, despite arguments, always done with good humour and laughter. G.J.V. Prasad was someone who I had not worked with before. Prasad readily agreed although it took time for him to start the work because of his busy schedule.

After he began to read the stories, our conversations slowly started. Being a writer and a poet himself, he understood the needs of a writer from another language to hold on to her metaphors and language nuances. Initially our conversations went somewhat like this:

August 13, 2019
C.S.L.: When do you think you can start translating?
G.J.V.: I have to let them sink in. This is going to be fun! For me!

August 30, 2019
C.S.L.: I am sure with a few fights thrown in!
G.J.V.: Absolutely
C.S.L.: How can we be friends without fighting?!
G.J.V.: That is the proof

By May 2020 we began to talk about specific colours and some other language words I had used in the stories.

May 10, 2020
G.J.V.: What is தளிர் பச்சை in English?
C.S.L.: Tender sprout green, tender leaf green
G.J.V.: I thought sprout green but doesn't come up in English. Will use it anyway.
C.S.L.: We can create the colour that does not exist in English!
G.J.V.: Of course.

May 27, 2020
G.J.V.: In which language does moongi mean dumb? In Hindi, we would say goonga or goonge baba
C.S.L.: Yes, good question. I think I went by the reference in Gujarati where Mungi means dumb. There is a Mungi mata (Dumb Mother) and also Parsis make a Vegetable Kichri which is rare for they always eat meat so they call it Mungi Khichri (Dumb Khichri)!
G.J.V.: Would that work in the hills? Should I check?
C.S.L.: Why don't you check? Otherwise we can change it to Goonge Baba and I can change it in the Tamil second edition....
Gunga is the Hindi word. Gungi will be a woman who is dumb. Maybe you should write Gunga and I can change it in the second Tamil edition. However I am also checking for usage in the Hillls....
In Uttarakhand the word for dumb is LaTo. So it won't work. I think we should keep it as Gunga. But you also check....
I don't know how I made that mistake! I am familiar with Gujarati so I must have written that. But mungi means ants in Marathi and Hindi! So it will not work. Let us say Gunga, Prasad.

G.J.V.: Do you want to write Goonga or gunga?
C.S.L.: Should be goonga
G.J.V.: Cool

Everything had started well but around 1 June came warnings of the cyclone *Nisarga* hitting Mumbai. It was expected on the night of 2 June. It had started raining. Our building was opposite the sea. Everyone in the area was asked to be ready to evacuate if necessary. Versova village had been evacuated. From the window the waves seemed very high, and it was all grey.

Packing those bags with all the documents and two sets of clothes and necessary medicines was the most painful and traumatic experience I had ever had. I wondered about all my books and my manuscripts more than anything else. Fortunately, the cyclone *Nisarga* changed its route. And when everything came back to normalcy, I could think again of matters like translation.

Since Prasad and I had an unwritten agreement that what the original is trying to convey should not in any way be tampered with for added explanation or changed to make it 'easy' for the English reader, the arguments that we had were not heated ones, involving the nature of the translation itself but were in terms of conveying the right meaning and giving the right emphasis for a word when it was needed. We arrived at a process of translation exchanging views and ideas and reaching an understanding that the original story will always remain a different experience of writing and reading. Translation can touch it, but it will never be an embrace. And with Prasad it was always an enjoyable exploration leading to this knowledge about translation. Right through the discussions and the arguments, I could relax and sense that there was no powerplay or hierarchy. As the translation was taking its final shape, there was no *apaswaram* or *besur*; all the notes were falling into place effortlessly: it was an equal music.

12

TRANSLATION, INTERPRETATION, AND TRANSCREATION

Texts and Contexts in the Indian Scenario

Somdatta Mandal

Like all serious academics, I begin with a comment by Walter Benjamin that Homi Bhaba quotes at the head of a chapter in his *The Location of Culture* (1994)*:* "Translation passes through *continua* of transformation, not abstract ideas of identity and similarity" (214). Whether cultural translation, which implies a language that is performative and active, or literary translation, where the language is formulative or enunciatory, the transformational process cannot (or possibly doesn't want to) ensure a sense of belonging. The separated textuality of the translated text is proposed by, among others, the new signifying and stylizing practices, and a new order of expression that put a lot of ground between the *ur*-text and the finished product. Translation from one language to another is burdened with difficulties at the best of times – even for a person who knows both the source and target languages perfectly. A good translator is a person for whom the language of translation is also the language of creativity. One cannot be a good translator in a language one has not mastered and made one's own. All good translations must convey not just the meaning of the original in another language but must exploit the resources of the target language to convey not an exact equivalent of the verbal pleasure of the original piece of writing but in an equitable way.

In a 2012 article entitled "Lost in Translation: What the First Line of 'The Stranger' Should Be," Ryan Bloom states how, over the decades, various scholars found it difficult to accept the translated first sentence of Camus's novel as "Mother died today":

> For the modern American reader, few lines in French literature are as famous as the opening of Albert Camus's "L'Étranger": "Aujourd'hui,

DOI: 10.4324/9781003399926-17

mamanestmorte." Nitty-gritty tense issues aside, the first sentence of "The Stranger" is so elementary that even a schoolboy with a base knowledge of French could adequately translate it. So why do the pros keep getting it wrong?

Within the novel's first sentence, two subtle and seemingly minor translation decisions have the power to change the way we read everything that follows. What makes these particular choices prickly is that they poke at a long-standing debate among the literary community: whether it is necessary for a translator to have some sort of special affinity with a work's author in order to produce the best possible text.

A similar problem is raised by Umberto Eco in *Mouse or Rat: Translation as Negotiation* (2003) when he says, "translation is always a shift, not between two languages but between two cultures – or two encyclopaedias. A translator must take into account rules that are not strictly linguistic but, broadly speaking, cultural." Based on a series of lectures on translation, these essays are thought-provoking and compelling discussions on the difficulties of translating faithfully. Using examples from classic literary texts including his own bestselling novels, Eco examines the rights and wrongs, the misunderstandings and the 'negotiations' needed in order to translate. He turns his eye on the subject of translations and the problems the differences between cultures can cause. A translation does not want to remain a mere mirror image of the original in a different language; it always aspires to appropriate elements of a new textuality to assume a new identity and to transcend strict similarities with the *ur*-text. Both of these images are abstract activities, but are now subsumed under a new language game – that of growth, not simply transformation. This 'growth' is largely a product of reading (or misreading) of culture in which the reader brings his own ingrained ideas and cultural perceptions. The textuality of the translated text, in that sense, is a composite in which a cross-cultural dialogue marks space of complicity and confrontation.

Even if we agree with all these propositions, a basic question remains unanswered, namely, who is an 'ideal' translator? With the problem of linguistic and cultural translation gaining predominance in postcolonial studies, this chapter attempts to evaluate practical issues and problems related to translation in the Indian context primarily in four categories. The first is when the author himself/herself acts as the translator of his/her own text. References to Rabindranath Tagore's own translation of *Gitanjali (Song Offerings)* in 1912, and 90 years later, Alka Saraogi's Sahitya Akademi Award-winning novel *Kalikatha: Via Bypass* (2002) illustrates this category to show that the basic problems of cultural translation have remained unchanged over almost a century.

I

Given that English, the only language in which Rabindranath Tagore translated his own work, was the language of his colonial masters, any evaluation of his work as translator is essentially a 'colonial discourse.' But the extraordinary circumstances under which the poet started translating his own songs need to be recapitulated here. In 1912, the intelligentsia of Bengal decided to rectify the neglect of their greatest poet by celebrating his fiftieth birthday in the Town Hall of Calcutta (a very rare honour for a nonwhite in those days). After a string of other jubilee celebrations, the poet felt physically and emotionally exhausted and decided to have his vacation in England. He was due to set sail from Calcutta on 19 March, but being taken ill the night before, he retired to his family estate in East Bengal for rest and recovery. It was there that he began to translate some of his *Gitanjali* songs into English. In a letter to his niece Indira, written a year later on 6 May 1913, he wrote:

> That I cannot write English is such a patent fact that I never had even
> the vanity to feel ashamed of it.... I had not the energy to sit down and
> write anything new. So I took up the poems of *Gitanjali* and set myself to
> translate them one by one.
>
> *(quoted in Kripalani, 221)*

As Faria Majid rightly points out, one should keep in mind the fact that these were not 'poems' as such in terms of Tagore's entire canon. Being the verbal parts of short musical compositions, their brevity was a factor singularly suitable for a novice translator's enterprise under the circumstances. In the West, however, this simplicity was conveniently seen as "the beauty and freshness of his Oriental thought," not as a distillation achieved by consummate artistry.

From the time he was well enough to travel and his arrival in London a few months later, Tagore had filled an exercise book with English renditions of the *Gitanjali* songs. He presented it to William Rothenstein who later showed it to A.C. Bradley and W.B. Yeats. When the India Society decided to publish a private edition of the book, Yeats was obviously chosen to be the editor and to write the preface. We are all aware of how the relationship between Tagore and Yeats later soured – the same man who was all praises for the Indian bard and was largely instrumental in introducing him to the Western audience parted ways, and in May 1935, he wrote to Rothenstein:

> Damn Tagore! ... he thought it more important to see and know English
> than to be a great poet, he brought out sentimental rubbish and wrecked

his reputation. Tagore does not know English, no Indian knows English. Nobody can write with music and style in a language not learned in childhood and ever since the language of his thought.

I quote so many well-known historical facts just to emphasize that the crux of all these interrelated matters lies in Tagore as a translator of his own work. Like many Bengalis of his time, and judging from his letters and speeches, Tagore had a good command of English. There are occasional phrases and lines in his own rendition that both capture the spirit of the original and are striking in English. Yet, *Gitanjali* is still the best, perhaps because Yeats and Sturge Moore were able to polish the English of translations that were made in the isolation of Tagore's village-estate in Bengal, with no other purpose than sharing some of his favourite songs with friends he would meet on his forthcoming trips abroad. There are inaccuracies and mistranslations in *Gitanjali*, but the apparent lack of any extra-literary motive makes these mistakes tolerable in the days when there was no serious challenge to the assumption that literary translation is an inexact art, and when mistranslations of Oriental literature were even welcome (as in the case of Edward Fitzgerald's *The Rubbaiyat of Omar Khayyam*) as a creative activity of a sort.

If ability or command of English were in question, one would not be wrong to expect *improvements* in Tagore's translating endeavours after the *Gitanjali* experience. Though there are indications of improved English in his letter to Rothenstein over this period, yet we find that things went from bad to worse in his subsequent translations. In one of these letters, Tagore stated:

Latterly I have written and published both prose and poetry in English, mostly translations, unaided by any friendly help, but this again I have done in order to express my ideas, not for gaining any reputation for my mastery in the use of a language which can never be mine.

(quoted in Kripalani)

The difficulties of translation range beyond knowing both the languages well. One must also know the cultures of both languages, the traditions of the people who read the writing in the original and those who will read it in the translation. Do writers who know both languages translate their own works well? There was Tagore whose own translations of *Gitanjali* have been criticized for monotony of style and diction, for retaining only about a third of the poems of the original *Gitanjali*, for drawing the rest from his earlier works, for only imperfectly paraphrasing the poems in the English version. Much of the force in the original was lost in the English. Tagore himself felt the weakness of his translation and had written to Amiya

Chakravarty that he had done great injustice to the translations and that he could be so careless and insolent simply because they were his own writings. Several years after translating *Gitanjali*, Tagore went to China in 1924 to deliver lectures at different fora. All the lectures were delivered in English, some impromptu and some written down earlier. Some of his selected talks were published as *Talks in China* after he returned to India. In one of the talks, he mentions about the difficulty of expressing his thoughts through another language and trying to read the poems of Dante, Goethe and Heine in translation:

> Languages are jealous. They do not give up their best treasures to those who try to deal with them through an intermediary belonging to an alien rival. You have to court them in person and dance attendance on them.... Poems are not like gold or other substantial things that are transferrable … You cannot receive the smiles and glances of your sweetheart through an attorney, however diligent and dutiful he may be.
>
> *(40)*

The problem of being an inefficient translator was not Tagore's alone. When a creative writer is good enough in another language to translate it himself/ herself, there is the understandable desire not to give it to someone else who might not understand the nuances of the writing. As per a private conversation with the author a few years ago, Professor Niaz Zaman of Bangladesh rightly points out that in the case of the Urdu writer Qurratulain Hyder when she was translating *Aag Ka Darya*, we find the writer taking liberties with the original text that a translator cannot. Hyder had written the novel in the 1950s, sitting in Karachi. When she came to translate it years later, she was back in India. She thus came to the work of translation a very different person from the one she had been when she wrote the Urdu original. Hyder – or her publishers – were aware of these changes: the title page notes that the book has been "transcreated from the original Urdu by the author."

Moving on to a similar phenomenon in much more recent times, the problem of self-translation manifests itself in a different form. Narrated in a chronological fashion, Alka Saraogi's novel *Kalikatha: Via Bypass* (2002) gives us a brilliant picture of the Marwari business community that migrated from Rajasthan and made their second home in Calcutta. The novel was originally written in Hindi and later translated into English by the author herself within a short span of time. In the Introduction of the translated version, Saraogi claimed that she had "rewritten" most of it and in the Acknowledgements section admitted that her self-translation was faulty, and she had "little confidence in [her] Hinglish." Though there is no perfect way of translating a text, one expected a little more finesse on the part of Saraogi, especially when she was confident that it was she who would be able to do justice to her novel. In spite of the help that she had received from her unnamed friend, it remains a great lapse on the part of the publishers to print the English version without correcting several grammatical errors and faulty literal translations. Phrases like "the weekly schedule of the his classes" (173); "the British have broken the back of Bengal" (202); "Kishore Babu was put in mind of a three-month-old foetus" (247); "Perhaps it her fate" (242); or "making a flag out of the front of your sari" (264) definitely lowers the charm of reading a Sahitya Akademi Award-winning novel. Thus, as both Tagore's and Saraogi's cases illustrate, the notion that the original writer is the best translator of his or her own work remains a myth.

II

Translating a work like Joginder Paul's *Sleepwalkers* by someone closely related to the author forms the focus of the second category of this discussion. First published in 1990 as *Khwabrau* in Urdu in Lahore, this novella was made available to Indian readers through its Indian edition in 1991. An excellent translation into English by Sunil Trivedi and Sukrita Paul Kumar (incidentally Paul's own daughter) now makes it possible for the non-Urdu-speaking readers to appreciate the story. Apart from being a labour of love, what moves the reader most is probably the theme of the story, which harps upon the universal ideas of pain, anguish, and trauma of separation following the Partition of India. Briefly speaking, it tells the story of one Deewane Maulavi Sahab, who, like the other *mohajirs*, migrated from Lucknow to Karachi after the Partition but transported the entire city "within the fold of their hearts." While some of the other *mohajirs* are shocked into insanity, the protagonist does not feel the pain of separation because he is a sleep-walker and finds security in the world of dreams. Others call him mad but it is his madness that helps him keep his sanity.

Apart from the gripping storyline what appeals to the readers is the epilogue entitled "On Writing Sleepwalkers" where Paul himself provides the background of conceiving such a tale. A visit to Lahore in the mid-1980s made Joginder Paul realize that "the situation itself is the meaning that inspired [him] to attempt the novella." He candidly admits, "Suffer did I no less than Deewane Maulavi Sahab, the suffering having driven the old man out of his wits, and me to an insane pursuit of premature sanity." Personal experience of the writer therefore made the translation of the feelings of the protagonist much more authentic. Again, the universality of the theme of the story is also reiterated when the author narrates how a German Indologist burst into tears after reading the story, managing to say between sobs, "But this is my story. This is the story of all of us living on either side of the Berlin Wall." Though the Wall has come down, the mental barriers still remain. Such a theme probably also helps to transcend the limitations of translation.

III

The third category comprises different versions of translating the same text by academics and freelancers. To illustrate this point let us focus upon different translated versions of Saadat Hasan Manto's famous Urdu short story 'Toba Tek Singh,' first published in *Savera* in 1953 and Jibanananda Das's eponymous poem 'Banalata Sen.' A comparative study of selected portions from the three translated versions of the Manto story reveals interesting details as the translation depends a lot on the qualification and background of the translator. Whereas the first version done by Tahira Naqvi in 1994 is more condensed with simple, direct sentences (with Naqvi, herself settled in the United States, probably having the Western readers as her target), the second translation done by Khalid Hasan in 1997 is more textual. The translator here seeks out more culture-specific words to remain as faithful to the original as possible. For example, instead of using just 'sweets' in the earlier version, he mentions 'rice crispies.' When M. Asaduddin ventured to translate the same story in 2001, he was already aware of the drawbacks of the earlier versions and therefore added a detailed explanation with notes at the end of his work. A quote from this note goes like this:

> Towards the end of the story, by a brilliant metonymic process, Bishen Singh becomes Toba Tek Singh; the person becomes the place where he was born and had his roots. They merge inextricably with each other, so much so, that towards the end of the story, at least in the Urdu text, it is difficult to distinguish one from the other. To my knowledge, no English translation of the story has endeavoured to retain this tension and ambiguity. I have endeavoured to retain it even if it meant sacrificing a bit of lucidity.

Thus the physical description of Bishen Singh or Toba Tek Singh changes from "ghoulish appearance" of the first version, the "frightened appearance" of the second, to "a fearsome look" in the third. Again, in another instance, the mention of Toba Tek Singh's daughter becomes much more explicit with details as one moves from the 1994 to the 2001 versions.

1) He had a daughter who was grown up now. As a child, she cried whenever she saw her father, and she continued to cry for him when she was a young woman. (Naqvi, 1994)
2) When he was first confined, he had left an infant daughter behind, now a pretty young girl of fifteen. She would come occasionally, and sit in front of him with tears rolling down her cheeks. In the strange world that he inhabited, hers was just another face. (Hasan, 1997)

3) He had a daughter who had grown up a little, every passing month, during these fifteen years, and was now a young woman. Bishen Singh could not recognize her. She used to cry at the sight of her father when she was an infant. Now a grown woman, fears still flowed from her eyes, seeing her father. (Asaduddin, 2001)

The climactic end of the story also focuses upon the personal interpretations of the translators:

1) But he was adamant and would not budge from the spot where he stood. When the guards threatened to use force, he installed himself in a place between the borders and stood there as if no power in the world could move him.... Before the sun rose, a piercing cry arose from Bishan Singh who had been quiet and unmoving all this time. (Naqvi, 1994)

2) The guards even tried force, but soon gave up. There he stood in no man's land on his swollen legs like a colossus.... Just before sunrise, Bishen Singh, the man who had stood on his legs for fifteen years, screamed and as officials from the two sides rushed towards him, he collapsed to the ground. (Hasan, 1997)

3) When they tried to move him forcibly to the other side, he stood on his swollen legs at a spot in the middle, in a posture that seemed to suggest that no power on earth could move him from there.... Just before sunrise, a sky-rendering cry emerged from the gullet of Bishen Singh, who till then had stood still and unmoving. (Asaduddin, 2001)

Thus the appreciation of the Manto story for non-Urdu-speaking readers will always be affected by the particular version of the translated text he/she is reading.

For our second example, we turn from the problems of translating prose to the more complicated problem of translating poetry. Way back in 1923, Walter Benjamin had mentioned in his famous essay *The Task of the Translator* (first printed as introduction to a Baudelaire translation) that translation is 'second life.' He had particularly used the term 'afterlife.' The idea itself is quite thrilling – something that is situated on the verge of death regains new life through the translation. In 1974, the American poet James Merrill had written a poem called "Lost in Translation" which suggested that what you have omitted during the process of translating a poem is the actual poem. Though translators did not appreciate his idea, the poem and its idea were appreciated by poets. Again, we find a poet like Octavio Paz who had literally scolded people who claimed that poetry cannot be translated at all. There are other theorists who opine that while translating a poem one has to pay due attention to the form and the rhyme scheme as well. So once again the translator becomes the villain. Does that mean that translating poetry will disappear from the world? Herein lies the paradox. The answer is not at all. Translation is now a full-fledged industry which is thriving.

One of the questions that perplex the reader of a translated poem is whether it is able to retain the culture specificity of the source text. Regarding translation of poetry in the Indian context, it is often believed that poetry cannot be translated at all. The 'Indianness' gets lost in the maze of the Queen's language. According to the poet Subodh Sarkar, it is often believed that after a lot of brainstorming what the translator produces is a watered-down version of the original poem. Though this is true, it is also not wholly true. Let's say fifty-fifty. There is risk on both sides. Take for example the 16 translated English versions of 'Banalata Sen.' Till today, scholars who can read the poem in original Bangla have been left dissatisfied with each of these translated versions including the one that was done by the poet himself. Some go on arguing about the loss of the onomatopoeic rhythm of the original poem; others feel the scent and smell of rural Bengal landscape in the poem cannot be recreated in English; while there are others who go on arguing that "*danay roudrer gondho muche fele chil*" is simply untranslatable. Let alone the metaphor, the argument arises even with the simple nomenclature of the bird '*chil*' – is it vulture, eagle, kite, hawk, or kestrel? Different translators have used each of these words and so who is closest to the original remains a million-dollar question.

Let us examine a few versions of 'Banalata Sen' to see how the problem manifests itself. Jibanananda Das (1899–1954) was one of the foremost figures of modern Bengali poetry, and his work combines the substance of international modernism with the timeless experience of rural Bengal, and both these with the complex and disturbing patterns of urban life and political upheaval of his time. Since Jibanananda's poetry has a major contribution to Bengali poetic idiom, his work becomes specially challenging for the translator. In his book *Translation as Discovery* (1994), Sujit Mukherjee compares six different versions of 'Banalata Sen' that had been published by 1981, including the translation by Martin Kirkman, as well as a "transcreation" of the poem by Mukul Sharma.

Published in 1935, 'Banalata Sen' may or may not be the best poem that the poet had written, but it is undoubtedly the most popular one. Built up through a series of opulent images of sea and island, lashing storm and quiet resting place, fragrant forests, and shipwrecked sailors, it captures the old fairy-land magic that merges the geography of mythical and historical times only to culminate in the frustration and hope of the modern age. Ashok and Vimbisara, Sravasti and Vidisa, the Malay Sea and the Sinhala Sea cease to be the luxurious backdrop of a romantic escape. Apart from heightening the contrast between the past and the present, and intensifying the pain and agony of modern man, the poem connects the narratorial voice with the ever-moving forces of history. In his "Translation Editor's Preface" to the volume *A Certain Sense: Poems by Jibanananda Das* (1998), Sukanta Chaudhuri tells us that the translations emerged out of a workshop where the 11 translators had agreed to do away with the rhymes but preserve "the general movement and impact of the original poems" (xvii). The translators, we learn, had decided to be pragmatic rather than consistent in using Bengali names of plants, birds, seasons, etc. The haunting rhythm, the rich imagery, the magic of proper names, and the ethereal beauty of the concluding sestet have contributed to its immense popularity. As mentioned earlier, a comparison of the translations of the original Bengali line *"danay roudrer gondho muche fele chil"* in the closing stanza of the poem helps us to understand the problem better. Sukanta Chaudhuri's translation reads as follows: "At the end of all the days, dusk comes like the sound of dew; / The kite wipes off the scent of sunlight from its wings." The American professor Clinton B. Seeley largely ignores the formal and tonal quality of the original poem and translates the lines in free verse as: "At day's end, like hush of dew / Comes evening. A hawk wipes the scent of sunlight / from its wings" (120).

In a note prefacing his translations, Chidananda Dasgupta, a distant relative of Jibanananda Das, in his book *Jibanananda Das* reveals that the poet had given his "blessings readily" to five of the poems he had rendered into English shortly before Das's death in 1954 (1972, 28). Moreover, Dasgupta informs us that the poet had agreed to the translator's decision to avoid too literal renderings. Apparently, the poet had allowed Dasgupta "a certain degree of sacrifice of the literal meaning" and even some tampering with the sense of the original to make the meaning of a poem "comprehensible in a foreign idiom." The poet seemed to have also consented to Dasgupta's decision to have "smoothed out to a clear flow ... Jibanananda's very complicated and apparently arbitrary syntax." Thus, Dasgupta decided to depart from the original as often as he felt necessary. Terming the tendency of translators in general to "convey all of the many layers of thought, feeling and rhythm of the original" as a "temptation" to be avoided and as the wrong kind of "enthusiasm," he describes himself as someone opting for "restraint" (28). Thus in his translation of 'Banalata Sen' we read that "The raven wipes the smell of [sic] warm sun / From its wings; the world's noises die" (31). Having a series of translations before him already, Fakrul Alam is more conscious about his method of translation of the same poem in 1999. In his translation the line reads as follows: "At the end of a long day, with the soft sound of dew, / Night falls; the kite wipes the sun's smells from its wings" (63).

In the detailed introduction to the volume of Jibanananda's poems that he translated, Fakrul Alam explains his modus operandi as well as the drawbacks in some of the earlier translated versions of the same poem. He also points out that Faizul Latif Chowdhury's collection of translations of Jibanananda Das's poems, *I Have Seen the Bengal's Face: Poems from*

Jibanananda Das (1995), is uneven in quality and significantly the better translations in the volume are the ones by the foreigners – an Englishman, an American, and an Australian. "The Bengali translators fail probably because in translating verse the translator must have a much surer command of the target language than of the source language" (19). Confessing that he knew full well that a lot of the poetry of the original has got lost in his renderings as well, Alam states that to think that "all or even much of the poetic qualities of Das's poems can be transmitted into another language is therefore to indulge in wishful thinking." For instance, the tonal qualities of a line such as this one from 'Banalata Sen' are uncapturable in translation:

Chul t<u>ar</u> kabek<u>ar</u> andhok<u>ar</u> Vidish<u>ar</u> Nisha

Even if one did not know any Bengali, one could still hear the rich music of these lines coming from the extensive sound patterning – the internal rhyme and the repetition of the "a" "h" "r" and "s" sounds (21). Alam further states that he has always worked on the assumption that translation of poetry should involve not only following the words of the source poem but also in recovering something of the poetic qualities of the original, in transmitting the tone of the poet, and in conveying as much as is possible of Das's formal experiments and idiosyncrasies as a poet. Another goal that he had set himself was that "the translated poem should be capable of being read as a poem in English in its own right."

Should we then believe that extraordinary poetry is written in Indian languages, but it cannot travel out of its linguistic boundary? Whatever the case might be, we must agree that translation, (albeit good translation), or as what Professor P. Lal had called 'transcreation,' which does not negotiate the nuances and niceties, is the only way out.

IV

To focus upon the fourth and final category that translates text from one medium to another, we will use cinematic translations of adapted texts – Mahasweta Devi's *Hazaar Churasir Ma* ("Mother of 1084") and the film as well as theatrical adaptation of her short story 'Rudaali' as examples. In the Indian context, the problem of authenticity acquires a newer dimension in the sense that often regional languages create more distance. The general problems pertaining to literary translation from SL to TL (source language to translated language) also becomes apparent in films. For instance, we can cite the example of *Hazaar Churashir Ma*. Told in simplistic terms, it narrates the story of an unsuspecting mother who faces the trauma and tribulations after the death of her young Naxalite revolutionary son in Calcutta when she is called upon to identify his corpse and the narration centres around how she gets involved in her son's political activities only after his death.

Though Govind Nihalani, the film director, was true to the spirit of the translated text, and though Mahasweta Devi herself had given a most heartening endorsement for the performance of Jaya Bachchan in the lead role of the mother, for serious viewers across Bengal, the film seemed to have failed in the haunting memories of the turbulent 1970s and the actual Naxalite movement seemed too insipid. Yet considered from the psycho-sociological angle, the film can be called successful in the depiction of the lead role of Sujata, the mother, who is the prototype of every urban Indian woman who pretends to have established a great channel of communication with her children but seldom digs deep to understand what might be bothering them. And after she does, she often gives up, saying that she cannot handle them anymore.

Another interesting variation of the same problem occurs when the original text as well as the filmic version involves masters in their respective fields. Take the case when Rabindranath Tagore's *Ghare Baire* (*The Home and the World*) is made into a film by the world-class filmmaker Satyajit Ray. Tagore's 1916 novel, written in the diary form of narrative, is a significant, yet rather complex, work of fiction. Embedded in it is a historical moment of the *swadeshi* in Bengal around the years 1903–1908 – a period in Indian nationalism when the concerted demand for self-government and the boycott of British goods seemed for a while to rock the very foundation of imperial administration in India. This theme is dealt in detail by juxtaposing the character of the fire-brand revolutionary Sandip with Nikhil, the noble but misunderstood hero who personally believed that each individual has a freedom to choose his own way of serving the cause of social and political emancipation. What is more significant is how Tagore portrays the invasion of this *swadeshi* political movement to "home" and ultimately brings in a threat to feminine virtue.

When such a complex story is made into a film, one is naturally interested to see how the symbolic meanings of the "home" and the "world" are analyzed. Closely following the text, Ray's statement that he "did not use a single line of Tagore's dialogue in the film…. The way people talk in the novel would not be acceptable to any audience" puzzles us. Again, though Tagore presents his introspective story through multiple points of view, shuffling through the narratives of the three main characters at random, Ray's straightforward narration in the film makes some critics feel that the film is structurally weak. One such view endorses that the film is divided into three separate watertight compartments. The first section deals exclusively with Bimala. The political involvement of Sandip and Nikhil covers the second section. The third section primarily focuses on the Hindu–Muslim riot and clash. These three sections do not seem to be well coordinated, or in other words, one section does not automatically lead to the other. Again, though critics and the viewers in general accept the changes when a work of art is transferred from one medium to another, from one set of codes to another, one of the most frequently raised questions regarding *The Home and the World* is that whereas Tagore left his novel rather "open-ended" (with the communal riots breaking out, Sandip runs away to safety and Nikhil rides off into the night to face the hostile mob), Ray makes his story rather "well-closed." In the film, Bimala is seen looking out of the window and she sees the people carrying in Nikhil's dead body in a procession and immediately the image of the widowed Bimala fills up the screen. The film, considered one of Ray's failures, is now merely referred to as a definite 'period' story. Much earlier, Tagore had come to realize that "cinema continues to be a sycophant to literature because no creator has yet liberated it from this servitude by the strength of his own genius" and Satyajit Ray attempted to do just that.

A deviation of medium and the problems of translations are also witnessed in the case of theatrical adaptations. Take the case of Mahasweta Devi's short story 'Rudaali.' The stark setting and Usha Ganguly's remarkable acting in the role of the protagonist Sanichari had made this theatrical production by the Calcutta-based Rangakarmee Group a memorable event. Though a Hindi production, this play had received rave reviews from all kinds of audience in Calcutta, which included the snooty Bengali theatre-goers who are used to viewing only avant-garde productions and are also not very conversant with Hindi. Years later, Kalpana Lajmi's directorial venture made the film version of the same story more a vehicle for presenting a matured Dimple Kapadia along with full support from Bhupen Hazarika's soul-rendering music ['*Dil hoom hoom karey, ghabraye*']. But we think since this film remains the only medium of approach to Mahasweta Devi's work for the pan-Indian audience, the positive side of any transcreation has to be accepted as an equally important genre. The only exception of course is the rare and enterprising viewer who would read up the translated English version of the text before landing up at the movie hall or vice-versa.

After considering all these various forms of translation, we are still confounded with the question "Who is an 'ideal' translator?" Though the choice of the medium alters the message, the question still remains how far the translator can construct those messages effectively. In an article, "Babel Now," the noted critic Susan Sontag opined:

> To translate means many things, among them: to circulate, to transport, to disseminate, to explain, to make (more) accessible. By literal translation we mean, we could mean, the translation of the small percentage of published books actually worth reading: that is to say, worth rereading.

... In what I call the evangelical incentive, the purpose of translation is to enlarge the readership of a book deemed to be important.

Sontag further explains that the translators were "the bearers of a certain inward culture" and that to translate "thoughtfully, painstakingly, ingeniously, respectfully, is a measure of the translator's fealty to the enterprise of literature itself." Though she propagated such values as 'integrity,' 'responsibility,' 'fidelity,' 'boldness,' 'humility,' and 'ethical understanding' in the translator, she does not define who an 'ideal' translator is. She just states that "literary translation is a branch of literature – anything but a mechanical task." This chapter thus ends with the naïve contention that since there are no immediate solutions in sight, there is nothing called an 'ideal' translator whether in the Indian or in the global context and the problem remains open-ended till date.

Note: A few sections of this chapter were published earlier in "The Writer as Transcreator: Are Comparisons Odious?" in Anisur Rahaman & Ameena Kazi Ansari (Eds.), *Translation/Representation*, Creative Books, New Delhi, 2007, pp. 66–74, and "Of Defining and Redefining an 'Ideal Translator': Problems and Possibilities" in Udaya Narayana Singh, P.P. Giridhar & Anjali Gera Roy eds. *Translation Today*, 1(2), Central Institute of Indian Languages, Mysore, October 2004: pp. 230–252.

References

Alam, Fakrul, *Jibanananda Das: Selected Poems with an Introduction, Chronology, and Glossary*, The University Press Limited, Dhaka, 1999.

Asaduddin, M. (Trans.), "Toba Tek Singh", in Ravikant & Tarun K. Saini, *Translating Partition*, Katha, New Delhi, 2001.

Benjamin, Walter, "The Task of the Translator", in Hannah Arendt (Ed.), *Illuminations*, (Trans. Harry Zohn), Harcourt Brace Jovanovich, New York, 1968, pp. 69–82.

Bhabha, Homi, *The Location of Culture*, Routledge, London & New York, 1994.

Bloom, Ryan, "Lost in Translation: What the First Line of 'The Stranger' Should Be", *The New Yorker*, 12 May 2012 at https://www.newyorker.com/books/page-turner/lost-in-translation-what-the-first-line-of-the-stranger-   should-be. Accessed on 15 January, 2018.

Chaudhuri, Sukanta, "Translation Editor's Preface", in *A Certain Sense: Poems by Jibanananda Das*, Sahitya Akademi, Calcutta, 1998, pp. xvii–xviii.

Chowdhury, Faizul Latif (Ed.), *I Have Seen the Bengal's Face: Poems from Jibanananda Das*, Creative Workshop, Dhaka, 1995.

Dasgupta, Chidananda, *Jibanananda Das*, Sahitya Akademi, New Delhi, 1972.

Devi, Mahasweta Devi and Usha Ganguly, *From Fiction to Performance*, Seagull, Calcutta, 1999.

Eco, Umberto, *Mouse or Rat: Translation as Negotiation*, Weidenfeld & Nicolson, London, UK, 2003.

Hasan, Khalid (Trans.), "Toba Tek Singh", in *Mottled Dawn: Fifty Sketches and Stories of Partition*, Penguin India, New Delhi, 1997, pp.1–7.

Kripalani, Krishna, *Rabindranath Tagore: A Biography*, Visva-Bharati, Calcutta, 1980, (revised 2nd edn).

Majid, Faria, "Tagore's Own Translations: Blindness and a Hindsight", in Fakrul Alam, Niaz Zaman and Tahmina Ahmed (Eds.), *Revisioning English in Bangladesh*, The University Press Ltd., Dhaka, 2001, pp. 85–100.

Mukherjee, Sujit, *Translation as Discovery*, Longmans, New Delhi, 1994.

Naqvi, Tahira (Trans.), "Toba Tek Singh", in Alok Bhalla (Ed.), *Stories About the Partition of India*, HarperCollins, New Delhi, 1994.

Paul, Joginder, *Sleepwalkers*, Sunil Trivedi and Sukrita Paul Kumar (Trans.), Katha, New Delhi, 2001.

Saraogi, Alka, *Kalikatha – Via Bypass*, Rupa & Co., New Delhi, 2002.

Seely, Clinton B., *A Poet Apart: A Literary Biography of the Bengali Poet Jibanananda Das (1899–1954)*, University of Delaware Press, Newark, 1991.

Sontag, Susan, "Babel Now", in *The Times Literary Supplement*, 12 June 2003 at http://www.the-tls.co.uk/story.asp?story_id=27334. Quoted in linguaphiles.li vejournal.com/397875.html. Accessed on 31 July 2019.

Tagore, Rabindranath, *Talks in China*, Visva-Bharati Book Shop, Calcutta, 1925.

13

TRANSLATING SOUTH ASIA

Women and Radical Textuality

Radha Chakravarty

This Death, how pitiless

(Kaul 2015: 74)

These words, from Rukhsana Jabeen's Nazm, articulate the anguish of mothers who have lost their sons to political violence in Kashmir. The poem describes how such bloodshed "devastates homes", consigning the dead to eternal sleep beneath "graveyard-earth" (Kaul 2015: 74). In He Is But a Child, Ayesha "Mastoor", another poet from the same region, laments the loss of innocent lives, snuffed out in front of a "caravan of widows", evoking a vision of annihilation where all life in the universe will be wiped out by a stroke of lightning:

May all turn upside-down

(Kaul 2015: 84–85)

These poems by two women writers from Kashmir confront us with the human cost of political turbulence, through poignant representations of the collective plight of bereaved mothers in a trouble-torn part of South Asia. In another powerful story, "The Sack" by Sri Lankan author Jean Arasanayagam, a mother struggles to carry her critically injured son to a hospital in order to save his life. Located in a "border village", the narrative recounts the story of innocent civilians, caught in the mesh of violence and bloodshed in the name of politics. The mother transports her son's body in a sack used to store grain during other, more peaceful times. The bleeding body in the sack becomes a powerful signifier for the burden of history that

DOI: 10.4324/9781003399926-18

she must unwittingly bear. These three texts, from different parts of South Asia, speak of the remarkably similar predicaments of women as mothers in turbulent worlds, the kind of experiences that generally don't figure in history books and newspapers. The two poems from Kashmir come to us through translation. It is through translation that readers from elsewhere can apprehend the commonality of situation and affect between the mothers of lost sons in Kashmir and Sri Lanka.

The significance of translating the works of women writers of South Asia forms the subject of the present chapter. It addresses the conspicuous gaps in our knowledge about the region and the lack of adequate archives of translations across the languages of South Asia, to question sanctioned silences about prevailing political, social, cultural, and linguistic hierarchies. It looks ahead to future roadmaps for translation as a practice that can interrogate these hierarchies through a collaborative will towards reaching out to our Others. Through a range of examples drawn from South Asian women's writing, the chapter demonstrates "how contemporary feminist translation has made gender the site of a consciously transformative project, one which reframes conditions of textual authority".[1] Feminist writing signals an emancipatory textual practice, but to translate such writing with interventionist intent implies a double radicalism. Here, I explore the creative and emancipatory potential of this double textual radicalism.

Ideas of identity, voice, and agency have much to do with location. Gendered identities are produced by particular histories, and modes of resistance and paradigms for change are also determined by their specific contexts. South Asia forms the context for this chapter, but the category "South Asia" itself needs to be regarded as a construct.[2] It is important not to essentialize the idea of a region that is marked by such geographic, linguistic, ethnic, cultural, and social heterogeneity. In fact, we may ask whether, by using such an umbrella term, we can afford to ascribe to the region an internal coherence it may not already possess, as if trying to impose an imaginary order on what is actually a shifting, mutable, diverse reality. Yet, the idea of "South Asia", however provisional, remains a useful analytical category for the consideration of the radical potential of women's writing in translation, for the term signals a fractured, diverse domain, but also a space for the articulation of common concerns, and the possibility of dialogues beyond national borders. In this chapter, therefore, "South Asia" signifies a complex, unstable, dynamic configuration, a geographical re-mapping that also functions as a re-articulation of regional and global power relations. Likewise, terms like "the West" and "women" are also used as conceptual shorthand, to refer to categories that are not essentialized, but regarded as provisional, mutable, and heterogeneous.

The idea of "South Asia" disrupts conventional binaries such as national/international, colonial/postcolonial, and local/global. It also challenges hierarchical formulations that carve up the world into First World/Third World or global North and South. This is in consonance with what Gayatri Chakravotry Spivak, in *Readings*, calls "self-worlding", which she regards as a task imperative for writers from once-colonized cultures: "[W]e have to make a world, rather than just complain about colonialism" (Spivak 2014: 74).[3] In the making of our own world, translation can play a vital role, connecting cultures in the process of imagining into being a new "South Asia", beyond the formulations of the official discourses of colonialism and nationalism.

Tejaswini Niranjana, in her book *Siting Translation* (1992), makes a plea for an "interventionist" approach to translation, which can resist the "containment" of colonial discourse. She says: "Translation as a practice shapes, and takes shape within, the asymmetrical relations of power that operate under colonialism" (2). Niranjana's call for an "interventionist" method can be extended beyond postcolonialism, to also consider the transformative potential of feminist approaches to translation. What can it mean, to translate the works of women writers from diverse locations in South Asia and make them visible across geographical and cultural boundaries? In what ways can such translation function as a mode of intervention that takes us beyond the limits of postcolonial discourse?

"I am a translator because I am bilingual ... I am a translator because I am a woman", declares Canadian translator Susanne De Lotbiniere-Harwood in *The Body Bilingual: Translation as a Rewriting in the Feminine* (1991). What is the relationship between being a translator and being a woman? Theorists highlight the parallel between the status of women in relation to men, and translations in relation to the original. For women are expected to be faithful and subordinate to men, and translations too are usually judged in terms of their fidelity to the original, and assumed to be inferior, secondary, and derivative. In *Gender in Translation: Cultural Identity and the Politics of Transmission* (1996), Sherry Simon detects a language of sexism in translation studies. She objects, for instance, to George Steiner's aggressively male image of translation as penetration, in his book *After Babel* (1975). She points out the images of dominance, fidelity, and betrayal in most translation theory, as in the phrase "les belles infidels", attributed to the 17th-century French theorist, Menage, who argues that translation, like women, can be either faithful or beautiful (Simon 1996: 10). To counter this sexism, Simon speaks of a committed translation project: "For feminist translation, fidelity is to be directed toward neither the author nor the reader, but toward the writing project – a project in which both writer and translator participate" (2). The issues are not straightforward, though. Does a woman translator experience a double marginalization on account of her dual role as a woman and a translator? Can a woman translator from a once-colonized nation find herself the target of multiple forms of prejudice?

Such questions acquire a special resonance when we speak of women and translation in South Asia.

Colonial discourse as well as postcolonial theory have largely ignored other intermeshing social structures that compose our contemporary reality. There has always been rich linguistic and cultural traffic across the borders that today define the different components of South Asia. Along with the high tradition of mainstream literature, there is also a long history of popular traditions that cut across geographical and linguistic boundaries. To this tradition, women poets from the past, such as Andal, Meerabai, Chandrabati, and Lal Ded, have made major contributions. Today, anthropologists also recognize oral traditions as a rich extra-archival source of history. These alternative traditions played a dynamic role in promoting the fusion of cultures and languages across different parts of South Asia. With the movement of people, stories and songs also migrated from one part of South Asia to another, adding to the storehouse of collective memory. To this process, women made significant contributions, but in colonial as well as nationalist historiographies, their voices have been largely excluded. Reading women's writings across linguistic and national borders can make us aware of an alternative discourse that often runs counter to the dominant patriarchal and nationalist discourses of the different regions that constitute "South Asia". To translate these writings in order to make them mutually intelligible is to place them in dialogue with each other, generating a more heterogeneous space where commonalities can be recognized and differences negotiated. For the "reworlding" of South Asia, a new literary historiography is urgently needed, where translation as transcultural mediation can spearhead the move towards drawing these marginalized voices into the mainstream and highlighting their interconnectedness.

Heterogeneities

In their introductory essay for a special issue of *Feminist Review* devoted to South Asian women, editors Firdous Azim, Nivedita Menon, and Dina M. Siddiqi write of "the cross-border solidarities and conversations defying dominant trends of nationalist politics that are a significant feature of feminist activism and scholarship in South Asia" (Azim et al 2009).[4] They remind us, however, about the historical, political, cultural and linguistic differences that also fragment the region, precluding any move to homogenize the idea of "South Asian women".

It would be simplistic to regard "South Asia" as a monolithic cultural entity, placing it in a dualistic relationship with "the rest of the world". The region is in fact fragmented by asymmetries of power both within and across the nations that constitute it and by tensions generated by differences in history, politics, religion, language, culture, practices, perceptions, and interests. There are histories shared across some of the nations – such as the legacy of Partition, experienced by India, Bangladesh, and Pakistan – that are not as relevant to the people of Nepal, Bhutan, and Sri Lanka, where there are other demographic and communitarian issues of concern. Hence, translating the literature of South Asia brings these pluralities and ruptures to the fore, for it involves the negotiation of multiple levels of difference. Such negotiations make us aware of the links between translation and structures of power. Gender issues in South Asia cannot be treated in isolation, because they are cross-hatched with other cultural factors, such as caste, class, language, region, and community. Their complex forms of intersectionality make it impossible to formulate sweeping generalizations about women in the region. Instead of a reductive homogeneity, writings by South Asian women highlight the discontinuities produced by their culture-specific contexts.

Feminism in translation is not merely a matter of textual manipulation or linguistic strategy. The question is much larger and has more to do with the circumstances framing the translation, such as the factors governing the production, dissemination, and reception of the translated text. If translation is seen as a form of activism, the focus shifts from *what* is translated to *why* it is translated in a particular context. For instance, *Women Writing in India: 600 BC to the Present* (1991–1993), a two-volume anthology edited by Susie Tharu and K. Lalitha, is a landmark in feminist literary historiography, reconstructing through translation of the rich and versatile tradition of women's writing in the region, from pre-modern to contemporary times. *We Sinful Women: Contemporary Urdu Feminist Poetry* (1991), an anthology of feminist poetry from Pakistan, edited by Rukhsana Ahmad, uses translation to foreground female resistance. Anthologies, in fact, offer a fruitful ground for translators who wish to underline women's overlapping concerns across different socio-linguistic contexts. My own anthology *Vermillion Clouds: A Century of Stories by Bengali Women* (2010) attempts to retrieve through translation, for a non-Bengali audience, the creative voices of these women, claiming for them a place in the literary history of South Asia. In *Bodymaps: Stories by South Asian Women* (2007) – another edited anthology – I try to highlight through selection and juxtaposition the differences as well as the common concerns found in South Asian women's writings on the body.

The publication of women's autobiographies in translation is another growing trend that privileges female voice, perspective, and history. Issues of caste and class intersect with gender in these narratives, to highlight the particularity of individual women's experiences and sometimes also the collective marginalization of women belonging to specific communities. *My Story and My Life as an Actress* (1998), the autobiographical works of the legendary Bengali actress Binodini Dasi, *A Life Less Ordinary* (2006), the personal narrative of Baby Haldar, a domestic worker who evolves into a writer, *Anthrjanam: Memoirs of a Namboodiri Woman* (2011) by Devaki Nilayamgode, and *The Weave of my Life: A Dalit Woman's Memoirs* (2009) by Urmila Pawar are some instances of such life writings in translation. Pawar's narrative can also be read as autoethnography, for it also seeks to reconstruct through the telling of an individual life story the history of an entire community and the position of women within it. In choosing to translate such works, the translators make the resistance of these marginalized voices audible to a wider readership in another language. Such an interventionist move constitutes the double radicalism that is the theme of this chapter.

In this process of dissemination, publishers and editors can play a pivotal role. Kali for Women, a feminist publishing house founded more than a quarter of a century ago (and now bifurcated into two parallel publishing houses, Women Unlimited and Zubaan), has a remarkable track record. Two of their early anthologies, *Truth Tales* (1987) and *The Slate of Life* (1990), are milestones in the history of women's publishing in India, showcasing women's short stories translated from diverse languages to affirm the presence of a female literary tradition in the region. Other publishing houses that undertake similar projects in translation include Stree (which published *Women in Concert: An Anthology of Bengali Muslim Women Writing 1904–1938* in 2008) and Katha, which has published several volumes devoted to South Asian women's writing in translation. Anthologies such as *Women Writing: 25 Short Stories* (2004), translated from Sinhala by Vijita Fernando from Sri Lanka, *Galpa: Short Stories by Women from Bangladesh* (2005), edited by Firdous Azim and Niaz Zaman, and *Arshilata: Women's Fiction from India and Bangladesh* (2007), edited by Niaz Zaman, to name just a few instances, have emerged from different parts of South Asia. Such publishing initiatives can go a long way towards creating an audience and generating public awareness.

Market forces, in fact, have a large say in promoting or suppressing certain kinds of writing. When it comes to women's writing, elements of censorship or self-censorship often come into play, due to public perceptions about what women are allowed to articulate, and how. The case of Taslima Nasreen, surviving in exile for her outspokenness about religious orthodoxy and patriarchy, is only one flagrant example of the price a woman writer sometimes has to pay, for speaking her mind. Much earlier, Ismat Chughtai was charged with obscenity for her Urdu story "Lihaaf" (The Quilt), a bold narrative foregrounding same-sex desire and a young girl's coming of age. Choosing to translate such "rebellious" women's texts for wider audiences constitutes a renewed challenge to conservatism in altered contexts and marks a double rebellion on the part of the translator.

Women's writings from South Asia often interrogate conventional notions of the "feminine". Such works, in translation, can be placed in conversation with each other, to map a network of common concerns between women from different parts of South Asia and from elsewhere in the world, without erasing their cultural specificities. A range of translations undertaken by Gayatri Chakravorty Spivak and others, for instance, highlight the Bengali author Mahasweta Devi's sustained political activism and her tireless championing of the indigenous people of rural India, beyond the private, domestic realm traditionally considered the appropriate sphere for women's writing. Rokeya Sakhawat Hossain's story "The Fruit of Knowledge" (Vermillion Clouds) combines feminist and anti-imperialist rhetoric to make a plea for women's participation in the public life of a nation-in-the-making. To translate such works into English is to place them in a "South Asian" frame but also to make them available to a wide, international reading public, inviting comparison with progressive writings from different parts of the world.

That is also the impulse behind *Translating Women: Different Voices and New Horizons* (2017), a collection of essays edited by Luise von Flotow and Farzaneh Farahzad, which brings together reflections on translations of and by women writers from diverse cultures across the world. "We must first see otherness before we can affect change in the treatment of others", the editors declare. "We are progressing towards transnational coalition building" (Flotow and Farahzad, 2017: xiv). One essay in this anthology, "Voices from the *Therigatha*: Framing Western Feminisms in Sinhala Translation", by Kanchuka Dharmasiri from Sri Lanka, describes the author's use of translations from the ancient songs of Buddhist nuns in the *Therigatha*, as a point of entry for the study of Sinhala translations of modern feminist texts from the "West", to make the "foreign" texts more accessible for university students in Sri Lanka. She describes this as a double manoeuvre: "We see here how translation operates in multiple directions. While the feminist texts offer a rereading of *Therigatha, Therigatha* offers a rereading of the feminist texts". Dharmasiri adds:

> It does not have to be a one-way process. Ideas of women's freedom do not have to travel from one direction to another either. Rather, a consideration of notions of women's bodies, gender, and freedom as they appear in different contexts could open up fertile space for dialogue.
>
> *(Dharmasiri 190)*

Such a vision of dialogue and alliances between women across different cultures can give special meaning to the translation of women's texts from South Asia.

Women's writing from South Asia tends to destabilize the conventional opposition between imperialist and nationalist discourses by highlighting the patriarchal underpinnings of both. In Selina Hossain's "Double War" (*Bodymaps*), Nurjaan, a young activist in the Bangladesh Liberation War, secretly delivers ammunition to the freedom fighters' camp. But her complicity in the ambush is detected, and she is tortured brutally by her Pakistani captors. The story ends with a graphic image of Nurjaan's naked, bleeding, and half-alive body, suspended in public view. The discourses of gender and nationalism intersect, but also collide in this narrative, for Nurjaan's is a dual rebellion, against women's exclusion from politics, and also against the oppression of *muktijoddhas* (freedom fighters) by the state. Translation moves this re-narrativization of history from a local to a transnational frame, to insert it into dominant discourses on women, history, and politics. Such a move is transformative, for mainstream histories often tend to marginalize the voices of women. Anthologies of Partition literature, such as *The Other Side of Silence: Voices from the Partition of India* (2000), edited by Urvashi Butalia, *Mapmaking: Partition Stories from Two Bengals* (2011), edited by Debjani Sengupta, and *Bengal Partition Stories: An Unclosed Chapter* (2006), edited by Bashabi Fraser, also mark, through translation, the special ways in which a historical watershed impacted the lives of diverse women in the region.

Translations of South Asian women's writings, when read in a comparative, transnational frame, have the power to undermine the universalizing tendencies of "international" feminisms that tend to presume a continuity of women's experiences across the globe. Feminist theories from the "West" challenge the binaries that govern the construction of gendered identities in patriarchal discourse. Such binaries work on hierarchical lines, assigning an inferior position to women: masculine/feminine, reason/emotion, culture/nature, and public/private. In South Asian contexts, however, the complex intermeshing of gender with other social factors generates a spectrum of patriarchal positions that cannot be so easily expressed in the same binaries. The public/private dichotomy, for instance, operates in South Asian societies in complicated ways. The politics of space and also of touch are based not on gender alone but also on other factors such as class, caste, religion and community and couched in the rhetoric of purity/pollution, legitimacy/illegitimacy, or containment/transgression. Fear of the "abject" governs these inclusions and exclusions, but women writers often appropriate the transgressive power of the abject to subvert the dominant discourse. Mahasweta Devi's *Bayen*, for instance, uses this power to stunning effect, in the narrative of Chandi, a cremation attendant, accused by her community of using supernatural powers to raise dead children from their graves, to suckle them. Later, Chandi is posthumously recognized as a martyr after she gives her life to prevent a disaster. In *Sindhubala* (from *In the Name of the Mother*) by the same author, a childless woman abandoned by her husband for her lack of beauty is exploited by her mother, who forces her to pose as a "semi-divine" healer with a magic touch. The story unmasks a society that exploits women in the name of deifying them, without allowing them to express their real needs and desires. Both narratives draw on local superstitions of a particular time and place. The "bayen" is regarded as different from other witches because killing her brings misfortune: *Sindhubala* deals with the stigma of childlessness, the beauty myth, and the villagers' naïve faith in the supernatural powers of a woman who is *devanshi*, semi-divine. Through translation, these culture-specific narratives enter into textual relationships with women's narratives from other languages, cultures, and traditions, to complicate and extend the discourse of women's critiques of patriarchy.

"Western" conceptions of gender, for a long time, tended to draw upon the Cartesian duality of mind and body, identifying men with the rational principle and women with the biological. In South Asian cultures, though, traditions of materialist thought have flourished alongside transcendental forms of spiritualism, and so have philosophical systems based on a recognition of the fundamental oneness of things, rather than on dualities. This is the context for Bhuwan Dhungana's daring story "The Bell", which uses the trappings of traditional prayer rituals to narrate the sexual coming of age of a young Nepali girl. The story boldly represents the sexualized body as the source and site of female subjectivity and self-empowerment, drawing its central tropes from local conventions and religious practices in Nepal. At the sound of a temple bell, the protagonist experiences a complex emotion: "When someone rings the bell in front of the temple, sin and virtue suddenly smile at that bell, that symbol of religion ... The bell reminds her of an image of male/female coupling" (Dhungana 2007: 27–28). Manjushree Thapa's English translation of the story draws attention to the narrative's assertion of a "modern" female consciousness framed by local codes even while contesting their orthodox underpinnings.

In their questioning of regulative hetero-normativity, writings by women in South Asia draw upon indigenous traditions that go back a long way. As Ruth Vanita and Saleem Kidwai point out in *Same Sex Love in India* (2000), sexual norms in the region were more liberal during ancient times than is often recognized, and it was only during the colonial period, especially after new laws introduced in 1857, that the homophobic voice assumed greater dominance (191). Male and female roles are not very markedly differentiated in the mythologies and ancient cultural practices of South Asia. Theories of reincarnation, for instance, reveal fluid gender identities, and the female gender is assigned a powerful position in ancient cosmologies. Contemporary South Asian texts that challenge the heterosexual norm can thus be framed within this long history. *The World That Belongs to Us: An Anthology of Queer Poetry from South Asia* (2020) highlights the continuity of this tradition. The editors Aditi Angiras and Akhil Katyal speak of the heterogeneities implicit in the term "queer": "we had chosen to break up this part-weird, part-convenient, part-phantasmatic word 'queer'. We let it disperse. We made it splinter".

"Chandanamarangal" ("The Sandal Trees"), originally written in Malayalam by Kamala Das, which narrates the disruption of a marriage by the female protagonist's memories of same-sex love, is an earlier text that interrogates hetero-normative paradigms of desire, dealing with "subjects which are imbricated in a variety of other sexual and affective economies" (Rajendran 2015: 7). Das's story belongs in the tradition of "rebellious" stories such as Ismat Chughtai's "The Quilt", Shobhana Siddique's "Full to the Brim" and Mumtaz Shirin's "Angrai". In Sarojini Sahoo's story "Behind the Scene", published in my edited anthology *Writing Feminism: South Asian Voices* (2010), the happiness of a lesbian couple in a railway compartment makes their female fellow traveller aware of the hollowness of her own marriage. "Playing with Dolls: A New Love Story", by Ahana Biswas (*Vermillion Clouds*), set in rural Bengal, focuses on a married woman who leaves the joint family to seek self-expression in a sexual relationship with another woman. The text at one point reflects ironically on the shifting meanings of *bhalobasha*, the Bengali word for love: "Love. What was love, damn it? ... Who loved whom in this village, ... such things were common knowledge" (Biswas 2010: 165). In all these stories, the reified categories of hetero-normative discourse are displaced by more fluid, non-essentialist ideas of gender embedded in diverse, specific, localized contexts. Translation of such narratives can involve a simultaneous questioning of conventions pertaining to language, gender, and power. It cannot be assumed, though, that translations into English, automatically adopt an interrogative stance, for there remains the risk that such translations will be absorbed into dominant "global" discourses on "queer" sexualities. To mark the cultural distinctness of South Asian sexualities in a transnational frame is the translator's special challenge. My translation of Biswas's story, for instance, uses a localized vocabulary to situate this queer narrative in the context of a joint family in provincial Bengal, retaining Bengali kinship terms such as *Deor* (husband's younger brother), *Sejobou* (the third brother's wife) and *Chhtobhai* (youngest brother), caste markers such as the names Bauri and Bagdi and mythological references to Goddess Durga and celestial *apsaras*. To a great extent, the radical potential of such translations also depends on the stance of the reader from the receiving culture, who must be willing to confront sexual/textual otherness in the translated text.

South Asian women's narratives often overturn the traditional nature/ culture binary in their representations of the body. In Marathi writer Asha Kardalay's story "The Abyss" (*Bodymaps*, 2007), the protagonist undergoes a sex-change operation, but in this representation of a body transformed by new technologies, Kardalay's narrative also represents the inhibiting effect of social prejudices, for the protagonist's bold choice does not alter the conservative social attitudes of those around her. Ismat Chughtai's Urdu story, translated by Anjana Srivastava as "The Flower Vase" (*Bodymaps*, 2007), touches upon the scientific "progress" that has made artificial insemination possible but also challenges what Foucault calls "biopower", the way medical discourse targets the reproductive body as an object of experiment, while stereotyping the reproductive woman as a dangerous "hysteric". These stories, which subvert the social traditions of their respective literary and cultural contexts, acquire an additional radical edge when they circulate in translation, as disruptive interventions in discourses of the body across and beyond South Asia. The trope of the body-in-transformation in these narratives may also be read as an analogue for translation itself, which deals with textual metamorphoses and translingual mutability.

Women, Language, and Power

Central to these metamorphoses are issues of language and power. To speak of South Asian women's writing in a global frame is to also invoke the major contribution of writers of the South Asian Diaspora, such as Anita Desai, Bharati Mukherjee, Shauna Singh Baldwin, Jhumpa Lahiri, Monica Ali, Manjushree Thapa, and Muneeza Shamsie. The fact that they all write in English (and Jhumpa Lahiri also in Italian) grants them a visibility generally denied to South Asian women who remain rooted in their home cultures and write in their mother tongues or other indigenous languages. It is in relation to this dominance of English in the global literary marketplace that the question of translating South Asian literature from other languages *assumes prime importance.*

Gayatri Chakravorty Spivak, in "The Politics of Translation" (1992), critiques feminists from the West who expect women's writing from the global South to be translated into English, the dominant "international" language. She sees this privileging of English as a "betrayal of the democratic ideal into the law of the strongest" (Spivak 2000: 399–400). Such translations, she complains, seek to over-assimilate, to make themselves more accessible to Western readers, deploying what she calls "translatese", a uniform idiom that erases the cultural specificity of writings from the "periphery". To counter this trend, Spivak exhorts feminists from the West to try to learn "other" languages, to show their solidarity with women from the margins.

Spivak's exhortation demands of the privileged Global "North" an active attempt to reach out to the marginalized cultures of the once-colonized world, regarded as the West's subordinate Other. Today, translators from South Asia often adopt a proactive role in this process, through their translational strategies. Often, instead of trying to "Anglicize" their style, contemporary Indian translations appropriate and "localize" the target language in ways that have transformed the English lexicon. For translators today are aware of a double audience. Instead of trying to "domesticate" their translations to make them palatable to a Western readership, they affirm the local particularities of their source texts, using strategies of foreignization that Venuti describes as "resistancy" (Venuti 1995: 25). Venuti argues for a "theory and practice of translation that resists dominant target language cultural values so as to signify the linguistic and cultural difference of the foreign text" (1995: 23). This constitutes a political act, drawing attention to the "translatedness" of the text, instead of trying to render the translation transparent by "domesticating" it.

The bulk of women's writing in South Asia continues to be translated into English, in a "vertical" move that allows marginalized languages to challenge what was once the "master" language. But there is also a growing recognition of the need for "horizontal" translations across South Asian languages. Sometimes, in the absence of translators fluent in both indigenous languages, another common language, very often English, is used as a "bridge" in such endeavours. Journals such as *The Little Magazine*, *Himal Southasian*, *Bengal Lights*, and *City: A Journal of South Asian Literature* offer platforms for the publication of contemporary South Asian writing in translation. Ajmal Kamal, the Pakistan-based editor of *City* (published in India), asserts the need

> to develop a common South Asian literary readership and shared cultural experience, by building works of collaborative translation both in English and between languages of the regions to take these writings to the vast publics that read only in their own language.
>
> *(Kamal 2019)*

The idea of collaborative translation is certainly an important way forward. A new bilingual journal, *Pashyantee*, conceived to promote women's collective vision of language, literature, and translation as sites of radical practice, marks another initiative to draw upon our polyglot culture. The project aims at archiving and showcasing inspirational writings by women of the region, emphasizing a multilingual ethos through a focus on women and translation.

The need of the day is to develop a body of polyglot translators who can work together, across the multiple languages of South Asia. Systemic changes in education, publishing, and the job market are needed, to redress the asymmetries of power that separate "international" languages like English from "indigenous" tongues. Yet, English can still remain instrumental as a link language in our multilingual culture and also as a medium for granting international visibility to writings from our world. While most translations in South Asia are from indigenous languages into English, there is also a need for more translations from international languages into the languages of South Asia, as a way of precluding narrow regional insularity by connecting the global with the local and regional. Arjumand Ara's Urdu translation of Arundhati Roy's new novel, *The Ministry of Utmost Happiness* (2017), translated as *Be-Panah Shadmani ki Mamlikat*, enacts such a move. So does Karuna Gokhale's Marathi translation (2010) of *The Second Sex* by Simone de Beauvoir.

Questions of addressivity and multiple audiences complicate such practices, for translations of South Asian literature address potential readerships across South Asia as well as the rest of the world. As Benedict Anderson points out, translation brings into being an imagined community of readers, some of whom may never meet or know each other (Anderson 1991: 6). Yet the act of reading connects them all. Such interconnections do not presume a smooth transcultural passage for these texts in translation. Fractures, divisions and "misunderstandings" haunt the perilous journey of migrant texts, but what drives the process is a will to clear the space for mutual discovery, negotiation, and dialogue.

Translating South Asian women's writing can be regarded as a political act, but also as an act of love. In "The Politics of Translation", Spivak gestures at two forms of alterity: the ethical and the erotic. The ethical involves a humanistic universalism premised on a recognition of the basic likeness of all human beings, "so that the agent can be alive, in a human way, in the world" (Spivak 2000: 399). But this liberal humanism does not allow for the distance needed for translation to acknowledge the irreducible quality of otherness. The awareness of difference belongs more to the realm of the erotic than the ethical (Spivak 2000: 398). The troping of translation as love enables an exploration of a relationship between self and other that demands a "surrender" but not an erasure. By this definition, the translator must earn the right to intimacy with the text, through the act of reading.

To claim South Asia as the ground for a radical literary practice is also to challenge the dominant discourse of "world literature", to ask whose world we are talking about. That was precisely Rabindranath Tagore's intention when, asked to deliver a lecture on Comparative Literature in 1907, he chose instead to use the expression *visva sahitya*, the Bengali term for "world literature". In his lecture, Tagore calls for a reconceptualization of the world itself as a less divided place:

[J]ust as the world is not merely the sum of your plough field, plus my plough field, plus his plough field—because to know the world that way is only to know it with a yokel-like parochialism—similarly world literature is not merely the sum of your writings, plus my writing, plus his writings. We generally see literature in this limited, provincial manner. To free oneself of that narrowness and resolve to see the universal being in world literature, to apprehend such totality in every writer's work, and to see its

interconnectedness with every man's attempt at self-expression —that is
the objective we need to pledge ourselves to.

(Tagore 2015: 288)

Tagore's vision is utopian. To translate the radical writings of women from
South Asia is also something of a utopian move, to reimagine "world literature" on our own terms.

Notes

1 Sherry Simon, *Gender in Translation*, Routledge, London, 1996, p. 167.
2 For some of my preliminary ideas on South Asian women's writings, especially
  on the body, see the "Introduction" to my edited volume *Bodymaps: Stories
  by South Asian Women*, Zubaan, 2007. Several textual examples of women's
  writing in translation, cited in this chapter, draw upon my own translations and
  edited anthologies of South Asian writing, including *Crossings: Stories from
  Bangladesh and India*, Indialog, 2002; *In the Name of the Mother: Four Stories*
  by Mahasweta Devi, Seagull, 2004; *Vermillion Clouds: Stories by Bengali
  Women*, Women Unlimited, 2010; and *Writing Feminism: South Asian Voices*,
  University Press Limited, 2010.
3 Gayatri Chakravorty Spivak, *Readings*, Seagull, Kolkata, 2014, p. 14.
4 Firdous Azim, Nivedita Menon, and Dina M. Siddiqi, "Negotiating New
  Terrains: South Asian Feminisms", *Feminist Review*, 91, 2009, pp. 1–8.

References

Anderson, Benedict, *Imagined Communities*, Verso, New York, 1991.
Angiras, Aditi and Akhil Katyal (Eds.), *The World That Belongs to Us: An Anthology
  of Queer Poetry from South Asia*, HarperCollins, Noida, 2020 at https://books
  .google.co.in/books?id=j6vrDwAAQBAJ&printsec=frontcover#v=onepage&q
  &f=false. (Accessed on 4 September 2020).
Azim, Firdous, Nivedita Menon and Dina M. Siddiqi, "Negotiating New Terrains:
  South Asian Feminisms", *Feminist Review*, 91, 2009, pp. 1–8 at https://doi.org
  /10.1057/fr.2008.54 (Accessed on 10 April 2020).
Biswas, Ahana, "Playing with Dolls and a New Love Story", in Radha Chakravarty
  (trans. and Ed.), *Vermillion Clouds: A Century of Women's Stories from Bengal*,
  Women Unlimited, New Delhi, 2010.
Devi, Mahasweta, "Bayen" (translated by Mahua Bhattacharya), in Geeta
  Dharmarajan (Ed.), *Yuvakatha: Unforgettable Short Fiction from Some of
  India's Master Story Tellers*, Vol. 2, Katha, New Delhi, 1995, pp. 35–62.
Dharmasiri, Kanchuka, "Voices from the *Therigatha*: Framing Western Feminisms
  in Sinhala Translation", in Luise von Flotow, and Farzaneh Farahzad (Eds.),
  Translating Women: Different Voices and New Horizons, Routledge, New York,
  2017, pp. 175–193.
Dhungana, Bhuwan, "The Bell" (Translated by Manjushree Thapa), in Radha
  Chakravarty (Ed.), *Bodymaps: Stories by South Asian Women*, Zubaan, New
  Delhi, 2007, pp. 25–28.

Kamal, Ajmal, "A Case of Collaborative Translation of Literary Texts in South Asia", *Economic & Political Weekly*, 54 (16), 20 April 2019 at https://www .epw.in/engage/article/case-collaborative-translation-literary-texts-south-asia (Accessed on 9 April 2020).

Kaul, Suvir (Ed.), *Of Gardens and Graves: Essays on Kashmir, Poems in Translation*, Three Essays Collective, Gurgaon, 2015.

Lotbiniere-Harwood, Susanne De, *The Body Bilingual: Translation as a Rewriting in the Feminine*, Women's Press, Toronto, 1991.

Niranjana, Tejaswini, *Siting Translation: History, Post-Structuralism and the Colonial Context*, University of California Press, Los Angeles, 1992.

Rajendran, Aneeta, *(Un)familiar Feminisms: Studies in Contemporary Lesbian South Asian Texts*, OUP, New Delhi, 2015.

Simon, Sherry, *Gender in Translation*, Routledge, London, 1996.

Spivak, Gayatri Chakravorty, "The Politics of Translation", in Lawrence Venuti (Ed.), *The Translation Studies Reader*, Routledge, London, 2000, pp. 397–416.

————, *Readings*, Seagull, Kolkata, 2014.

Tagore, Rabindranath, "Visva Sahitya" (Translated by Rijula Das and Makarand Paranjpe) in Debashish Banerji (Ed.), *Rabindranath Tagore in the Twenty-first Century: Theoretical Renewals*, Springer, New Delhi, 2015, pp. 277–288.

Vanita, Ruth and Saleem Kidwai (Eds.), *Same Sex Love in India: Readings in Indian Literature*, Palgrave Macmillan, New York, 2000.

Venuti, Lawrence, *The Translator's Invisibility: A History of Translation*, Routledge, New York, 1995.

Fiction, Language, and Context

14

ARE THE GHOSTS IN HENRY JAMES'S *THE TURN OF THE SCREW* REAL?

Tabish Khair

Of what use are canonical texts, and that too by dead white males, in today's world? And what if the text is about something of no topical relevance at all – say, a kind of ghost story? That too, written by an author who was such a master of the complex and the compound sentences that he is at times almost unbearable in our accelerating age of digital snippets and, at best, fast and simple sentences!

Henry James's *The Turn of the Screw* fits all the above categories – or shall we say objections? First serialized in *Collier's Weekly* in 1898, this novella followed in the wake of another major work by James, *What Masie Knew*, and was subsequently issued in four other authorized forms. Of course, James is notorious for "mulling" over his works for years – so much so that it is usually difficult to place them within the customary brackets of 'starting' and 'finishing' dates. The 'germ' of the idea that became *The Turn of the Screw* is noted by James as far back as 1895. Whatever the process of its writing, the novella, though 'faster paced' than most of James's other, longer, works, shares the kind of retrospective style, partly a creation of his use of Proustian sentences, that we associate with the author. It is not a writing style that, however much we might admire it, is likely to be replicated by contemporary writers, or not unless they wish to give their narratives a 'period' note.

Moreover, the tale is set in a country house and concerns the possible haunting of two orphans by a ghost, or so their new governess imagines. This ambiguity – are the children haunted or not? – is the one question that still attracts contemporary readers, and with considerable force at times. But, if one looks at it in the light of matters like the Iraq–Syria crisis, oil spills,

DOI: 10.4324/9781003399926-20

climate change and, positively, the Black Lives Matter movement, one can ask if a vague tussle between Jehovah and Freud is enough to justify heavy intellectual investment in the novella? More so, in academic circles where religion will not be taken as seriously, or literally, as it was even among the literati in the 19th century.

Let us start with that question, then: Are the ghosts in Henry James's *The Turn of the Screw* real? This online survey was conducted by a colleague of mine in a BA first-year class of 62 students in Spring 2020. Eighteen students said the ghosts were real, 29 said they were not, and 15 remained undecided.

Having taught the text for a number of years now, I feel that this is not an unrepresentative division, though of course the percentages shift in keeping with the teacher's position. To use Tzvetan Todorov's terms, teachers who prefer an uncanny reading usually get more students saying that the ghosts are not real. Those who prefer a marvellous reading tend to convince more students about the reality of the ghosts. And teachers who stay suspended in the fantastic, as Todorov defines it, get students who remain undecided too. In my classes, for reasons that will become clear in this chapter, most students bend towards the 'fantastic' – where the explanation remains undecided and suspended between the natural and the unnatural. However, there is no doubt that the text of James's novella lends itself to all three interpretations.

This is also borne out by critical responses to the novella. It has invited strong, sometimes even combative, argument in favour of especially the first two positions: that the ghosts are real or that the ghosts are not real and instead demand a psychological explanation. There is enough 'textual' evidence on both sides. The non-ghost side points out various psychological manifestations. These are too many to be listed, but they always include the obvious romantic fascination that the governess exercises on Douglas (the man who passes on her manuscript account of the events to the unnamed author, who then gives it its title, 'The Turn of the Screw', and a preface), and the children's flamboyant, rich uncle exercises on the governess. The governess's small-town religious background, her need to prove herself, her urge to impress the uncle and her tendency to read events in ways that confirm her own hypotheses are elements too. As is the underplayed but obvious desperation of the two children, who have recently lost their parents and then two other guardian figures, Mr Quint (the butler) and Ms Jessel (the previous governess), and have been essentially abandoned in comfort by a fashionable uncle. Another obvious 'psychological' factor is the housekeeper, Ms Grose's "under the stairs" sensibility, which makes her agree with the governess and stay very critical of Mr Quint and Ms Jessel for transgressing social and perhaps, moral norms in her countryside world. Finally, the role of seeing and not seeing has been discussed in great detail by various non-ghost critics, all of whom note that only the governess sees the ghosts, and she tries to get others to see them without success – until the last moment when Miles, the boy, dies in her arms of sustained perturbation or perhaps even suffocation. The last paragraph, in its subtle ambiguity, which is an effect of James's language, needs to be quoted in its entirety, and I will return to it later:

> But he had already jerked straight round, stared, glared again, and seen but the quiet day. With the stroke of the loss I was so proud of he uttered the cry of a creature hurled over an abyss, and the grasp with which I recovered him might have been that of catching him in his fall. I caught him, yes, I held him – it may be imagined with what a passion; but at the end of a minute I began to feel what it truly was that I held. We were alone with the quiet day, and his little heart, dispossessed, had stopped.
>
> *(p. 85)*

The matter of seeing and non-seeing has also been taken up by adherents of the ghosts-are-real thesis. They stress, for instance, the fact that the governess, even before learning about the existence of Mr Quint (and, later, Ms Jessel), describes seeing a man who is identified from her description by Ms Grose as the dead butler. There are other similar indexes of the 'reality' of the ghosts, though all can be doubted if one attributes a certain kind of character to Ms Grose: a person who defers to authority and respects the status quo. This is also indicated by the narrative.

In his retort to "sly Freudian readers" of the story, Robert B. Heilman correctly notes that, in his letters about the story,

> James speaks continually of the ghosts as if they are objective manifestations, and there is no sign whatever of a knowing wink to the rationalists. He is concerned almost entirely with defining his technical problems and with observing, almost gaily, how satisfactorily they have been met.
>
> *(p. 178)*

Actually, it might be a good idea to return to this matter of "defining his technical problems" by looking at the 'Preface to the New York Edition' that James wrote, and which essentially contains all his positions on the novella. The sections on *The Turn of the Screw* were part of a larger preface that James provided to volume XII of *The Novels and Tales of Henry James*, published in 1908, exactly ten years after the publication of the novella under discussion.

Almost the first thing that James says about *The Turn of the Screw* is revealing: he describes it as "this perfectly independent and irresponsible little fiction" (p. 123). He moves on, very quickly, to talking about how the novella arose: a recapitulation that reminds the reader of the frame of the narrative. James notes that it started "one winter afternoon" as the kernel of a narrative told in response to the general sentiment that the real ghost stories "appeared all to have been told" and the "mere modern 'psychical' case" was not really capable of the old terror (p. 123). As his account proceeds, it is clear that James is solidly on the side of the 'Yes, the ghosts are real' contingent, despite the fact that most readers today do not associate with it. While he is fully aware that the governess's "explanation" of the events is a "different matter" than her "crystalline" account (p. 126), James has no doubt that he set out to write a real ghost story, not a psychological horror story. The nature of the 'ghosts' in the novella is left undefined, but their supernatural import is not contested by James: "Peter Quint and Miss Jessel are not 'ghosts' at all, as we now know the ghost, but goblins, elves, imps, demons as loosely constructed as those of the old trials for witchcraft" (p. 127).

It looks like the judge, in this case James, is against the general verdict of the readers' jury today: that the ghosts are not real or at least that the matter cannot be settled, that it is ambiguous. Of course, in these days of the death of the author and simplistic celebrations of the reader's response, we can dismiss the judge and insist on the democratic privilege of the jury's reading. But, actually, there is no need to go so far. Because, very soon, James writes something that, perhaps inadvertently, clears up not only this matter but the larger matter of what literature might or might not be and why the classics 'matter'.

James goes on to write that he wanted his supernatural agents – ghosts or imps or demons or whatever they might be – to contain not just "villainy of motive" and "evoke [...] predatory creatures", but also signify "the depths of the sinister" and "[p]ortentious evil" (p. 127). At the same time, he was aware – and suggests that this is the fault of many contemporary ghost stories – that the evil could not be "feebly or inanely suggested" (p. 127).

In short, James has put his finger on a major twofold problem: our conception of something so extreme and undefinable as 'absolute evil' is liable to vary from person to person, and language is not sufficient to suggest 'absolute evil'. Whatever we describe, as horror films (once you get over the technical shock effects) so aptly illustrate, is liable to fall short. Hence, James wisely finds a way out: "Only make the reader's general vision of evil intense enough [...] and his own experience, his own imagination, his own sympathy (with the children) and horror (of their false friends) will supply him quite sufficiently with all the particulars" (p. 128).

This works admirably in *The Turn of the Screw*. By avoiding "weak specifications" in the language of the text, James makes the reader "think the evil" (p. 128). This explains the difference between the 'yes', 'no' and 'maybe' contingent. Readers, of different types and in different ages, are likely to imagine their own kind of evil: what seems to be the evil of ghosts/ imps to James can end up – because James has not defined and narrated it in language – being the 'evil' of a repressed and manipulative governess. Our sympathy with the innocent children can lead us to blame not the 'ghosts' as their "false friends", but the governess and the uncle as their false friends. The only way James could have avoided this would have been by illustrating the evil, defining it in language – and that, as he wisely realizes, would have made the novella a much weaker work, even as a ghost story.

James, being the kind of writer he was, and even more the kind of reader of his own writing that he was, is talking in technical terms. He convincingly illustrates to us why and how *The Turn of the Screw* 'works' and inadvertently reveals why we are not likely to find real ghosts or imps or demons in it, regardless of what James intended. Since our conception of the nature of evil has shifted: more of us are liable to attribute it to natural causes, and even many of those who believe in the supernatural are unlikely to see the operation of supernatural evil untinged by the natural in our world. Even for many of the religious today, the Devil has his agents and the agent is more likely to be a human being, rather than a ghost or an imp.

But James does something else, and quite inadvertently. He illustrates the nature of literature; because, as I have been arguing for years now, literature is not just written in language about whatever might or might not exist outside language. Literature presupposes a certain understanding of language and its relationship to 'reality'. We know today that the signs of a language do not have a natural relationship to their referents and that, after Ferdinand Saussure at least, even signifiers and signifieds are artificially matched. Languages, in other words, are systems of differences, not natural and given emanations from 'reality'. In other words, language is not sufficient to talk about the world – and yet it is the only way we can talk about it. Not just talk, but think, because talking and thinking, language and reason, cannot be delinked.

We live with this knowledge, and yet almost all uses of language insist on its transparency. That is what language is supposed to do: communicate, with as little loss as possible. This is the assumption in medical literature, in legal works, in sociology, in university history, even in contemporary institutional philosophy (as contrasted to traditional philosophy, which, well into the 19th century, was a version of literature). Those aspects of language that retard communication are left out of the construction of discourse in these fields: hence, the focus on terms and the danger of jargon. This, as you can imagine, also infects literary criticism in modern times.

What happens then to those aspects of 'reality' that cannot be communicated, either because of historical circumstances or ontological ones? James's *The Turn of the Screw* provides evidence of both. 'Absolute evil', like the concept of God, is impossible to bottle in words; this is an ontological matter that evades language and will probably continue to do so as long as language exists. On the other hand, the difference between James's reading of the 'ghosts' in his text ('yes') and our tendency to read it ('no' or 'unde-cided') is, as illustrated above, a historical matter. We tend to think differently than James's generation often did: language says different things to us. This is where literature steps in. Literature implies a particular use of language, which is *not* premised on transparency. It is language used with the full awareness that language is both essential and not sufficient. Both these aspects play into the creation of literature, and hence the role of not just 'words' but also silences, paradoxes, noise, contradictions, etc. in literature. It is essential to note that literature is not necessarily 'ambiguous', though it might be. The inordinate stress on the ambiguity of literature might be more of a reflection of our own socio-political and hence moral state as largely middle class readers who, by definition, need to sit on the fence regarding many matters. It is evident, for instance, that James is not 'ambiguous' about his aims in *The Turn of the Screw*: he is writing about ghosts, imps, demons. There is no doubt in his mind, and none whatsoever even ten years after publishing the novel, when more or less 'Freudian' readings were already available.

What makes the text 'ambiguous' to many of us is the fact that James knows, as the great writer he is, that language will not suffice. He knows that he has to use language but allow space for silence, slippage, difference of imagination, etc. He knows that great evil slips the net of language and that different readers will imagine it differently. It is in negotiating this "technical" problem that he creates what we like to call 'ambiguity' at times. But the description is misleading, because there is finally nothing ambiguous about the novella: James has achieved exactly the end he sought to achieve. We close the novella burning with rage at a great wrong, an absolute evil: it is only that we attribute it either to ghosts or to the governess or to some combination of the two. And this happens because James knows what literature *qua* literature can do – and that what it can do arises from its distinctive usage of language and its awareness, occluded or bracketed in other fields, of the relationship between language and 'reality'.

Let us just look at that last paragraph again. Even right at the end, James knows that he cannot show the 'evil' or define it in any way. Hence, he concentrates on two elements: the scene itself and the governess's apprehension of the scene. The 'evil' is not even shown as appearing to the boy, because if a subjective matter like 'great evil' appears to any two people simultaneously, it turns objective: it is reduced to and trapped in language. Hence, the violent struggle depicted. The boy, held tightly by the governess, "jerks", turns, glares, cries out, collapses ("falls"), etc. The governess is not depicted as unconsciously suffocating the boy – we know that nothing was further from James's intention, as expressed even ten years later. However, the same factors can allow us to consider it a possibility, because we notice not just that the boy is physically overwhelmed by the governess but also note the governess's "grasp", "catch", "hold", "passion", all of it leading to the fatal gap during which the governess is looking for something else and the boy might well have been gasping for something quite different (p. 85).

In conclusion, reading James's novella as above, one can say that, actually, there is no real justification for literature, unless it is read as literature. In that sense, literature is not so different from other fields: who justifies reading a medical treatise as history, or a history book as philosophy? Literature, unfortunately, tends to be read as everything but literature. There are good reasons for it: we are still fighting against the tyranny of 'taste' that had once read literature, no, not as literature, despite the claims, but as accomplishment, culture, refinement, tradition, etc. In the process of snatching literature away from such refined hands and thrusting it back into the grimy world – the world not just of taste but also of poverty, money, violence, change, history, ideas, domesticity, women, minorities, slaves, conflict, workers, etc. – we have often stopped reading literature *qua* literature.

This needs to be countered. Because, finally, returning to literature as literature might not just be the best way to appreciate 'classics', even by dead white males, but also to break the predefined, language-bound stranglehold of the 'market' or the 'nation' or the 'people' on ideas. This is necessary to return literature to what it always was and what it still is at its best: a distinctive way to think.

References

James, Henry, *The Turn of the Screw, Second Norton Critical Edition*, Deborah Esch and Jonathan Warren (Eds.), W. W. Norton and Company, New York, 1966 (1999).

15

MARGINALIZATION AND DISPOSSESSION IN THE KASHMIRI NOVEL

A Look at Mirza Waheed's *The Collaborator*

Meenakshi Bharat

Kashmiris are one of world's most 'muted, marginalized, misrepresented' people. How then can we be surprised that sermons on participation and development mean nothing to a generation born and raised in a garrison state, who have all their lives known only the end of a barrel?

Shama Naqushbandi[1]

For Kashmiris, the concept of marginalization has deep, confoundingly complicated reverberations. Relentlessly sidelined in all spheres, the aggravated torment of insistent exclusion from the broader 'Indian' identity in a decidedly troubled political scenario has engendered a perpetual and compelling sense of being exiled from their own country. Weighed down by an ineradicable sense of insecurity imposed by circumstances beyond their control, Kashmiri youth find themselves caught in a limbo, tortured simultaneously by a burning desire to do something to alleviate the situation and a despondent recognition of the fragility of the effort. In the highly fraught political scenario which has had a lasting impact on the culture of the state, sidelined, marginalized and pushed to the corner, Kashmiri youth, whether Muslim or Hindu, are no longer in a mood to accept authority unquestioningly. Contemporary Kashmiri writing in English has taken on the difficult task of representing and interrogating the pressures and uncertainties of living in this beleaguered space; of digging deep into the recesses of the tortured Kashmiri soul chafing at the uncongenial environment.

It is one of history's ironies that an entire populace has been relegated to disputed margins in their own land, in the land of their forefathers, by their own people with whom they share a national affiliation and an overarching

DOI: 10.4324/9781003399926-21

national history. This is the utterly untenable situation in which Kashmiris have found themselves ever since the initial unthinking, insensitive, controversial partition of the Indian subcontinent. Time has buffeted them, ousted them out of their own land to other parts of the nation, even the globe. They have been trundled into situations, the result of which is a succession of displacements.

As the bone of contention between uneasy neighbours, India and Pakistan, the idyllic border state of Kashmir has become fertile, even if negatively generated, creative space. Islamic fundamentalism and state reprisals have set in motion an unprecedented 'dispossession' by coercive physical displacement that has skewered power equations in the state time and again. This simultaneous marginalization and displacement has been especially noted by Kashmiri writers in the various indigenous languages but has only lately been declared to the wider world through comparatively recent writing in English. Recognizing the invisibilizing silence that threatens to annihilate Kashmiri identity, internationally renowned fictional and non-fictional texts like Basharat Peer's *The Curfewed Night* (2010) and Mirza Waheed's *The Collaborator* (2011), Siddhartha Gigoo's *The Garden of Solitude* and Rahul Pandita's *Our Moon Has Blood Clots* (2013) sensitively take on this feeling of loss and dispossession under which the common Kashmiri is reeling. Labelling Kashmir as a 'conflict zone,' Basharat Peer's impulse to writing was 'the absence of our own telling.' He bemoaned the fact that while 'people from almost every conflict zone had told their stories,' the books about the embattled Kashmiri existence were 'unwritten'[2] (*Curfewed Night*, Basharat Peer). Consequently, the literature from this area represents the malaise resulting from this marginalization, with the writer trying to wrest authority for the Kashmiri identity through his word, combatively and profoundly engaging with the explosive situation.

Kashmiri fiction contests the expectation of the dominant political imagination that Kashmiris ought to remain passive and penetrable in the peripheries. Any effort to seize authority for the embattled self is seen as a threat to the 'centre.' It demands immediate and necessary quashing and containment with the unspoken but obviously intended result of petrifying an imaginary in which subalterns will never be able to speak. Kashmiri writing in English committedly confronts these concerted efforts of the suppression and silencing of Kashmiris by doggedly engaging with the resultant dispossession and marginalization of the people of the Valley.

Geographically and politically, the ideas of dispossession and peripheralization imply a clearly marked space which can be claimed as one's 'own,' but which is, unfortunately, also one over which one is denied control. This is particularly pertinent in the case of Kashmir because the idea that the border, to use Navtej Purewal's words, 'territorializes and nationalizes local populations and identities' and which is employed as 'a site for the construction of a dominant national consciousness' (Purewal 2003: 547) completely collapses. Instead of plainly signifying the beginning and end of nation-states, as borders normally do, the border between India and Pakistan in Kashmir suffers from a precarious lack of clarity and certainty. The peculiar circumstances of Kashmir imbue the notion of borders and claim to borderlands with a tenuous and contentious piquancy. Despite mapped borders, the denizens of these spaces are in no position to assert their rights over them and consequently are not entitled to the national identity-instilling attributes of normal borders. On the contrary, and rather ironically, the demarcating lines emphasize the gnawing sense of dispossession that shadows the native Kashmiri. With both India and Pakistan claiming the territory for themselves, the Kashmiri claim takes a backseat. In fact the discomfiting overlay of borders, of borders within borders, of a truncated area called Pakistan-Occupied-Kashmir within the greater Kashmir further exacerbates the problem. In this context, to which nation does the ordinary Kashmiri align himself to and to which land lay claim?

The ongoing, constantly asimmer turmoil of conflicting claims of identity within border-bound territory allows Kashmiris neither an easy, clear-cut allegiance to either nation-state nor a sense of entitlement to either space or identity. This problematic location at the heart of discordant, dividing national pulls, leaves them with an overpowering sense of loss: despite occupying 'Indian' space, despite therefore being theoretically able to lay overt claims on 'Indian' nationality, their emotional inclination towards Pakistan does not allow them to lay claims to a sure, ascribable identity. Torn between acrimonious and contesting allegiances, the border becomes blurred and the resultant toxic, corrosive sense of liminality, emotionally sapping and disruptive. Every time Kashmiris lean towards one or the other side, they lose out on the certainty of cultural belonging to the other side. Every time, Kashmiris stake their alignment with one or the other side, they find themselves thrown back into a liminal zone of marginalization. Concerted hegemonizing tactics by both centres mark Kashmiris as occupying a peripheral space which is yet outside the 'mainland.' To use the Gibson-Graham model of the 'hegemony of the hegemonic formation,' it, as if the act of preserving the centre/peripheries binary and the effort to liberate and grant subjectivities to the 'peripheral' Kashmiris, actually ends up robbing them of the chance of staking a straightforward alliance with one or country.

It is the hope that 'crossing over' will sort out all their problems and give their claims to a distinct Kashmiri identity some solidity that prompts Kashmiris to repudiate one national affiliation in favour of another. Marginalized from any fruits accruing to citizenship, they are unable to claim national allegiance to the Indian state: Kashmiris may live on 'Indian' space and may therefore be officially named as 'Indian' nationals, even as they harbour deep emotional sympathies for Pakistan.

Historically, the sense of divided allegiance which had its seeds in the partition of the subcontinent and the creation of Pakistan continued to fester till it came to a head in the turbulent developments of the 1990s. Discontentment with the step-motherly treatment meted out to the contested region of Kashmir and to Kashmiris lay at the core of the turbulence and political turmoil in the state. This peaking of political and social unrest in the stormy, last decade of the twentieth century saw young unhappy Kashmiri youth thronging into Pakistan-Occupied Kashmir (POK), to train in terrorist outfits under the misguided notion that they were fighting for Kashmiri sovereignty and thus to gain legitimate control over their land and to wrest a meaningful independent identity for themselves.

Fleeing from what, to them, were the draconian marginalizing and displacing tactics of the Indian state, Pakistan now came to be seen as a benevolent and safe haven by the troubled Kashmiris. Yet paradoxically, far from instilling a new, substitutive sense of national affiliation to Pakistan, it actually marked the awakening of the Kashmiri populace to the reality of a distinct 'Kashmiri' identity, emerging from the recognition of belonging to a particular land, the space of Kashmir. This was the time that the campaign for an independent Kashmir began, and the operative slogan *'hum kya chahte, azadi'* (What do we want? Freedom!) went on to become a veritable anthem for the separatist movement in the region. This had the effect of completely submerging any notion of alliance with either India or Pakistan, the sense of *being Kashmiri* now coming to far outweigh any sense of belonging to any nation.

It is this growing malaise and anger at the coercively imposed marginalization and dispossession of power and control in the 1990s that the writing in English from Kashmir covers. Up until the first decade of the new millennium, the physical displacement forced by Islamic fundamentalism and state reprisals had been an aspect of Kashmiri cultural and political identity that had largely remained at the level of ground reality of messy and unequal power equations. But the peaking of the hurt exacerbated by violent political underpinnings made the Kashmiri youth sit up to take cognizance and react. Young Kashmiri scribe and analyst, Basharat Peer too woke up to the gaps in the recording and telling of the plight of Kashmiris and sought to recover Kashmiri space and identity by putting his ability with the written word to use, deploying it to represent the malaise that had resulted from this apprehension of marginalization and dispossession. As participant-commentators, young Kashmiris like Peer and Mirza Waheed, reacting sensitively to the plight of the common Kashmiris, gave renewed bite to Adorno's tortured conclusion that '[P]erennial suffering has as much right to expression as a tortured man has to scream' (Adorno, *Negative Dialectics*, 362–363) in their internationally celebrated texts *The Curfewed Night* (2010) and *The Collaborator* (2011), respectively. Kashmiri youth growing up in these terrifying times were compelled in large numbers to opt for crossing over the physical border by this growing marginalization and forced displacement and dispossession. Others, seared by the intensity of the experience, traversed the metaphoric margins between silence and articulation by taking up their pens. More and more young writers in English took it upon themselves to give visibility to their troubling truth in narratives that memorialized this decade of unrest, insurgency and turmoil, all implied in this apprehension of displacement and exile. The simmering dissent in most Kashmiri writing of this period feeds on the powerful play of these themes, all building up to a complex dynamic that marks all post-terrorist writing.

Concertedly, Kashmiri writers focus on events that are peculiarly local and particular to Kashmir, their 1990s novels, all questioning and weighing the ideas of nation and nationality, of owning and no-longer-owning, whether from the perspective of government agencies or terrorist forces. With the breakdown of the normal, accepted developmental trajectory of history, Kashmiri fiction in English comes as a definite disruption, each successive novel marking a deepening focus and amplification of the issues and the hurt involved in the growing alienation. The literature from Kashmir becomes a narrative enactment of the ruination of the notions of fraternity and the loss of fellowship. It seeks to uncover the hollowness of the mainstream political endorsement of cultural differences within the subcontinent. It is ironic that the erosion of identity and loss of control over Kashmiri space and polity brings home the niggling apprehension of sameness, of identity, as Kashmiris. The Kashmiri-English novel seeks to make sense of these complex and harrowing contraries in the recent historical events that have shaped the region.

Mirza Waheed's *The Collaborator*, the eponymous protagonist of *The Collaborator* (2011), battles with just this disconcerting sense of alienation and loss. One of the most sensitive novels written on the unrest in Kashmir, Waheed's novel comes as a first-person narrative from the mouth of a 19-year-old, who has grown up in these grim conflict-ridden times in the ravaged paradise. Unceremoniously being divested of all that he holds dear as a Kashmiri, he is forced to look hard at the physical movement of locals constantly taking place in the state: travel across the border from one space to another, from Indian Kashmir to POK and further thence to Pakistan. Gnawed by the feeling of torn loyalties, he has to face the accompanying realities that mar his teen years: lost friends, unrealized love and a total breakdown of the community.

This divestiture of a loved scene, a cherished space fuels the desire to do something about it and the youth, driven into a cul de sac, seems to think that the only solution lies in fighting for it. Thus it is that *The Collaborator* follows Kashmiri youth (sometimes with families) to the border, and we see them disappear across to unknown and unspecified terror training camps.

It is not surprising that the dividing border, a veritable trope for the division of the soul and the denudation of a wholesome sense of self, also becomes symptomatic of the awareness of marginalization and dispossession that has pushed them across the line. The border simultaneously seems to dangle the dream of re-possession and re-authorization of control even as it carries on shattering them:

> There was this time, not too long ago, just two or three years ago, when everyone wanted to go *sarhad paar,* to cross over and become a famous freedom fighter. Hordes and hordes went in the early days, everyone wanted to return and be a commander, a masked legend in their own right, a liberator of the Kashmiri people.
>
> *(17)*

The realization is soon forced upon him that the dream of attaining either 'heroism or martyrdom' (17) will never be realized. Souring even before it can be fully dreamt, the dream has the ultimate effect of depressing him with the persistent dread that all is lost. He is sometimes even pushed to the brink to contemplate suicide, to take a 'nice plunge' (19) into the stream, his 'personal Hades' (19), that runs through his ill-fated land.

Traumatized by a sense of betrayal, young Kashmiris move across into POK, spurred by the possibility of a better life and a restitution of all that has been lost, and a desire to right the ills that have overtaken their beloved land. Thus, it is that the novel essays a serious negotiation of the issue of stolen and lost rights of the sidelined community of poor, powerless villagers of the borderlands of India and Pakistan in Kashmir, by unsympathetic politically powerful people who can direct and regulate the fate of the borders and its people. Men like the Juggernaut Governor and the army officer, Kadian, are in complete directional control over the lives of the common Kashmiris, including those of the Collaborator and his family. This move away and across the border sees homes being transformed into ghost habitations in ghost villages. In the course of this displacement, everyone—the ones that leave, as well as the ones that stay behind 'in desertion, in abandonment' (11)—is assailed by an unnerving, overwhelming sense of loss.

Thus, if life is difficult for the ones who go away, it is even more fraught for the unnamed collaborator, the one young man who has not joined them. This teen narrator-protagonist is forced into an untenable region of in-betweenness, of being neither emotionally aligned with the Indian army nor ideologically allied with the militants; of neither owning a clear-cut identity—admirably indicated by his 'namelessness'—nor having the gumption or the freedom to make a definite effort to take control. Yet, even though he is pushed to a corner and forced to become a collaborator with the army, in choosing to become a witness to the events in the valley and to give them word, he critiques it from the inside. Paradoxically, this insider location represents an oblique staking of claim. Pressurized into 'picking stuff off dead people' (8) by the 'pig of a captain' from India, the Collaborator, by becoming a dramatic embodiment of the Kashmiri love–hate relationship with both India and Pakistan and of the accompanying lack of any definitive sense of belonging to any nation-state, ironically names and claims Kashmir as his only emotional homeland. Embracing and otherizing both the Indian and the Pakistani in the same breath, and with thus invoking the ideas of 'nation' and 'nationality' problematically, the Collaborator and all Kashmiris are left with an overpowering sense of loss and marginalization, of displacement and exile in their own land.

Clearly, as the Collaborator shows by his example, they do not have to physically step over the border to experience this alienation; they do not have to be distanced from the land to feel the loss. The literalization of the border and borderlands as danger zones of violent death in *The Collaborator* makes 'being alive' a continuing painful confrontation with their reality of peripheralized existence. The ongoing tussle for territorial control, coming hand in hand with the large-scale abuse of human rights and principles, by both displacing and alienating the Kashmiri populace, transforms the paradise into a living hell. This becomes the central trope of the novel. The only land that is open for uncontested claim is the 'corpse-land' border, both a physical reality and a symbolic space, a last degrading haven for youth who are denied any respect in death, their cadavers subjected to brutal pillage and stripping by the state apparatus through their collaborators.

In this scenario of dispossession and exclusion, the novel thus pitches this no-man's land as both symbolic of the Collaborator's situation and a trope for the situation of Kashmir itself. Overrun by death, stench and hovering carrion birds, this sombre, unhappy space is not very different from the death that pervades the land. Visually marked in the novel by a narrow valley with a stream flowing through it, it is a 'corpse-field' of dead 'terrorists' apparently killed in the course of their subversive operations. Aggression and transgression from within throw up this liminal space as representative of the death of all that is meaningful to Kashmiris, alienating the Kashmiri/the Collaborator, completely pre-empting any sense of belonging and weighing down on them with a permanent sense of exile.

More and more, Kashmiri youth are realizing that neither India nor Pakistan has Kashmiri interests at heart. Consequently, it is more a feeling of hate for both the countries and their representatives and a powerful sense of belonging to Kashmir which forces the youth to move across the border to train for the fight for Kashmiri *azadi*. Even as he 'collaborates,' the Collaborator is inwardly seething with anger at the army man who has conscripted him. He wants him:

to come and inspect his crops, his harvest of human remains, I so want him to come and see the putrid trench he's turned *my valley* into.

(my italics, 13)

A deep unsettling sorrow overtakes the Collaborator when he recognizes how he has been denied ownership and the chance of doing something for his beloved Kashmiris. This has the direct effect of paralyzing him both physically and emotionally: he wants to 'cross over into Pakistan' (68) but he can't. Instead, he goes on to become a collaborator! Traumatized by the sight of his beautiful paradise converted into 'corpse-land' in which 'they have fake-encountered some poor boys in some far-flung areas' and dragged the bodies and mutilated their faces, makes 'him cry ... want to run away, to disappear' (16). He dithers; he seesaws. He decides to kill Kadian; he can't. Buffeted around by the middle-class representatives of the state, the border-land residents are exiled from meaning, forced to flounder in their efforts to keep a foothold in the land to which they belong. The sense of lost-ness is textually amplified by the determined naming of villages, towns and people. By furnishing historical and geographical specifics, the exclusion from these is given a pointed reality. Waheed thus particularizes the unfortunate hap-penings in Kashmir by listing names of people and places in conjunction with the crimes committed by the ones in power: *Rouf Qadri* of *Sopore* is sodomized; *the widows* of *Poshpur* are raped; *the women* of *Shopian* are both raped and murdered; and *Gowkadal* is linked with the massacre of *innocents*. In this thus very identifiable edifice of a war-torn state, the vocab-ulary associated with militancy proliferates. The centre imposes curfews and declares and conducts crackdowns. The Kashmiris, on the other hand, talk of martyrdom, sacrifice, freedom, war, tyrants—of *shaheed, azadi, jung* and *zalim*—of 'laying down their lives for Kashmir' (163) a land that is now peopled with curfew mothers, curfew women and jihadis.

Turning the stream of consciousness technique to advantage, Waheed accesses the keen, impassioned interiority of the Collaborator's wracked soul. His lyrical evocation of a despoiled paradise is backed by the in-text factual pile-up of atrocities perpetrated by the Indian army, by the politi-cians from both the sides and by the militant groups, to give specific bite to the loss of home and hearth. He concludes with his narrator that the only ones losing out are the Kashmiris and that Kashmir is 'a compromised state' and its representative, the Collaborator, a compromised citizen of Kashmir (188). The Kashmiri novel represents one attempt of the Kashmiri people to negotiate and overcome the feeling of being compromised and displaced that assails those living in these borderland spaces through the particular Kashmiri perspective.

Even as the movement, forced or preferred, leads to exile from Kashmir, from home, even the ones, like the *Collaborator*, who remain behind are irretrievably assaulted by a matching feeling of loss. Abandoned by his friends, he is left with an overpowering sense of being exiled, of being dispossessed, even though he has not moved physically at all. Without the alleviating presence of the people he loves, the people with whom he had shared a history and identity, his Kashmir no longer seems like home. It is now peopled and controlled by those who have little or no sympathy with the Kashmiri situation, textually represented by tyrannical rulers like the demolition Governor and Captain Kadian, all of whom resort to physical force and the rule of the gun.

The Kashmiri novels thus become sophisticated reflections on the issue of exclusion from a proud and comforting national identity. They offer nuanced presentations of the difficulties of inhabiting border zones, attempting a sensitive portrayal of the traumas of familial separation, of political and cultural marginalization caused by the imposition of borders. In a space of messy or absent values, principles are tested through the decisions and actions of the power players in the region as *The Collaborator* shows:

> You know, sometimes I wonder—for Kashmir there is always an Indian and a Pakistani version of everything—what if they have their own pasture of dead boys on the other side of the border? Their own stash of the infiltration residue? Young men who lost their lives while learning to walk the perilous path to freedom. Treachery is a word everyone should learn.
>
> *(15)*

Thus the significant amount of Kashmiri writing with concerted focus on the circumstances of the tense spaces of Kashmir seems to play out Navtej Purewal's suggestion that borderlands can become sites of creative cultural production. With cross-border movement bringing displacement and intimations of exile in its wake in the Kashmir borderland, a key development in the history of the beleaguered land is the rise of resistant creative intervention. Novels like Waheed's *The Collaborator* represent and engage with the dispossession implied by the drawing of the Indo-Pak border (Purewal 2003: 541). The literature from Kashmir emerges as a painstaking and poetic construction that not only mirrors the sense of displacement and exile that threatens to overpower and annihilate the common Kashmiri but appropriates this location in marginality to wage a considered war against its imposition by oppressive structures from the outside. If, as Noam Chomsky avers, 'As long as people are marginalized and distracted [they] have no way to organize or articulate their sentiments,' then the Kashmiri novel in English becomes a first rare and open enunciation of the organized resistance to the consistent marginalization and dispossession of the Kashmiri people.[3]

It is one of the greatest ironies that while the geographical and political entity of the state of Jammu and Kashmir is seen as being essential to the identity, integrity and pride of the nation, the people who populate it are, for the most part, disregarded. In fact, the recent history of the land and the people is not a grand one. It is, rather, a deeply conflicted history of marginalized people, the 'neglected people'[4] that Kashmiri journalist Pervaiz Bukhari bemoans. These novels, in recognizing this imposed subalterneity, this sidelining and pain of the Kashmiris, become an important acknowledgement of a distinctive identity. In fact, in facilitating the surfacing of the suppressed narrative of the state and its people, these fictional tales become identity-imbuing. In a state where journalists and politicians have been wilfully and combatively 'muzzling and misinterpreting'[5] the people, the creative writer becomes one of the few who can be trusted to paint the truth, to really feel with the people, and to give them voice. The creative writer, who had till recently skirted participation in the Kashmiri struggle, now realizes that his word could be a first effort at representing, and so of making, some sense of their muddled and chaotic reality. Where both media and government are conspiring 'to deny any legitimacy to protests in Kashmir,'[6] these novels submit themselves as the only proxy protests that are managing to see the light of day, to reach the public—however limited the reach may be. 'Life under political oppression,' to use Pankaj Mishra's insightful and prophetic utterance, 'has begun to yield, in the slow bitter way it does, a rich and artistic harvest ... There are more works to come.'[7]

Notes

1 Shama Naqushabadi, "Kashmiris Are One Of World's Most 'Muted, Marginalized, Misrepresented' People", *Counterview, Current Affairs* at https://www.counterview.net/2019/09/kashmiris-are-one-of-worlds-most-muted.html.

2 Basharat Peer, *Curfewed Night*, HarperCollins, New Delhi, 2010, p. 95.

3 Noam Chomsky, *Media Control: The Spectacular Achievements of Propaganda*, An Open Media Book, 1991, this edition 2002, p. 32 at https://chomsky.info/mediacontrol03/ (Accessed 30 Oct 2020).

4 Pervaiz Bukhari, "Politics and Nation: Kashmir's Young, Educated, Angry and Politically Aware", *The Economic Times*, 9 August, 2010, p. 2 at http://m.economictimes.com/news/politics/nation/kashmirs-young-educated- angry-and-politically-aware/articleshow/msid-6277584,curpg-2.cms (Accessed 25 June 2013).

5 Ibid.

6 Pankaj Mishra, "Introduction", in Tariq Ali, Hilal Bhatt, et al., *Kashmir: The Case for Freedom*, Verso, London, 2011, p. 5.

7 Ibid., p. 6.

References

Adorno, Theodor Wiesengrund, *Negative Dialectics* (Translated by E. B. Ashton), Continuum, New York, 1973.

Chomsky, Noam (this ed. 2002), *Media Control: The Spectacular Achievements of Propaganda*, An Open Media Book, 1991.

Gibson-Graham, J. K., 'Identity and Economic Plurality: Rethinking Capitalism and "Capitalist Hegemony"', *Environment and Planning D: Society and Space*, 13 (3), 1995, Sage Journals, pp. 275–282 at https://doi.org/10.1068/d130275. Accessed 9 July 2020.

Peer, Basharat, *Curfewed Night*, HarperCollins, New Delhi, 2010.

Purewal, Navtej, 'The Indo-Pak Border: Displacements, Aggressions and Transgressions', *Contemporary South Asia*, 12 (4), 2003, pp. 539–556.

Shama, Naqushabadi, 'Kashmiris Are One of World's Most "Muted, Marginalized, Misrepresented" People', *Counterview, Current Affairs* at https://www.counterview.net/2019/09/kashmiris-are-one-of-worlds-most-muted.html. Accessed 9 July 2020.

Waheed, Mirza, *The Collaborator*, Viking, London, 2011.

16

CALLING LOCAL/TALKING GLOBAL

The Cosmopolitics of the Call-Centre Industry

Jisha Menon[1]

This chapter considers dramatic performances of cosmopolitan encounters within the transnational framework of the call-centre industry in India. Have the virtual intimacies generated by new media and market technologies ushered in a cosmopolitan connectivity? What utopic gestures do we glimpse from portrayals of cross-cultural contact in the age of the copy? The four works that I consider dramatize cosmopolitan encounters between differently situated consumers and labourers. More specifically, I consider *Alladeen*, a collaborative venture by Builders Association and MotiRoti; *Call Cutta in a Box*, produced by Berlin-based Rimini Protokoll; *John and Jane*, an experimental documentary by Mumbai-based Ashim Ahluwalia; and *Dancing on Glass*, written by Bangalore playwright Ram Ganesh Kamatham. These works are not only produced through global artistic and financial alliances, they also take as their subject transnational circuits of production and consumption, labour, and leisure. By considering the intersection of consumer fantasy, global capital, and the neoliberal state, this chapter tracks the affinities between economic globalization and cultural cosmopolitanism.

Discourses of cosmopolitanism evoke ways of being and acting beyond the local, of having affective attachments in multiple spaces beyond the boundaries of the resident nation-state. Indeed the call-centre agents and the actors who portray them inhabit multiple places simultaneously and have imaginary investments in places that transcend and transgress their immediate environs. By invoking cosmopolitanism here, however, I consider its deep entrenchment within circuits of capital. Craig Calhoun reminds us that cosmopolitanism – though not necessarily cosmopolitan democracy – is

DOI: 10.4324/9781003399926-22

now largely the project of capitalism. Indeed as Craig Calhoun warns, cosmopolitanism "runs the risk of substituting ethics for politics" (2003, 107).

Moving beyond the binaries of virtuality and materiality, which dominate critiques of technology and mediascapes in late-modern capitalism, this chapter focuses on the material and social life of virtuality. The lives of the call-centre workers exemplify the ways in which disjunctures between fantasy and lived experience, discourse and embodiment, are negotiated, contested, and inhabited through impersonation. In considering impersonation I am specifically interested in the social, cultural, and political implications of impersonation within the context of intercultural and racialized economies of empire and power. The rich body of work in the context of colonial encounters by intellectuals such as Franz Fanon (2008), Roberto Retamar (1989), Homi Bhabha (1991), V. S. Naipaul (2002), and Derek Walcott (1980), among others has enabled us to consider the multivalent associations of mimicry in the production of a (gendered, elite) colonial subjectivity as violated authenticity, as weapon of resistance, as a register for the ambivalence of colonial discourse, as an index of nothingness, as a defiant act of imagination. The historical context of the multiple valences of mimicry is important to bear in mind while considering the ways in which neoliberal regimes of global capital harness this "flexibility" to facilitate multinational corporate agendas.

The political economy of colonial education in India offers an important point of entry to this particular genealogy of impersonation in India. Lord Macaulay's famous 1835 "Minute on Indian education" advocated English as the medium of instruction in colonial India for the specific purpose of constituting a class of English-speaking Indians, the "bilingual natives," or cultural intermediaries, who would facilitate the smooth functioning of empire within India (Macaulay [1835] 2000). This geopolitical history reminds us that mimicry has long been deployed, to repressive and subversive effects, to negotiate the psychic neurosis and disjunctural doubleness of colonial and postcolonial subjectivities.

The call-centre employees, the bilingual natives, are in many ways Macaulay's offspring, the products of English education in India. The large English-speaking population made India an attractive location to outsource low-end information technology functions in the early 1990s. The shift to digitization produced new regimes of labour that provided a range of services in the areas of data management and processing, mortgage, credit bureau, travel and hospitality, healthcare, and management, among others. The transmittance of large quantities of data across territorial boundaries ensures new modes of "labour arbitrage," a form of cost-cutting where a company outsources labour and pays one labour pool in a different geography less than it would another labour pool in its own country for accomplishing the same work.[2] The salaries for the call-centre employees are dramatically lower in India. For example, if an employee in the US is paid an annual income of $22,000–$32,000 (an hourly wage between $10 and $15/hour), his/her counterpart in India will make roughly $5,000 per year (about $2/hour). This considerable difference in salary, adjusted against the "fully loaded cost" to company per employee, creates net savings for the company in the range of 60%–70% per employee, providing the impetus for outsourcing.[3]

What are the material ways in which global capital enters into, disrupts, and rearranges a complex terrain of cultural, social, political practices? After all, even the "cyber coolies," as they are disparagingly referred to, are located somewhere, must negotiate traffic, readjust their body clocks to serve customers halfway across the globe, and contend with the unrelenting tedium of their jobs. (They take roughly 500–700 calls a night.) To begin with, then, let us travel to a call centre in Bangalore, a postcolonial city that retains the undisputed status of the outsourcing capital of the world.[4]

Material City

Driving down to Whitefield, the IT hub located on the outskirts of Bangalore in Southern India, to visit and interview employees at a leading call-centre firm was challenging: the bustling thoroughfare was crammed with cars, autorickshaws, buses, motorcycles, and cycles. Flanked on either side by tons of businesses, glitzy malls, small shops, and Internet cafes all crowded together, the streets of Whitefield catered to a conspicuously consuming middle class. Sprawling campuses called "IT parks" housed leading technology companies such as Microsoft, SAP, and Accenture.

If the glass-and-chrome buildings in Whitefield left me wondering whether I was in Silicon Valley, Singapore, or Bangalore, the rupture with "the real" was heightened when I entered the "hyper-real" world of the call-centre industry.[5] After waiting at the security desk and wearing a badge that identified me, I was escorted upstairs to visit the executives, the voice and diction trainers, and finally the call-centre employees, who were seated in rows, with headsets on, a flickering computer screen in front, and a telephone beside them. One of the executives invited me to pick up the telephone and listen in on the conversations. The "agents," as call-centre employees are called, conducted surveys with British customers on the other side of the telephone. Their greatest challenge was to ensure that customers stayed on the line. This was confirmed by a telephone exchange I witnessed: a young, urbane man conversed in a clipped British accent with a British woman across the line, who abruptly hung up on him. While he was probably familiar with such a scenario, the agent, somewhat embarrassed, expressed surprise. Although aware of my presence, he did not meet my gaze.

When I asked the Chief Operations Officer and the trainers what they thought about the practice of impersonation in call-centre industries, they were quick to point out that impersonation was getting more attention in the media than warranted. Some of these representations border on caricature, they argued. But despite the rhetoric, the trainer I spoke with offered six- to eight-week training programmes that included "accent neutralization," and voice and diction, as well as information on American sports and weather, and political and popular cultural scenarios. This, he tried to convince me, was not to perpetrate any deceptions on the American public but rather to facilitate smooth "small talk" between Indian employees and their American customers.

Many of the agents I spoke to referred to their jobs as interim positions before they moved on to something better, more lucrative, more permanent. While the pay was good, there was little potential for career growth, they claimed. Some insisted that it was the glamour of the call centres that drew them. In the words of one employee: "You're talking with a complete stranger from a part of the world you've only seen in movies. There's a sense of connection."[6] Another employee remarked: "Our call centre does work for really big global brands, we get a feel of what it's like to be working abroad by working for a big, multinational firm."[7] While some employees romanticize telephone conversations as a mode of travel, others evinced more pragmatic concerns. "I'm much more worried about how I will get home at night than if someone in the States believes I am from Texas or not," said one employee, while for another: "What I mostly think about is how I don't have a social life any more, how I can't hang out with friends because we work from 4 pm to 3 am … and of course I really miss my sleep."[8] In addition, customers' racist invective, when the agents' faltering American accent aroused suspicions, unnerved many call-centre employees, who were eager to move to a less abusive work situation.[9]

These divergent and contradictory responses not only heterogenize otherwise simplistic and uniform representations of the call-centre youth as enamoured of the West, but they also signal the lure and limits of consumer fantasies in the fashioning of emergent citizen consumers in urban India. More importantly, these variable perceptions of the call-centre industry remind us that cosmopolitan encounters register not only intercultural differences but also intracultural differences of class, gender, and regional diversity, destabilized by rapidly shifting techno-finance-media-scapes of urban India.

How do dramatic performances mine the call-centre industry to imaginatively work out ethical quandaries within late capitalism? How, in this moment of neoliberal globalization, do we imagine the lives of others? This is not only a question that propels the cosmopolitan imaginations of call-centre employees, who aspire to an "unbound seriality" of entrepreneurial youth, but also that of international artists who use performance to critically frame corporate practices of impersonation and in the process delve into the call-centre industry as a repository of data about "the other."[10]

Alladeen and "Global Souls"

I watched the Obie-winning production of *Alladeen* at the REDCAT (Roy and Edna Disney/Cal Arts Theatre) in Los Angeles in March 2004. The artistic collaboration between the UK-based multicultural performance group, MotiRoti, and New York-based experimental company, Builders Association, produced a mesmerizing experimental work that takes up questions of virtual identities and transnational impersonation within the call-centre industry.

Alladeen juxtaposes electronic music, innovative video imagery, and live performance to explore postmodern travellers' tales. Built in two dimensions, the set straddles a wide screen that rises to reveal the sterile and hyper-efficient interior of the call centre. Various images are projected on the back wall that merge into each other, carpets morph into highways, and abstract Islamic art morphs into images of American popular culture, thus reiterating the power of transformations evoked in the title of the play. The performance dramatizes through sound, spectacle, video, and new media the crisscrossing of global flows between various metropoles located in the global North and South. In the words on MotiRoti's official website: "*Alladeen* explores how we function as 'global souls' caught up in circuits of technology, and how our voices and images travel from one culture to another." It is this notion of disembodied "global souls" that I want to draw attention to here.

The collaborative "triptych" production of *Alladeen* enacts a tale of three cities, triangulated between the urban centres of New York, London, and Bangalore that are not only the key sites of transaction in a global outsourcing industry but also provide the source material for the transnational production of the performance. Displaying the tenacious relationship between capital and empire, this triangulation exposes American corporate hegemony as both continuity and rupture of British imperial history in India. The spectre of British imperial history lends it a sense of historical depth by reminding us that, despite the presentist rhetorics, globalization partakes in a much deeper history of transnational capital and empire.

The production insists upon using the Arabic pronunciation, Alladeen, instead of Aladdin, in order to de-Orientalize and re-appropriate the medieval Arabic folk character. Its critical mimesis of Orientalism with its evocations of flying carpets and genies offers the backdrop for flexible Aladdinian transformations. The scenic design reinforces the phantasmatic transformations: images from Hollywood and Bollywood movies alternate; blue globes turn in the workspace, green lamps float through black space. In addition, the screen projections of maps, video footage of "real" call-centre employees from Bangalore, images of the sitcom series *Friends* meld and morph into each other.

The pedagogical training and work sessions of the call-centre employees in Bangalore are at the heart of this play. The didactic indoctrination is juxtaposed with clips from a video called, "How to neuter the mother tongue." The segment illustrates the ways in which multiple media of instruction, from classroom teaching to American sitcoms, *mediate* the subjects of the call-centre industry. Language training within call-centre agencies focuses not only on re-training speech patterns that require dropping Indian regional inflections but also on acquiring facility and ease with spoken "global English."

Alladeen's focus on "accent neutralization" within call-centre industries raises the questions: in order for capital to be flexible does it need to neutralize culture? Does culture get in the way of capital? What is the culture of capital? The "global English" that renders agents placeless is a variant of metropolitan American English without regional markers. The efficiency of economic performance lies in the uninterrupted flow of global communication, which necessitates the indoctrination of a replicable, standardized set of practices and procedures that efface all traces of contextual specificity. This pedagogical indoctrination into American tongues, lifestyles, and popular cultural references becomes an important part of the training of call-centre employees.

The telephonic exchange between American consumer and Indian employee impersonating an American identity offers a crucial moment to consider both the racialization of imagined cosmopolitan identities in India as well as the territorial claims and articulations of citizen entitlements in the US. Call-centre employees engaging in a sort of "neo-colonial mimicry" play right into the desire of global capitalists for a reformed, recognizable Other as a subject of difference that is in Bhabha's formulation, "almost the same" (i.e., can do the same work) "but not quite/not white"[11] (i.e., gets a fraction of the pay). If, for Bhabha, "the gaze" offered the possibility of subversive re-articulation where colonial surveillance is returned in the displacing gaze of the colonized, in the context of the call-centre industry, the "vocal mimicry" plays upon the ambivalence of global capitalism that turns call-centre employees' mimicry of American identity into the "menace" of outsourcing American jobs to the Third World. The vocal mimicry presages the menace of highly mobile capital detaching entitlements from territorialized claims of citizenship and re-attaching them to the neoliberal market.

While *Alladeen* depicts the ways in which call-centre agents imagine the lives of others through a re-training of speech, corporal, and cultural sensibilities, it stops short of drawing the privileged and invisible spectator into the circuit of transnational labour. While for the call-centre employee fantasy, identification and impersonation are crucial technologies for the cultivation of a "flexible" self, the means through which to aspire to a better life; for the spectator, the native is unidentifiable, nothing like the self. The comforting colonial certitudes of master/native consolidate the "western subject's" self-image and structure his gaze. The disintegrating mutation of the native mimic on stage becomes the occasion to reinforce the binaries of us/them, First World/Third World, consumer/labourer, and augment the stability, desirability, and authenticity of the spectating subject. In this way, *Alladeen* re-inscribes the entrenched conceptual geographies of power and difference, leisure and labour, original and copy.

Cosmo-utopia of *Call Cutta in a Box*

Rimini Protokoll, a German/Swiss theatre collective, created *Call Cutta in a Box*, from their earlier work, *Call Cutta Mobile Phone Theatre* (2005), which staged a transnational performance encounter between Kolkata and Berlin. In *The Mobile Phone Theatre*, Rimini Protokoll casts call-centre employees as performers; the "actors/participants" spatially orient tourists in Berlin through their role as sedentarized, cyber-mobile expert tour guides. What ensues is a choreography where, via "virtual migration," the sedentary Kolkatan leads travellers through the streets of Berlin and Kolkata while also initiating a "coded," spontaneous cosmopolitan conversation.[12] However, the walking-tour project, while promising, was also technically distracting due to tenuous phone connections, thus disabling an engaged dialogue between two people located across the globe. To conduct a "real" conversation while simultaneously attempting to find your spatial bearings proved too challenging. Wetzel contemplates: "We asked ourselves what would happen if we reduced the complications and offered the option to really talk?" (2008). Thus emerged their second call-centre performance piece, *Call Cutta in a Box*.

In *Call Cutta in a Box*, Rimini Protokoll moves the mobile phone theatre within the precincts of a closed room, where the solitary audience member now engages in a one-on-one transnational telephone conversation with a call-centre employee in Kolkata. For the project, Rimini Protokoll contracted the services of Descon Limited, a software call centre in Kolkata which provided them with 15 workstations and free technical and maintenance services. Each performance is thus a joint venture between Rimini Protokoll and Descon Limited, a company situated in Salt Lake City, a satellite township and IT hub built on a reclaimed salt water lake in the city of Kolkata in West Bengal.

Call Cutta in a Box cordons off the artistic project from the concurrent rhizomatic political shifts in Kolkata.[13] In Rimini Protokoll's aesthetically bounded performance, the audience/customer enters into a room where a phone rings; she picks it up and begins her conversation with the call-centre agent.[14] The cosmopolitan encounter is enacted through discrete scenes: the agent offers her customer a cup of tea, to provide "the Indian touch." Immediately, an electronic boiler automatically switches on, and the customer enjoys the tea. More "synchronized surprises" follow that demonstrate the increasingly algocratic organization of social relations in the transnational marketplace.

The conversations in *Call Cutta in a Box* range from strained intimacy: "Can you feel the distance between us," asks the female agent to which her male customer responds: "You are very far but your voice is very near;" to overt flirtation: "I am very alone. Come here … You can marry me," says the male customer to the female agent; to more serious engagements, "What is a big mistake that you have made in your life?" asks the agent to which the customer replies, "I've learned something from all my 'mistakes' so I wouldn't call them mistakes, just experiences that brought new understanding"; to sentimental encounters: one customer begins to weep as she hears the agent sing a Hindi song. "Sometimes you don't need to understand the words to get the feeling," says the customer.

The agents steer the conversation by asking fairly direct and personal questions – "Are you lonely? Do you have a boyfriend? Are you healthy?" – to more probing ones: "Are you satisfied with your life?" Reminders of cultural difference punctuate the exchange: the agents insert the topic of reincarnation, sing Indian songs, share pictures of their domestic help, serve *Chutki* (Indian peppermint), display the map of Kolkata and a picture of the generic glass-and-chrome Descon building where they are located, and conclude by presenting a kitschy altar of Kali, the Hindu goddess, which the customers discover in a drawer while they are taken on an imaginary ride through the city of Kolkata. The scene of mutual revelation closes the intercontinental phone play: agent and customer gaze at each other's faces on their computer screens, promise to stay in touch, and bid farewell.

Rimini Protokoll is critical of the ways in which global capital, seeking a higher rate of return, enters into and disrupts the life worlds of labourers. So their cosmo-utopic project attempts to redress the dehumanizing effacement of the identity of call-centre employees. The DVD documentation of the film that I viewed demonstrates heterogeneous conversations that take place between agent and customer, but the blueprint of the script that the cheery agents follow ensures that the chat takes predetermined turns.

Call Cutta in a Box programmes a series of surprises into the dialogue that manifests the significance of code in enabling transnational commerce. Revealing the power of programming codes in the organization of transnational labour, A. Aneesh advocates "algocracy," where authority is embedded in the technology of the code itself, thus rendering older hierarchies obsolete (2006). Programming and coding are intrinsic to the emerging transnational labour regimes, he argues; through optimal algorithms that mediate code and capital, programming codes organize transnational labour. For example:

> The fields on a computer screen can be coded to allow only certain kinds of texts or digits. Software templates provide existing channels that guide action in precise ways. This guidance suggests that authority does not need legitimacy in the same sense, because either there are no alternative routes to the permissible ones or the permissible routes are themselves programmed.
>
> *(Aneesh 2006, 110)*

The rule of the algorithm presages a new neoliberal governmentality. While structured as a transnational conversation to give insight into the life of the call-centre agent, the inter-continental play ends up reifying cultural difference and obscures the algocratic programming of cosmopolitan encounters. The engrained polarities of pleasure and work, leisure and labour, consumption and production are reinforced through algocratic programming that codes cosmopolitan encounters.

In an interview with Barbara Van Lindt, Rimini Protokoll director, Daniel Wetzel, remarks: "[the] theatre of service hides the reality of globalization ... but this theatre of service also forces the Indian performer to hide his identity" (Wetzel 2008). Here Wetzel evinces an anxiety that corporate globalization requires practices of subterfuge to facilitate the smooth uninterrupted global flow of service/capital. *Call Cutta* offers an opportunity for a conversation between two people

> who don't know each other, who are literally situated in different worlds, without any business-related reasons, and trying to just get a glimpse of who and where and what the other one might be ... the play offers you an opportunity to talk to subjects on the backstage of the globalization process.
>
> *(Wetzel 2008)*

The theatre performance of Rimini Protokoll's *Call Cutta in a Box* attempts to redress the damage caused by such mediations by enabling the consumer to glimpse the Indian behind her American persona. The algocratic design of the transnational encounter ensures that the agent steers the conversation to deliver local colour, "authentic" ephemera, and touches of cultural difference to provide the audience with a coded intimacy.

Call Cutta's ingenuity in staging a transnational conversation that moved from the *Mobile Phone* theatre version to the one *In A Box* allows the audience member to enter into a "coded" spontaneity that enables differently situated cosmopolitan subjects to "just talk." But does the promise of a "real connection" deliver? Is it possible to access the presence of the Indian, behind the European persona, without recourse to more mediation? If the call-centre industry provides an intensified glimpse into the performance of roles in the everyday life of the corporate workplace, does having an Indian affirm her Indianness put an end to role-playing? Or is she now, in *Call Cutta in a Box*, playing the Indian? Does not the persona structure the person? Rimini Protokoll's redressing of capitalist dehumanization ends up reifying cultural differences into a programmed and *a priori* fact of identity.

John and Jane: Copies in the Age of Capital

If *Alladeen* and *Call Cutta in a Box* demonstrate the utopic potential for cosmopolitan contact in the global marketplace of the copy, then Ashim Ahluwalia's experimental documentary, *John and Jane*, depicts the ways in which consumer desires inscribe new habitations of selfhood in the neoliberal marketplace. Here consumption becomes the key mode through which call-centre workers aspire towards and enact cosmopolitan selfhoods. Shot in 35 mm images, the film explores the dystopic ramifications of the psychic and social disjunctures produced in the lives of call-centre workers. An experimental filmmaker, Ashim Ahluwalia deterritorializes his viewers through the film's unsettling sonic score, unstable visuals, and uncanny narrative.[15] *John and Jane* takes the viewer on a dark tour of the fantasy lives of its protagonists. Set against the frenzied rhythms and glimmering nightscape of neoliberal Mumbai, *John and Jane* tracks the ways in which the six call-centre agents step into the city's iridescent field of vision.[16]

Described by Ahluwalia as "part observational documentary and part science-fiction," *John and Jane* follows the stories of six call-centre agents who answer American 1-800 numbers in a Mumbai call centre. The trope of the replica propels the filmic narrative and is established in the opening shots where flickering lights of Mumbai's nightscape illuminate mannequins in a display window. The double life of the call-centre agent is presented through a series of three dyads, three versions of John and Jane. Traversing the spectrum of subject positions, Ahluwalia's narrative begins with agents most tethered to the material every day and depicts increasingly abstruse accounts and concludes with a story with only the faintest grip on reality.

The narrative of the six agents is punctuated by scenes of pedagogical training: instructors train call-centre aspirants to speak "neutralized English" and impart data on the values of the average John Doe, which include individualism, achievement and success, privacy, progress, and the pursuit of happiness. If the repetitive rehearsals of rhyming couplets to neutralize accents infantilize the adult trainees, the cultural education disparages India. Leafing through shopping catalogues, the instructor not only kindles the consumer appetites of her trainees, she insidiously indoctrinates the trainees into the cultural, social, and economic superiority of America. These scenes demonstrate the subtle ways in which corporations inscribe consumer desire within the trainees.

The first agent, Glen, while derisive and critical of his job, continues to labour under its gruelling work night in the hope that it will eventually pave the way for him to model for fashion giants such as Gucci and Cavalli. Smoking joints, drinking at local pubs, and ranting to his friend about his "disgust" for his job enable Glen to endure its degrading inanity. Even his sense of humour does not alleviate the increasing dehumanization that Glen experiences in this job. "Am I talking to an answering machine?" berates one caller. "No sir," comes Glen's curt reply, "We're some fucking human beings here." Intermittently Glen resists, then yields to, the algocratic programming of his embodied nightly labour.

Training dancers in decrepit rooms, applying mascara on his fellow dancers, and shopping at glitzy, high-end stores enable Sidney, a queer dancer (Jane, in this dyad), to withstand the dreary monotony of his job. Unlike Glen though, the uncertainty of the job, the constant surveillance and insecurity generated by the performance matrix begin to erode Sidney's self-confidence: "They record your calls, and they grade you. If the call was bad, you lose your incentives for the whole month." The exasperation of working through the unrelenting tedium and stress of his job generates a feeling of inferiority. "I'm stupid," he says, "because an inner feeling within me says: no, you can do better." The dyad of Glen and Sydney sharply criticize, even despise their jobs, but stick with it because they believe in its promise of cosmopolitan mobility.

If, for Glen, the insidious demands of capitalist labour are indoctrinated into workers through embodied practices that tame and train them into answering machines, for Osmond these bodily habits are precisely what enable him to cultivate a "principled" lifestyle. Osmond re-trains his personality, through carefully cultivated habits, to move from his earlier slovenly lifestyle to a brisk, corporatized one, or, as he puts it, from "a negative to a positive." As Osmond prepares himself an English breakfast in his tenement-style one-room home, we observe the images that adorn his walls – a house in a gated community, an Aprilia motorcycle, images of celebrity role models – all indexing the cosmocratic lifestyle he yearns for. He surrounds himself with timetables that account for every minute of his day and self-help books. He even sleeps to the incessantly reverberating tape-recorded mantra that repeats, on a loop: "Now I am wealthy, now I am wealthy ..." A careful re-training of embodied practices facilitates the fashioning of an entrepreneurial subjectivity: "Now when I'm talking about business, there's more to it than products," explains Osmond. "Like, for example, my breath. A small thing like my breath can turn people away. My business teaches me to improve upon those things." Through the embodied cultivation of successful corporate persona, Osmond lives the American dream in India.[17]

Nikki Cooper, the other half in the dyad, evinces more altruistic and sentimental desires. Inspired by new-age spiritual classes, Nikki convinces herself that her role in the call centre is not merely to sell products to customers but, more importantly, to assuage their gloom. She persuades lonely Americans to re-connect with friends and family by purchasing cheaper phone plans. "No one calls me. I call no one. That's just fine. I'm satisfied with it just like it is," admits one caller. But her missionary desire to rescue these abandoned souls makes her try harder to sell cheaper calling cards. "You want to do so much for others. It's love, and giving. It's so beautiful," she insists. For both Osmond and Nikki, orphans without the nurture of parents, call centres become their home. Nikki finds a surrogate family in the call centre; while for Osmond, Amway builds him up, just like a mother.

Nicholas and Naomi are the last in the series of dyads. For Nicholas, working at a call-centre firm promises to transform not just his exterior habits but re-arrange even his inner sense of self. The call centre offers the ground for courtship and conjugality. He meets, falls in love with, and marries a fellow call-centre worker. The call centre also promises to transform him from a Hindi-speaking Mumbaikar to an urbane, sophisticated American:

> I was a person who used to speak in Hindi, but then English started coming into me, where I would always like to speak in English … it was kind of an American feeling that I started having … I don't want to be an Indian any more.

This is no scene of accent neutralization, rather language is the means through which to escape the "vernacular" provincialism of Hindi to English, the language of the global elite.

Finally, we meet Naomi, a young woman whose racialized fantasy to be not just American, but specifically a blonde American, leaves her with only an indistinct grasp on her immediate surroundings. Speaking through a sleep-deprived haze, Naomi giggles: "I'm totally, naturally blonde. I'm looking for an ideal guy. Blondes get attracted to blondes. That's very natural, of course." If in her waking hours she fantasizes in colour, then as she sleeps, she dreams in numbers. "I'm doing data entry. My fingers move in my sleep," she murmurs. Unable to break the programmed reflexes of her embodied nightly labour, Naomi attempts to re-claim some control over her body through her consumer practices. Naomi languidly wanders through spaces of consumption: she tries on skin-lightening make-up at shopping malls and keeps an eye out for blonde men at nightclubs. In the racialized scenarios that play out in her head, we see a case of the other threatening to engulf the self. The film ends on this dystopic, post-human-ist note.

Ahluwalia etches out these "proletarian dreams" against the maniacal, pulsating canvas of the Mumbai nightscape, which glitters between the rush and flow of incessant traffic and the calcified images of dummies in window displays. Social ties wane as their nightly labour and daily sleep shift their temporal clock, leaving them increasingly more dislocated. We watch the agents as they navigate their day, in a slightly dazed manner, and the increasing hold that cosmopolitan aspirations, fuelled by consumer fantasies, have over their everyday lives. Ahluwalia insightfully demonstrates the continuous feedback loop between labour and leisure, production and consumption that structures the every-night life of the agents. By revealing the tenuousness of their hold on their material social worlds, he demonstrates the ways in which global capital subsumes and erodes social relations.

The six characters here are abandoned by their author and play predetermined roles within an algocratic imaginary with little scope for individual agency. As they shuttle between actor and character, person and persona, the dichotomy between the two begins to dissolve. But like Pirandello, Ahluwalia also insists that theirs is a play-within-a-play. The role-playing is not limited to their work nights: Ahluwalia exposes a range of habituated performances of globality, urbanity, gender, sexuality, charity, class, and race. There is no "authentic" agent who dons an inauthentic mask; Ahluwalia's six characters flicker between given and imagined roles, even as they resist and yield to the algocratic programming of their bodies and their dreams.

Cosmopolitanism from Below: *Dancing on Glass*

Ram Ganesh Kamatham's *Dancing on Glass* (2004) moves the focus from disembodied practices of global impersonation to a consideration of the social and cultural displacements experienced by call-centre workers. The title, *Dancing on Glass*, reinforces this point by calling attention to the material, mortal body, simultaneously in rapture and in pain.

I watched *Dancing on Glass* directed by Preetam Koilpillai in July 2004 in Bangalore, and in October 2010, I viewed Vidhu Singh's production of the same play in San Francisco's Counter Pulse theatre.[18] *Dancing on Glass* tracks the life of Megha, a.k.a. Megan, a young, confident, call-centre employee who gradually descends into a vortex of depression and gloom. In addition to the repetitive tedium of her job, the racist and sexist abuse she encounters over the telephone, she contends with the challenges of working through the night. The nocturnal working hours produce resultant ailments: she develops a skin disorder from the lack of exposure to the sun, her hormones act up because of her irregular sleep patterns. The temporal disruptions produced by the nightly demands of labour not only created physical ailments but also plunged them into quarantine work lives. *Dancing on Glass* exemplifies how somatic rhythms of the call-centre workers are disordered as employees work nightly to service American and European customers.

Displaying aggression through her language, Megha constantly exceeds the proper place of the idealized Indian middle-class woman in urban India. And yet, she is not invulnerable to the widespread sexual threat women experience in public spaces in India. For example, Megha narrates a fairly routine incident that occurs in the city:

> So I fall and some ten fuckers come running from all goddamn directions and surround me. One fucker lifts me up, like … like this … *(gestures).* The guy is supposed to help me up and instead he's feeling me up. And the remaining nine bastards stand around watching. I told them all to fuck off, got on my bike and got out of there.

Kamatham portrays the ways in which acute conflicts between culture and class are mediated through women's bodies. When global consumer desires are displaced onto intracultural scenes of material aspiration and cultural belonging, they generate unstable and volatile fields of social power. Recently, a spate of attacks in Mangalore and Bangalore in early 2009 and 2012 by members of Hindutva right-wing groups targeted middle-class women for wearing "Western clothes," drinking or smoking in public, and even speaking English.[19] The rapidly proliferating images of women as consumers and women to consume destabilize older tropes of the middle-class woman who embodied Indian culture. In addition, "independent women" with greater purchasing power are perceived as emasculating to lower-class men who redress economic emasculation by asserting masculine power.

To consider a more extreme case: on 13 December 2005, roughly a year and a half after *Dancing on Glass* premiered in Bangalore, Pratibha Murthy, a 24-year-old call-centre employee was kidnapped, raped, and killed by the company-hired cab driver.[20] The incident exposed the precarious conditions of labour that undergird the professional aspirations of Bangalore's young call-centre workers and punctured a hole in the gleaming façade of Brand Bangalore. For critics of the high-tech boom in Bangalore, this case reinforced patriarchal common sense about women's place being within the home, the dangers of the urban nightscape, and the threats awaiting "call girls," the epithet disparagingly used to refer to women workers in this industry.[21]

Dancing on Glass opens with a conversation between Megha, a.k.a. Megan, and a hostile American customer on the other end. The customer demands to know her real identity and then hurls a stream of invectives at her for taking his job. The opening immediately sets the context of social and economic anxieties about the flight of American jobs to India and China, among other places. Consider, to begin with, the following exchange between Megan and her American customer over the telephone:

> *Voice-over:* You're not Megan. You're Jamilla or Sushma or something right?
> *Megha:* Dan, I'm here to help you with any problems you have with your account. I'm just doing my job. And I'm here to ...
> *Voice-over:* Naw bitch. You're doing my job. Sitting in front of a computer, and takin' calls. That's my job. That's what I feed my family with, yeah? And you took it away.

Kamatham reverses the Orientalist fantasy of "white men saving brown women from brown men" (Spivak 1994, 93).[22] The rage and panic in the voice of the American man on the other end of the phone signals that it is not merely his job that the faceless Indian woman has usurped but more importantly, his entitlements as an American citizen, his American dream, his very sense of self. If a faceless woman halfway across the world usurps his role in the global economy, then what is he left with, indeed, who is he? The loss of his role as a knowledge worker produces a crisis in his understanding of himself and unsettles the very coherence of his sense of self.

The proliferation of call centres in cheaper, Third World locations indexes the disarticulation of entitlements from citizenship and re-connects them instead to cheaper labour with the requisite technological savvy and cross-cultural skills. As Aihwa Ong reminds us, it is not only "territorialized citizenship" that is fragmented by capitalist imperatives of transnational exchange, accumulation, and disenfranchisement. Further: "In this digitalized network, not only cognitive skills are being floated away. Also arbitraged, is some notion of American masculinity tied to technical know-how, as low-cost and high-quality versions can also be found offshore" (Ong 2006, 162).

The death of her lover, Pradeep, a fellow call-centre employee, precipitates Megha's descent into despair. On his way home from "the graveyard shift," a telling epithet for night labour, Pradeep, sleep deprived and disoriented, crashes to his death after he falls asleep behind the wheel. In a state of shock, Megha turns to Pradeep's roommate, Shankar, a small-town migrant infatuated with her. The play explores the class and gendered tensions within the city between lower-middle-class male migrants and their more "liberal" and urbane middle-class female counterparts. *Dancing on Glass* charts the gradual prohibitions of freedoms as the protagonist loses her sense of sexual, social, and personal freedom. *Dancing on Glass* pivots around the disjuncture between liberty and liberalization.[23]

Megha's inability to express her grief at her lover's demise alarms her friends, co-workers, and Pradeep's family. When Shankar chides her for not showing up to the funeral, she argues that her "schedule is messed up" and that his death has caused "inconvenience" all around. Kamatham stretches the limits of neoliberal rationalities of expediency, convenience, and opportunity. His portrayal leaves ambiguous whether Megha, caught within her role as the foul-mouthed, urban young woman, is simply unable to grieve, or if, more disturbingly, she views grief as an opportunity for renewed romance. *Dancing on Glass* depicts characters whose precarious techniques of self-management in the wake of grief presage new arrangements of selfhood and sociality in neoliberal India. While the critique of Euro-American corporate exploitation of Third World labour structures the cosmopolitan encounters in both *Alladeen* and *Call Cutta in a Box*, in *John and Jane* and *Dancing on Glass* self-management and intracultural differences shape the volatile encounters. The coded intercultural binaries we witness in the first two productions are re-programmed in the second two cases onto the psychic terrain of the agents. The latter two productions trouble binaries between self/other, consumer/producer, pleasure/labour, and economy/culture by exposing the precarity of the subject under neoliberal regimes of subjection. *John and Jane* and *Dancing on Glass* move us beyond entrenched conceptual binaries of West/East, First World/Third World, consumption/labour to renewed and dispersed mappings of the First World in the Third World and vice versa, of inextricable loops of consumption and production, of rhizomatic shifts of culture, class, and gender in the volatile and unstable fields of power and desire. Neoliberal cities are crucial cosmopolitan contact zones that offer important insights into the fractious problem of how to live with cultural difference. The city is crisscrossed by complex global dynamics that destabilize the certitudes offered by older geopolitical binaries.

This chapter considers the effects of an aesthetic cosmopolitanism that partakes in a deterritorialized discourse of cultural encounters. While artists are eager to redress the dehumanization of corporate globalization, their gestures of cosmopolitan connection, grounded in liberal individualism, offer only a thin conception of lived experience. In order to mount a robust critique of neoliberal globalization, it is essential to partake in cosmopolitanism from below, one that takes into account the thick textures of social, material, and political struggles. Cosmopolitanism from below allows us to move from a disembodied discourse of placeless, replicable, uniform workers in a generic globalized economy to a consideration of the lived contradictions and non-fungible particularity of virtual labour in late capitalism.

Notes

1 This chapter was first published in *Women & Performance: A Journal of Feminist Theory*, 2013, Vol. 23, No. 2, 162–177, http://dx.doi.org/10.1080/0740770X.2013.823011.
2 See Ong (2006).

3 Costs of operation include: mandated insurance, retirement, healthcare, disability, and other benefits paid to the employee; costs of infrastructure such as building and materials; costs of training employees, bandwidth and communication, security and transportation, etc.

4 In August 2007, the city was officially re-named Bengaluru, the name that Kannada speakers use to refer to the city. "Bangalore," the Anglicized version of Bengaluru, was adopted after the British took over the ancient kingdom of Mysore in 1831. The name change provoked quite a bit of debate, with proponents for the name change arguing that Kannada speakers have always referred to the city as Bengaluru, neoliberal elites claiming that the name change would affect the city's will to global power, and still others arguing that the change was an effort to erase colonial history.

5 I draw from Baudrillard's discussion of simulacra, hyper-reality, and the dominance of the sign in late-capitalist modernity. For Baudrillard (1994), the hyper-real is the *telos* of a world that has displaced the stability of material commodities with the value of self-referential signs.

6 Personal interview, 2008. All interviews were conducted confidentially, and the names of interviewees are withheld by mutual agreement.

7 Personal interview, 2008.

8 Personal interview, 2008.

9 These responses shift over time. For instance, in a 2007 interview conducted by *Time* magazine, employees spoke candidly of the demise of the call-centre dream, "Earlier it was considered cool to work at a call center," said Nishant Thakur, 19. "That died out quite quickly." Another employee, Vishal Lathwal, 19, corroborated: "If you work at a call center today people will think you don't have anything else to do or were a bad student" (Thanawala 2007).

10 See Anderson (1998) on unbound seriality.

11 See Bhabha's classic essay, "Of Mimicry and Man" (1991).

12 On "virtual migration," see Aneesh (2006).

13 From roughly 2006 to 2008, the trajectory of neoliberal aspirations was seriously challenged by disenfranchised peasants and sharecroppers in West Bengal, where Left governments promoted rapid urbanization of the city's peripheries. Two events re-shaped the electoral politics in West Bengal: first, the collusion of state and private capital led the Left government to seize land from peasants and provide massive subsides to Tata Motors to set up a factory for the world's cheapest car, Nano, at Singur, a site on the edge of Kolkata. Second, the Left government's plans to cordon off village land into a profitable Special Economic Zone (SEZ) at Nandigram, a village in West Bengal, sparked a peasant uprising, which was met with extreme police reprisals. The exposure of its imperialist designs, in its bid to make the poorest sections of society finance the neoliberal aspirations of the country's middle classes, discredited the Left government as a champion for social justice. It is telling that Rimini Protokoll's cosmopolitan gesture of aesthetic connection refuses to grapple with the concurrent democratic struggles on the ground.

14 This description is built on viewing the DVD of the production *Call Cutta in a Box*.

15 The ominous soundtrack in the film, created by Masta Juicy, heightens the disquieting sense of the uncanny.

16 Mumbai straddles multiple urban imaginaries: as the cosmopolitan nerve of the nation, as hostage to homegrown and terrorist violence, as a network of cinematic fantasies, and as the future Shanghai of urban planners. (Increasingly, other Asian cities, Singapore–Dubai–Shanghai, are replacing New York–London–Berlin as the mimetic models through which Indian cities imagine their participation in world-city projects.)

17 In her insightful essay on the entrepreneurial subjectivities of Indian call-centre employees, Purnima Mankekar details the ramifications of re-training bodily practices during employee training sessions. "Being American involves not just talking like an 'American' but also learning to inhabit an American body and learning anew how to move through space like an American" (2010, 218).

18 The Bangalore production drew a fairly homogeneous crowd of trendy, urbane, English-speaking theater-going youth. The encouraging cheers during the show from the cosmopolitan audience extended the sensuous camaraderie beyond the stage. The San Francisco production drew a more eclectic crowd which was made up of Indian software professionals, San Franciscan theatergoers, and older diasporic Indians, invested in a nostalgic and frozen idea of India. The divergent responses during the talkback discussion at the San Francisco production ranged from comments that addressed actors as native informants on all things Indian to vociferous objections to the "call girl" portrayal of Indian womanhood in the play.

19 See *Indian Express*, 13 February 2009. www.indianexpress.com/news/manga-lore-pub-attack/422961/0.

20 See Sharma (2006) for a detailed and probing discussion of the incident.

21 See Patel (2010). Through a gendered "mobility–morality" paradigm, Patel considers how discourses regarding morality circumscribe women's mobility. She argues that while enabling some women to expand their mobility, the onus of protecting the body of the middle-class woman inadvertently restricts her mobility.

22 I thank the anonymous reviewer for pointing this out to me.

23 According to the *Wall Street Journal* journalist Joanna Slater (2004): "For many young people, especially women, call-center work means money, independence and an informal environment where they can wear and say what they like. Along with training in American accents and geography, India's legions of call-center employees are absorbing new ideas about family, material possessions and romance … In a culture where women rarely wear shorts or skirts above the knee, the work itself was an eye-opener … Sometimes, it is all too much for a generation that still decries public kissing." Slater invokes the civilizing mission of the call-centre industry in India as her patronizing argument suggests that having flooded the Indian market with images, commodities, lifestyles, and fantasies, liberalization has ushered in liberty. The conflation of liberalization and liberty is unsurprisingly played out upon the body of a woman.

References

Alladeen. 2004. Created and directed by Builders Association and Moti Roti. Los Angeles: REDCAT (Roy and Edna Disney/Cal Arts Theatre).

Anderson, Benedict. 1998. "Nationalism, Identity, and the World-in-Motion." In *Cosmopolitics: Thinking and Feeling Beyond the Nation*, edited by Pheng Cheah and Bruce Robins, 117–133. Minneapolis: University of Minnesota Press.

Aneesh, A. 2006. *Virtual Migration: The Programming of Globalization*. Durham: Duke University Press.

Baudrillard, Jean. 1994. *Simulacra and Simulation*. Michigan: University of Michigan Press.

Bhabha, Homi. 1991. *Location of Culture*. London: Routledge.

Calhoun, Craig. 2003. "The Class-Consciousness of Frequent Travellers: Towards a Critique of Actually Existing Cosmopolitanism." In *Conceiving Cosmopolitanism: Theory, Context, and Practice*, edited by Steven Vertovec and Robin Cohen, 86–109. Oxford: Oxford University Press.

Call Cutta in a Box. 2008. Created by Rimini Protokoll. Berlin.

Fanon, Franz. 2008. *Black Skin/White Masks*. Trans. Richard Philcox. New York: Grove Press.

John and Jane. 2005. Directed by Ahsim Ahluwalia. Mumbai: Future East Films.

Kamatham, Ram Ganesh. 2004. *Dancing on Glass*. Unpublished manuscript.

Macaulay, T. B. (1835) 2000. "Minute on Indian Education." In *Norton Anthology of English Literature*, edited by M. H. Abrams and Stephen Greenblatt, 1610–1611. New York: W. W. Norton & Co.

Mankekar, Purnima. 2010. "Becoming Entrepreneurial Subjects." In *The State in India after Liberalization: Interdisciplinary Perspectives*, edited by Akhil Gupta and K. Sivaramakrishnan, 213–231. New York: Routledge.

MotiRoti Website. Accessed 2 February 2012. http://www.alladeen.com/content.html.

Naipaul, V. S. 2002. *The Middle Passage*. New York: Vintage.

Ong, Aihwa. 2006. *Neoliberalism as Exception: Mutations in Citizenship and Sovereignty*. Durham: Duke University Press.

Patel, Reena. 2010. *Working the Night Shift: Women in India's Call Center Industry*. Stanford: Stanford University Press.

Retamar, Roberto. 1989. *Caliban and Other Essays*. Minneapolis: University of Minnesota Press.

Sharma, Ravi. 2006. *Frontline*, 22 (27).

Slater, Joanna. 2004. "Call of the West: For India's Youth, New Money Fuels a Revolution; as Foreign Goods, Jobs Flood the Country, Young People are Spurning Tradition; Little Gentleman Loosens Up." *Wall Street Journal*, 27 January, A.1. http://search.proquest.com/docview/398866014? accountid=14026.

Spivak, Gayatri. 1994. "Can the Subaltern Speak?" In *Colonial Discourse, Postcolonial Theory: A Reader*, edited by Patrick Williams and Laura Chrisman, 66–111. Hertfordshire: Harvester Wheatsheaf.

Thanawala, Sudhin. 2007. "India's Call-Center Jobs Go Begging." *Time*. New Delhi, Tuesday, 16 October. Accessed November 11, 2012. www.time.com/time/business/article/0,8599,1671982,00.html.

Walcott, Derek. 1980. *Pantomime*. New York: Farrar, Straus and Giroux.

Wetzel, Daniel. 2008. "Call it *Call Cutta in a Box*." Interview by Barbara Van Lindt. *Call Cutta in a Box* program book. Accessed November 11, 2012. www.rimini-protokoll.de/website/en/article_3656.html.

17

AN EMERGING LITERARY TRADITION

An Overview of Writings in English from the Northeast

K.B. Veio Pou and Achingliu Kamei

Introduction

In recent times, there have been attempts at answering the question "What is Northeast writing?"[1] or more specifically "What is Northeast writing in English?" And because it is a later development, there is more curiosity than an attempt at answering it. In fact, the term "Northeast" did not come into use in the literary field until the last decade of the twentieth century. Before that it was used primarily as a political and administrative terminology. The expression Northeast India entered the Indian lexicon with the formation of the North Eastern Council (NEC) in 1971, following the Government of India's decision to affect administrative changes in the region. The Northeastern states comprising Arunachal Pradesh, Assam, Manipur, Meghalaya, Mizoram, Nagaland, Sikkim and Tripura share only 2 per cent of their boundary with other Indian states. The other 98 per cent are international boundaries bordering China, Bangladesh, Myanmar, Bhutan and Nepal. Sikkim was added as the eighth state in 2003, but since it is not contiguous with the other seven states called the "seven sisters" nor shares a history of turmoil like the other states, it somehow stands apart.

In literature, the evolution of a literary body called the North East Writers Forum (NEWF) in 1996 effectively gave rise to the term "Northeast writing". Recognized as the first literary body, the NEWF comprises writers writing in English from all the seven states of the Northeast. Their objectives include encouraging creative writings in English, translation of literature into English and to promote literature from the region to other parts of the world. The Forum also publishes an annual journal, *NEWFrontiers*, whose editorship rotates from state to state for a two-year stint. It has also been

DOI: 10.4324/9781003399926-23

successful in promoting translations of local works. The Forum also, in collaboration with some of the leading publishing houses like Penguin, Zubaan, Katha and HarperCollins, has published several authors from the region. The new millennium also saw the arrival of several publishing houses taking interest in ushering the region's writers into the limelight. Undeniably, however, this is partly an impact of India's liberal policy of "looking east" for new ventures that necessitated engaging the Northeast as a "gateway" to the East. Within no time, the region became a hotbed of literary sources. As of today, major publishing names like Speaking Tiger, Aleph and others, besides the ones mentioned above, are actively publishing many well-known writers from the region.

At the same time, it is also important to see how the various locales of English education centres in the region contributed to the growth of these literary personalities and intellectuals. Shillong has long been the centre of the Northeast for various developments. It was made the headquarters of the colonial Assam province and also the capital of undivided Assam after independence until 1972 when Meghalaya was created as a state with Shillong as its capital. Being bestowed with many mission schools and colleges, it became the hub of education within a short span of time and continues to be so even today. It also became the natural point of creative experimentation. When the Shillong Poetry Society was founded around 1988–1989; it gave the city more credibility as the centre of literary growth. The Society also started the bi-annual poetry journal called *Lyric* in 1992 but could not sustain "mainly due to financial contingencies". Nevertheless, Shillong continued to be the home that nurtured many writers and poets who have made a name in the literary world, the Shillong poets since the early 1980s being a case in point. Undeniably, Shillong will be remembered for its literary traditions in the Northeast, particularly English writing.

Although the region saw a fairly long history of vernacular writing in Assamese and Manipuri (Meitei) languages, the readership of these writings in these two languages has been limited. It is the new phenomenon of writing in English that has caught from the imagination of the reading public in the country. Interestingly, there are a lot of translations of Assamese and Manipuri literature into English which are also read in conjunction with the works originally written in English.

Needless to say, the seed of the English language in the region was sown during the colonial period, as was also the case with the rest of India. The expansion of the British Empire towards the Northeastern Frontier in the beginning of the nineteenth century also paved the way for the arrival of Christian missionaries. And wherever the missionaries went, they set up schools and healthcare facilities. Thus, within no time the printing presses ushered in primers in local languages in conjunction with the introduction of the English language for instruction in educational institutions. This helped produce a new educated generation who quite comfortably took to the language of the missionary enterprise. But the absence of a common language led to the introduction of English language as the *lingua franca* in the region, at least among the intelligentsia. And in the case of the communities of the hills whose traditions were passed on primarily orally, the Roman script was introduced to initiate a written culture in education. Today, the spawning of the various newspapers and magazines (both web-based and print) in English from the region testifies to the popularity of the language. Being schooled in English-medium institutes, colleges and universities, therefore, it was also expected of the following generations to find their creativity expressed in the language in which they were instructed.

Different genres of literature written by writers from the region have found their way into the bookstores of the metro cities and among research scholars in several universities across the country. However, there is also a visible resistance to the use of such a blanket term for all writers who are from the region, as it is seen as "stereotyping" and limits their growth. Besides, not all their writings necessarily portray the region or speak of its people. Whatever the case, somehow, the body of literature from and by writers of the region gets identified as one and projected as regional literature by virtue of it being from a particular geographical location. Perhaps, being linked to the rest of the country by a narrow strip of land, the Northeastern states marked themselves out by becoming India's "periphery", away from the "mainland", where real political power rested. Or just like the term "Northeast" is a construct that has stayed on to refer to anything and anyone from the region, the term "Northeast writing in English" also has become the umbrella term under which all writers from the region are clubbed under (Dutta 2018; Phukan 2013; Borpujari 2011; Ngangom 2010).

But one may, again, ask, "Are there any distinguishing features in these writings that mark them apart from the existing literatures of India?" I think, if we scan through the popular literary works across the states, it is most certainly a "yes". And that is primarily a thematic difference. This chapter, therefore, is mainly an overview of the issues and themes emerging from the writings in English from the Northeast. And since this chapter is a part of the *Festschrift* in honour of Prof. G.J.V. Prasad, it would be fair to mention the huge influence he has had on the scholars who walked into CLE/CES. During his long tenure at JNU his interest in the cultural studies from the region was admirable. We are truly indebted to him for guiding us through our PhDs. And we're sure this would be the testimony of many scholars from the Northeast who have greatly benefited from having him as a teacher with vast knowledge about literature from the region.

Politics of a Protest Literature

Many of the writings, particularly by writers who are based in the region, have a strong political undercurrent that runs deep. It is the uniform political unrest throughout the region since the early years after India's independence that gets reflected in the literary works. Somehow, the region quickly became one of India's "postcolonial others". The problematic political relationship that many ethnic communities of the region have with the Centre continues to find expression in the various writings of the region's writers. Many a time, therefore, literature from the region tends to be categorized as different from the rest of the country because it is overtly political.

In fiction, there are those who directly narrate political conflicts or set conflict at the backdrop of their narratives. Temsula Ao's *These Hills Called Home: Stories from a War Zone* (2006), Siddhartha Deb's *The Point of Return* (2004), Mitra Phukan's *The Collector's Wife* (2005), Bijoya Sawian's *The Shadow Men* (2010), Dhruba Hazarika's *A Bowstring Winter* (2006), Easterine Kire's *Bitter Wormwood* (2011), Aruni Kashyap's *The House with Thousand Stories* (2013), Jahnvi Barua's *Next Door* (2008), Veio Pou's *Waiting for the Dust to Settle* (2020), etc. come to mind. Likewise, in poetry, there is clear articulation of political unrest in the poetry of Desmond Kharmawphlang, Kynpham Sing Nongkynrih, Robin S. Ngangom, Mona Zote, Temsula Ao, Easterine Kire, and Monalisa Changkija, among others.

Many of these writings point to the Centre's negligence of the region for the many unfortunate turns of events in recent history. In an interesting article titled "Anthology Making, the Nation and the Shillong Poets" (2008), Prasanta Das alleged that poets from the Northeast were overlooked even in the world of Indian writing in English. He argues this while critiquing Jeet Thayil's omission of the well-known Shillong poets in his anthology *60 Indian Poets* (2008) and said that it, "is analogous to New Delhi's neglect of the [N]ortheast" (p. 19). Somehow, to prove that not much has changed since, a recent news item added fresh wounds to the discomforting relationship that the periphery has with the mainland. The popular daily *Mint* compiled a list of books by Indians originally written in English, on 15 August 2020, commemorating the country's Independence Day. The list did not include a single author from the Northeast. The next day, an incensed Aruni Kashyap took to Twitter thus, "Not a single book from Northeast India here. What a shame this list is. Erases not only a unique region but a unique literary tradition. Can't accept this racist erasure" (Menezes 2020). Such stray incidents only point to the fact that the mainstream often tends to erase, misread and misinterpret the peripheral region despite the bustling richness of a body of literature in English. Some might argue that such a thing as a separate category of writing from the Northeastern region need not be asserted; after all, we have the larger body of Indian writing in English. But, the fact is, sidestepping the region's literary tradition only goes on to accentuate its difference from so-called mainstream literature.

And so, with the non-visibility of the region in the discourses of the mainstream, a sense of alienation pervades the minds of the people. As such, there is already a sense of unfair treatment meted out by the Centre, any additional mistake only aggravates the situation. There is a good deal of poetry that is very political in its articulation against the injustices prevalent in the region. Desmond Kharmawphlang poetically captures the historical and cultural colonization in his poem "The Conquest" where he talks of a different kind of conquest even after the British colonial powers left – "But in the wavering walk of time / There came those from the sweltering / Plains, / From everywhere". The poem brings out the different epochs in the steady subjugation of the geographical landmass that his people inhabit. It finds resonance in similar stories from other people's groups of the region. Often, the large mongoloid stock that makes their homes in the majority of the states, face racial slurs, especially when they move out of the region for educational or various other purposes. Writing against this discrimination, Cherrie L. Chhangte sardonically comments that "The 'largest democracy in the world'" sounds good only on paper because many feel "Sidelined, side-tracked, side-stepped, a minority in a majority world" ("What Does an Indian Look Like").

Often stereotyped for being a periphery of violence and conflict, it is undeniable that the Northeast continues to be afflicted by many unfortunate tales of death and trauma. Being highly militarized, stories of the human rights violation by Indian armed forces also fill the pages of books. Monalisa Changkija expresses the anguish of the people's reality thus – "Stop, please stop this endless nightmare / wherein I read of another shot dead, / another apprehended, another tortured and maimed" ("Stop This Nightmare"). While these lines obviously project the plight of the Nagas in their struggle with the Indian state, the irony is that the poem can easily be also a rant against the perpetrators who have emerged from within. The latter-day movement for sovereignty is marred by factionalism and more bloodshed among the Nagas themselves. And so, the poem acts as a satire on the unfortunate turn of events in contemporary times. Using the imagery of the dust, Nini Lungalang writes of the everyday terror and madness – "I saw a young man gunned down / As I shopped in the market place. / Two thuds and then he fell" ("Dust"). The boldness of the cold-blooded murder that took place in public view – "market place" – tells a tragic story of the Nagas that started off with high idealism.

Intertwined in all these tensions is the ethnic conflict that has deeply wounded many communities of the region. Lamenting at the heart-wrenching episodes of strife in his homeland Manipur, Robin S. Ngangom describes a state that has seen many ethnic conflicts and says, "First came the scream of the dying / In a bad dream, then the radio report" and as such news continue to haunt the everyday news, he articulates – "I hardened inside my thickening hide, / Until I lost my tenuous humanity" ("Native Land"). So, as one would see, the poets and writers of the Northeast not only write against the state but also articulate against the various kinds of injustices and violence in the region. In this sense, they are very outspoken in taking the literature to the public realm. They become the voice of protest and their writings, the literature of protest.

Culture and Identity

Another theme that is similar to the theme of protest literature is that of culture and identity. Even though the regions differ from each other in tradition, culture, languages, etc., identity and identity crisis is a distinguishing theme in the writers from the region. Take for instance, Jahnavi Barua, Arnab Jan Deka, Siddhartha Sarma, Nitoo Das, Janice Pariat, Nabanita Kanungo, Mona Zote, Ankush Saikia, Bijoya Sawian, Aruni Kashyap and Uddipana Goswami.

Their work scrutinizes the mainstream style of dominating or sidestepping the writers from the region. Their work explores the traditional value system in quest for personal and cultural identity. The writings, especially from the Naga writers, express strong political awareness, necessitated by the administrative neglect of the region to the growing sense of instability because of various anti-social elements. Anjum Hasan, in her debut novel, *Lunatic in My Head* (2007), she talks about roots, identity, clash of culture and the idea of home. Narratives of outsider/insider conflict found prominence in the novel. The outsider identity crisis, born out of a fear of losing their originality, was explored. The divide between the two binaries of belonging could also be seen as the postcolonial distance between the "self" and the "other". An atmosphere of doubt and distrust is created by the polemics of power between the "insider" and the "outsider".

Naga people's struggle for independence and their continuing search for identity provided the background to the stories in *These Hills Called Home: Stories from a War Zone* (2006) by Temsula Ao. The stories are based on real-life events of violence and bloodshed. Sanjib Baruah's book *Durable Disorder: Understanding the Politics of Northeast India* (2005) also addressed the issues of the search for identity, ethnicity and aspirations for new homelands. It talked about the crisis of displacement and about the geopolitics of the region.

Not only do the authors of novels explore the themes of identity and identity crisis, but the poets from the region also continue to pen down the need to find one's roots; the search for roots going back to the native tradition in search of identity. The poets strongly advocate preservation of culture and tradition. Amidst political hegemony, asserting one's identity and culture is an effective form to preserve self-respect. Contemporary poetry too plays a pivotal role in the search for identity. In a searching poem called "Mymensingh", the poet Ananya Guha expresses the deeply ingrained memory – "straggling roots Mymensingh / I'll never dig them out / But let them remain growing like cacti / On the opal shore of history". There is a sense of nostalgia as well as loss in these lines. The poet, while talking about his roots in Mymensingh, refers to it as a place that she can never get back to. That part of her roots will forever remain history, something of the past never meant to be recovered. For the mother, the sense of "desolateness" will mark her present state. This poem also powerfully brings out the disruption that was caused by Partition in the Northeast. In India, often, the discourses on Partition tend to be focused only on what happened in the western frontier of the country. The impact it had in the eastern part of the country, and particularly in the Northeast region, is less talked about. And yet, the uncomfortable reality of dealing with the pains of conflict due to Partition continued to be played out viciously even today in different ways. The huge Assam agitation of the late 1970s and early 1980s is largely surrounding this identity crisis, the insecurity of the indigenous population, following the huge influx of immigrants from Bangladesh, especially after the creation of the country. The present-day debates on National Register of Citizens (NRC) and the controversies around it are only manifestations of the deeper fissures in the socio-political fabric of the region, particularly Assam. What we see in the writings of the region is a desire to actively engage with the issues of the society as a major theme of their literature.

Revival of the Oral: Writing Orality

Another important theme that emerges prominently is the synthesis of the written with the orality in the literary production of English writings from the region. The rich storytelling tradition finds resonance among many writers; take, for example, Mamang Dai's *Legends of Pensam* (2006), Janice Pariat's *Boats on Land* (2012) and Easterine Kire's *When the River Sleeps* (2014). Besides, various collections like *Fresh Fictions: Folk Tales, Plays, Novellas from the Northeast* (2005), *The Heart of the Matter* (2004), *Where the Sun Rises When Shadows Fall: The North-east* (2005), *Anthology of Contemporary Poetry from the Northeast* (2003), *Earth Songs: Stories from Northeast India* (2005), etc. have created new interest in the region.

With a rich history of oral culture, the writers from the Northeast finds their oral tradition a good source of inspiration, or as Mamang Dai puts it, "for many of us the legends and stories are still a wellspring of thought and emotions that are restored in a peculiar blend of myth and memory unique to the region" (2005: 5). Her book *Legends of Pensam* (2006) clearly captures the dynamics of her own people's oral culture wherein the reality of the folk is woven into a tapestry of the historical narrative. And her poems recreate the natural world in its wonder, because the mountains, the rivers, the clouds, etc. still breathe life just as human beings do.

And it is in this light that Temsula Ao rightly points out that there is "a subtle conceptual shift" in the writings from this part of the region because they borrow a lot of the "elements from the oral traditions" (2007: 107–108). Temsula's own poems speak of this truth. Her poems are sourced from the rich oral tradition of her own people, and the retelling of the stories enables the readers to reimagine folktales and songs as dynamic and not something obsolete. There is the obvious use of narrative techniques borrowed heavily from oral traditions. We find similar trends from other poets and writers of the region. In her poem "Stone-People from Longterok", Temsula Ao poetically retells her people's mythical belief of their origins from the six stones found at Lungterok – "Where the progenitors / Of the stone-people / Were born / Out of the womb / Of the earth". In a similar vein, Mamang Dai also wrote, "We are the children of the rain / Of the cloud woman / Brother to the stone and bat" ("Birthplace"). The rich imagery is rooted to their oral tradition, describing their origins and attachments to the land they belong to. The expressions are pregnant with meaning as they sing of how natural elements are personified beautifully.

There is, certainly, a recognition of the importance that one's culture and tradition have on the making of the self and the community, as we see from these writings. Unfortunately, their negligence for long of them since the encounters with modernity since the nineteenth century has led to a point of loss. Tilottoma Misra aptly puts it: "An intense sense of awareness of the cultural loss and recovery that came with the negotiation with 'other' cultures is a recurrent feature of the literatures of the seven [Northeastern] states" (2011: xiii). But there is also a visible effort for "recovery" in the way writers are able to revive the storytelling traditions of the region. In an interview in August 2020, Easterine Kire spoke about the importance of culture-specific stories in this way,

> For me, my culture is what I know, what I grew up imbibing from what I was taught, what I saw around me, and what I lived and experienced … Stories are so essential to our spirits … And the stories would carry cultural knowledge because that is one of the ways how our culture is transmitted. Not the only way, but one of the ways.

Ecological Concerns

Alongside sustenance, Nature is an extension of identity and roots for the Northeastern states. Both in poetry and in novels, there is an undeniable presence of Nature. Human culture is connected to the physical world and draws extensively from it for their understanding of being. Mamang Dai, in her poem "An Obscure Place", speaks of the mountain not only as landscape but as a site of history. The mountains are the bridges to lead the people back to their ancestral roots. In her quest for identity, she has used mountains, rivers and forests as metaphors.

Temsula Ao attempted to trace back her ancestors' long-lost identity by invoking the spirits of Nature in her poem "Blood of Others", by saying that they believed their God lived "In the various forms of nature", but their faith was shaken by strangers who came with just a "book" and promise of a "heaven". Several writers of the Northeast deal with eco-critical texts on ecological concerns like deforestation, loss of flora and fauna, pollution, etc. After independence, some Assamese writers like Nabakata Baruah, Harekrishna Deka, Hiren Bhattacharya, Nilim Kumar, Jiban Narah, Kushal Dutta, Pranay Phukan, Bijay Sankar Barman, Kamal Kumar Tanti and others focused on environmental issues.

In the poem "Eyat Nodi Asil" (There Was a River), Nabakanta Baruah makes readers aware of how rivers turn into desert. His other poems represent environmental and mental degradation in contemporary times. Nilim Kumar in his poem "Oxygen Cylinder" wrote about the positive and negative impact of science and technological developments. The short story of Sahitya Academy Award-winner Mahim Bora, "Ekhan Nodir Mrityu" (Death of a River), talks about a weir in Kalang River. The author reflects on the environmental problems that occurred because of the unexpected weir and how people suffered because of vested interests. Ram Gogoi in "Pothar" (The Paddy Field) described Nature both as a soothing and dangerous element. The farmers dreamt about a rich harvest on seeing the field filled with crops in the rainy season, but soon all the crops were washed away by the floods.

There have been novels in Assamese, like that of Prabhat Goswami's *Xukula hatir khuj* (2012) and Gobin Kumar's *Rumyang* (2016), that focus on eco-critical perspectives powerfully. *A Bowstring Winter* (2006) by Dhruba Hazarika portrays life in Shillong, with all its ecological aspects. Indira Goswami expresses strong ecological concerns in her novels like *Pages Stained with Blood* (2002) and *The Man from Chinnamasta* (2006). The biodiversity of the region with a rich flora and fauna has been a recurrent theme in her writings. She also wrote about the peaceful co-existence of man and animal. Another notable writer, Mitra Phukan in her novel *A Collector's Wife* (2005) narrated a touching story of Rukmini, a young lady. Even though the main theme of the story was the violence and insurgency prevailing in Assam during the agitation of the 1970s and 1980s, she also wrote about ecological issues. Ecological concerns run through in almost all the works.

Among the Naga writers, Temsula Ao and Easterine Kire share the same ecological concerns. What stood out prominently is their love for the mountains, hills, forests, waterfalls, ravines and deep gorges: in short, love for the land. The writers are able to transmute the chaotic into the sublime. Most of the writings from the region have ecological concerns that transcend the local. Writings on daily experiences, trauma, bloodshed, roots and land, have become a new force amidst the current ecological disasters and those that are forecast for the future. Disparate authors from the region shared a common thread through a united concern for the environment and land. Literature from the region is able to broaden cultural perspectives and encourage alternative ways of perceiving the world. Works of Easterine, Mamang, Temsula and others challenge the assumption that Nature is merely something for humans to conquer and misuse, even the native inhabitants. In *When the River Sleeps*, Easterine puts Nature back where it belongs – at the forefront. She has exalted rural life which is untouched by modernity and unadulterated by technology. Nature is presented as empowered and not oppressed. The wilderness in the novel is the "new wilderness", just as Gerrard's division of the representation of wilderness in his literary works. It is not as a place to fear, but a place to find sanctuary. The river gives the power stone to the one who will never misuse its power – to Vilie. By the end of the novel, the stone finally comes under the custody of Ate, a woman. Easterine seems to suggest that Mother Nature favours the women to be its custodians. The need Nature and humans have for each other was brought out by the relationship between Vilie and the forest. They protect each other. Nature is the antidote for the ills of this world.

The Sahitya Academy Award winner and Adi writer Mamang Dai's novel *The Legends of Pensam* deals with the ecology of Arunachal Pradesh. She merges the history, myth, tradition and memories of the Adi tribe into her narrative. Eco-feminist ideals were visible in the clash between tradition and modernity. Biakliana, the writer of the first-ever Mizo novel *Hawilopari*, also deals with ecology in her short story "Lali". Ecological concerns like the age-old bond between the human world and the world of Nature were deftly dealt with. In her story, there are references to traditional ways where Mizo rites, rituals, myths and legends are woven together. Manipuri playwrights G.C. Tongbra and Ratan Thiyam are much concerned about the erosion of human values resulting in the degradation of ecology and try to expose the anomalous conditions in society. Ratan is also an activist who is acutely aware of contemporary issues.

Conclusion

Whether one sees it or not, the writings in English from India's Northeast are forging their own literary tradition. Given the different historical and cultural experiences that the region has witnessed for a long time now, it makes sense to see the emerging new writings as an independent category. As far as cultural factors are concerned, the region has more commonality with the rest of Southeast Asia. Mark Bender (2012) has even concluded an interesting study to show how the literary works of the Northeast have high resonance with those of South China. Cultural proximity certainly plays a big role in literary tradition.

At the same time, one needs to be cautious, as the writing of a literary history somehow "imposes a sense of order" and hence a kind of "closure" (Valdes and Hutcheon, 1994). However, we would argue, the recognition of the writings in English from India's Northeast as an emerging literary tradition is not seeing it necessarily as a "canonization" of certain literature. It is an acknowledgement of the development of a new body of literature which shows signs of potential growth. With the rising interest shown in the region in the last few decades, these writings can serve as the window to understand the region's cultural heterogeneity, which has been much wanted in the study of India's Northeast.

In conclusion, this chapter, as the title suggests, is meant to provide an overview of some of the emerging themes from the literature in English from the region. However, the themes brought under discussion here are not necessarily exhaustive, and there are many potential areas of research. We hope to see more interest in the study of the region so as to understand its people, culture and tradition.

Note

1 There are a few differing terms used to refer to the Northeast of India, such as "north east", "North East", "North-east", "north-east", "northeast", "Northeast", etc., but they all refer to the same geographical region. For the sake of conformity we have used the compound term "Northeast".

References

Ao, Temsula, *These Hills Called Home: Stories from a War Zone*, Zubaan, New Delhi, 2006.
——, "Stone-people from Lungterok", in Robin S. Ngangom and Kynpham S. Nongkynrih (Eds.), *Dancing Earth: An Anthology of Poetry from North-East India*, Penguin, New Delhi, 2009.
——, "Writing Orality", in Soumen Sen and Desmond L. Kharmawphlang (Eds.), *Orality and Beyond: A North-East Indian Perspective*, Sahitya Akademi, New Delhi, 2007, pp. 99–112.
Baral, Kailash C., *Earth Songs: Stories From Northeast India*, Sahitya Akademi, New Delhi, 2005.
Baruah, Debashis, "Contemporary Writing in English from India's Northeast: A Study in Ecopolitics", PhD Thesis submitted to Nagaland University, 2009 at

http://www.nagalanduniv.ndl.iitkgp.ac.in/bitstream/handle/1/59/T00045.pdf
?sequence=1&isAllowed=y, 25th September 2020.

Bender, Mark, "Ethnographic Poetry in North-East India and Southwest China", in *Rocky Mountain Review*, Special Issue: Border Crossing, 66, Summer 2012, pp. 106–129 at https://www.jstor.org/stable/10.2307/rockmounrevi.66.106, 30th August 2015.

Borpujari, Utpal, "Recognition for North East Writers", *The Times of India* (The Crest Edition), 5 February 2011 at http://www.timescrest.com/culture/recognition-for-north-east-writers-4689, 25th September 2020.

Changkija, Monallisa, *Monsoon Mourning*, Write-on Pubications, Dimapur, 2007.

Chhangte, Cherrie L., "What Does an Indian Look Like", in Tilotoma Misra (Ed.), *The Oxford Anthology of Writings from North-East India: Poetry and Essays*, OUP, New Delhi, 2011, p. 76.

Dai, Mamang, "On Creation Myths and Oral Narratives", in *IIC Quarterly*, "Where the Sun Rises When Shadows Fall: The North-East", Moonsoon-Winter, 32 (2 & 3), 2005, pp. 3–6.

————, *The Legends of Pensam*, Penguin, New Delhi, 2006.

————, "Birthplace", in *River Poems*, Writers Workshop, Kolkata, 2013, p.54.

Das, Prasanta, "Anthology-Making, the Nation, and the Shillong Poets", *Economic & Political Weekly*, 43 (42), 18–24 October 2008, pp. 19–21.

Das, Jyotishman, "Ecological Concern in Assamese Literature: An Introduction", *International Journal of Advanced Research*, 7 (5), pp. 147–149, at http://www.journalijar.com/uploads/26_IJAR-27352.pdf, 25th September, 2020.

Dutta, Nandana, "Northeast India: A New Literary Region for IWE", OUP Blog at https://blog.oup.com/2018/09/northeast-india-new-literary-region/, 25th September 2020.

"Ecocriticism (1960 – Present)", Purdue University at https://owl.purdue.edu/owl/subject_specific_writing/writing_in_literature/literary_theory_and_schools_of_criticism/ecocriticism.html, 25th September 2020.

Hasan, Anjum, *Lunatic in my Head*, Zubaan, New Delhi, 2007.

Kire, Easterine, *Bitter Wormwood*, Zubaan, New Delhi, 2011.

————, *When the River Sleeps*, Zubaan, New Delhi, 2014.

———— "'Years of Listening to Stories Grows a Wealth of Knowledge within Your Spirit': Easterine Kire", Interview with Veio Pou, 23 August 2020, Scroll.in at https://scroll.in/article/971141/years-of-listening-to-stories-grows-a-wealth-of-knowledge-within-your-spirit-easterine-kire, 20th October 2020.

Lungalang, Nini, "Dust", in Kynpham Sing Nongkynrih and Robin S. Ngangom (Eds.), *Anthology of Contemporary Poetry from the Northeast*, NEHU, Shillong, 2003, pp. 224–225.

Menezes, Vivek, "Why is Writing from the North East Often Ignored by the Mainland Literary Culture?", 23 September 2020 at https://scroll.in/article/973821/different-ways-of-belonging-literature-from-indias-north-east-states, 10th October 2020.

Misra, Tilottoma, *The Oxford Anthology of Writings from North-East India*, I & II, Oxford University Press, New Delhi, 2011.

Ngangom, Robin S., "Alternative Poetry of the Northeast", *Muse India* (32), *Focus: English Poetry of the North-East*, July–August 2010, at http://www.museindia.com/focuscontent.asp?issid=32&id=2014, 24th July 2020.

———, *The Desire of Roots*, Chandrabhaga, Cuttack, 2006.

Nongkynrih, Kynpham Sing and Robin S. Ngangom (Eds.), *Anthology of Contemporary Poetry from the Northeast*, NEHU, Shillong, 2003.

Phukan, Mitra, "Writing in English in the North East", in *Muse India* (48), March–April, 2013 at https://museindia.com/Home/ViewContentData?arttype=feature&issid=48&menuid=4026, 20th October 2020.

———, *A Collector's Wife*, Zubaan, New Delhi, 2005.

Pou, K. B. Veio, *Literary Cultures of India's Northeast: Naga Writings in English*, Heritage Publishing House, Dimapur, 2015.

The Heart of the Matter, Katha, New Delhi, 2004.

The North East Writer's Forum. *Fresh Fictions: Folk Tales, Plays, Novellas from the Northeast*, Katha, New Delhi, 2005.

Valdés, Mario J. and Linda Hutcheon, "Rethinking Literary History – Comparatively", in Occasional Paper No. 27, 1994, American Council of Learned Societies, at http://archives.acls.org/op/27_rethinking_literary_history.htm, 20th October 2020.

For Product Safety Concerns and Information please contact our EU
representative GPSR@taylorandfrancis.com
Taylor & Francis Verlag GmbH, Kaufingerstraße 24, 80331 München, Germany

www.ingramcontent.com/pod-product-compliance
Lightning Source LLC
Chambersburg PA
CBHW061918130726
47908CB00017B/2044